Memories of An Old-Time Tar Heel

Memories OF AN OLD-TIME *Tar Heel*

By *Kemp Plummer Battle*
PRESIDENT OF THE UNIVERSITY OF NORTH CAROLINA
1876-1891

EDITED BY HIS SON *William James Battle*
PROFESSOR OF CLASSICAL LANGUAGES IN THE UNIVERSITY OF TEXAS

Chapel Hill
THE UNIVERSITY OF NORTH CAROLINA PRESS
1945

Copyright, 1945, by

THE UNIVERSITY OF NORTH CAROLINA PRESS

Van Rees Press, New York, PJ

SECOND PRINTING

Editor's Note

Having finished his History of the University, my father set about recording the memories of his life. He made a general outline but he did not write consecutively and he did not complete what he had planned. Still less did he revise what he had written. So it came about that there was in his manuscript a good deal of repetition, and there were slips both in facts and in style. These I have endeavored to remove and have sought to make a coherent story. I have even added a sentence here and there where it seemed needed for proper sense. In short, I have tried to do what I believe my father himself would have been glad to see done. The manuscript came into my hands after the death on July 3, 1929, of my brother Herbert B. Battle of Montgomery, Alabama, main author of *The Battle Book*, which was published in 1930, but only now has it been possible for me to work it over. My father had not shown me any of it but from many a talk with him I was familiar with most of the subject matter. Needless to say *The Battle Book* has been of great help.

William James Battle

University of Texas,
Austin, Texas.
July, 1943.

Kemp Plummer Battle: Biographical Sketch

KEMP PLUMMER BATTLE was born December 19, 1831, near Louisburg, Franklin County, North Carolina, the son of William Horn Battle, later an associate justice of the Supreme Court of North Carolina, and Lucy Martin (Plummer) Battle, his ancestors on both sides being pioneer settlers of Virginia and North Carolina. His early training was received in private schools at Louisburg, Raleigh, and Chapel Hill. Entering the University of North Carolina in 1845, he was graduated with first honors at the age of seventeen in the class of 1849 and delivered the valedictory. For the session of 1849-1850 he was Tutor in Latin at the University, then for the four years 1850-1854 Tutor in Mathematics. Meantime he studied law and then, being admitted to the bar, settled in Raleigh. In 1855 he was married to a distant cousin, Martha Ann Battle, of Edgecombe County. In 1857 he was made one of the directors of the newly re-chartered Bank of North Carolina. In 1861 he was chosen a delegate from Wake County to the State Constitutional Convention and signed the Ordinance of Secession although a strong Union man prior to Lincoln's call for troops to coerce the seceding states. During the years of war he was president of the Chatham Railroad Company organized to build a road from Raleigh to the Chatham County coal fields in order to supply the Confederate munitions factories.

In 1862 he was elected by the General Assembly one of the trustees of the University and served till the whole board was displaced by the Republican General Assembly of 1868. Again elected a trustee in 1874, he served by successive re-elections till his death, a total of fifty-one years. In 1866 he was elected State Treasurer and held the office till 1868, when the whole existing State Government was replaced by the United States military authorities under Congressional Reconstruction. Because of his large farming interests and his conspicuous advocacy of improved agriculture, he was made in 1869, 1870, and 1871 president of the State Fair Association at Raleigh. For many years also he was a member of the State Board of Agriculture, and it was primarily on his initiative that a State Agricultural Experiment and Fertilizer Control Station was established at the University in 1877. In 1875 he was largely instrumental in re-opening the University, closed since 1870. By personal solicitation he secured large private contributions for the repair of its buildings and was one of the leaders in persuading the General Assembly to vote to the University the income from the Federal Land Grant Act of 1862. In 1876 he was made President of the University and held the office for fifteen years, resigning in 1891 to become Professor of History. In 1877 he was chiefly responsible for the establishment of a State Summer Normal School at the University, the first school of the kind in the South. In 1881, mainly through his persistence, was made after bitter opposition the first legislative appropriation to higher education in the history of the State. In 1885, again owing chiefly to his efforts, the appropriation was quadrupled.

In 1881-1882 he was a leading spirit in the building of the State University Railroad, connecting Chapel Hill with the North Carolina Railroad, and was for some years its president. As Professor of History he served sixteen years, retiring on a Carnegie grant in 1907 at the age of seventy-five. Twice he received the degree of LL.D.: in 1882 from Davidson College, in 1910 from the University. The manifold services he rendered to the University caused him to be called its Second Founder and the affection of his old boys gave him for years before his death the name of the Grand Old Man of North Carolina. A prolific author of addresses and lectures and monographs, his chief published work is his *History of the University of North Carolina* in two volumes. The first volume was published in 1907, the second in 1912. He died at Chapel Hill February 4, 1919, and was buried in Raleigh. Both houses of the General Assembly adjourned in his honor and his funeral was attended by many of the most prominent men of the State.

Contents

Editor's Note	v
KEMP PLUMMER BATTLE: *Biographical Sketch*	vii
1. My Childhood at Louisburg	3
2. My Father, William Horn Battle	12
3. My Mother, Lucy Martin (Plummer) Battle	15
4. My Uncles and Aunts	21
5. School Days at Louisburg, Raleigh, and Chapel Hill	32
6. Phases of My Life as a Boy in Raleigh	43
7. My Brothers and Sisters	48
8. Amusements of My Boyhood and College Days	57
9. Life as a Student and Tutor at the University	73
10. A Trip to the Mountains in 1848	87
11. Eminent Men of My Youth	96
12. A Lawyer in Raleigh	108
13. Courtship and Marriage	113
14. My Wife's People	118
15. Our Home in Raleigh	123
16. Plantations and Slaves in Edgecombe	125
17. Children	132
18. The Courts in Wake County	140
19. Practice in Wake County	143
20. Old-Time Treatment of Criminals	148
21. Practice Outside Wake County	153
22. Extra-Legal Activities in the Fifties	157
23. Running for the General Assembly	160

Contents

24. My Part in Secession — 168
25. President of the Chatham Railroad Company — 172
26. War Pictures — 179
27. Trips to Richmond in War Time — 186
28. Last Days of the War in Raleigh — 191
29. Battle, Heck, and Company — 201
30. My Term as State Treasurer — 204
31. Northern Missionaries to the Negroes — 216
32. The Special Tax Bonds — 220
33. Revival of the State Fair — 224
34. Commissioner of the City of Raleigh — 226
35. Oakwood Cemetery, Raleigh — 228
36. Visits to Lenoir, Boone, and Three Summer Resorts — 231
37. Revival of the University — 241
38. Back at the Old Home in Chapel Hill — 245
39. The University Loses the Land Grant Money — 247
40. Speech at a Banquet in Honor of Col. L. L. Polk: The University, the Farmers, and the Agricultural and Mechanical College — 250
41. Unpleasant University Duties — 255
42. Visits to My Brother William at Lilesville — 259
43. Educational Addresses — 266
44. Visit to New York in 1884 — 270
45. Visitor at West Point in 1886 — 274
46. Visits to William and Augustus Van Wyck in 1886 — 277
47. An Address at Round Lake, New York, in 1888 — 279
    Chronology of Kemp Plummer Battle — 281

Illustrations

	Facing page
Mrs. William Horn Battle. From a portrait of Kemp Plummer Battle's mother, painted by William Garle Browne about 1860	4
William Horn Battle, father of Kemp Plummer Battle. From an engraving after a portrait by William Garle Browne about 1860	5
James S. Battle, father of Mrs. Kemp Plummer Battle. From an engraving after a portrait by Thomas Sully	5
William S. Battle, brother of Mrs. Kemp Plummer Battle. From an engraving after a photograph taken about 1900	5
Richard H. Battle, brother of Kemp Plummer Battle. From an engraving in Van Noppen's Biographical History of North Carolina	5
The Capitol at Raleigh, burned in 1831. From a rare print of a drawing by W. Goodacre, Jr., published in London August 15, 1831	20
Faculty of the University of North Carolina in 1878, with President Battle in the center. From an old photograph	21
Mrs. Kemp Plummer Battle. From a daguerreotype taken about 1865	36
Kemp Plummer Battle. From a daguerreotype taken about 1865	37
Allen Battle. For many years, as slave and free man, overseer of Mrs. Kemp Plummer Battle's plantation "Walnut Creek." From a photograph taken about 1870	52
Easter Snipes. Senlac cook for some thirty years. From a photograph taken in 1917	52
The Chapel of the Cross, Chapel Hill. From a photograph by Bayard Wootten	53
Senlac, the home of Kemp Plummer Battle in Chapel Hill. From a photograph taken about 1884	76

Illustrations

	Facing page
A Family Group at Senlac. From a photograph taken about *1893* Following page	76
Senlac. View from the front walk toward the woods (later Battle Park). From a photograph taken about *1903*	77
Senlac. View from the front porch toward the campus. From a photograph taken about *1903*	77
Campus of the University, Cameron Avenue, looking west. From a photograph taken about *1888*	148
Cameron Avenue, looking east. From a photograph taken about *1888*	148
Dialectic Society Hall at the University. From a photograph taken about *1885*	149
Faculty Group on the Campus. From a photograph taken in the early spring of *1888*	164
Kemp Plummer Battle. From a photograph taken about *1900*	165
Mrs. Kemp Plummer Battle. From a photograph taken about *1900*	165

Memories of An Old-Time Tar Heel

1. My Childhood at Louisburg

ON THIS DECEMBER 19, 1912, ON WHICH I reached the age of eighty-one years, I begin the writing of my memories. My ambition is to do more than chronicle my personal history. I wish to throw light on the history of the state during my time, having respect to the character of the public men whom I have met and the changes in our institutions.

I was born at Oakendale, the country place near Louisburg to which my father brought his wife soon after their marriage, and lived there two years prior to the removal of the family to Louisburg. I have no memory of my country life, but learned some incidents from my mother. At this time there was a fever for emigrating to Tennessee. My father and Uncle William Plummer concluded to make an inspection of the country in order to decide whether to join the emigrating throng. They went on horseback as far as Nashville. I was amused years afterwards at my father's arms. His weapon of defence was a short single-barrelled flint and steel pistol. The cock was in the middle of the breach, so that it was impossible to take aim. Still, the bullet was large and at close quarters good for one robber. We boys occasionally practiced with it. We could hit the side of a house or even a large tree at ten steps. I grieve at its loss.

We have a letter from Mother to Father while he was in Nashville, Tennessee. She counsels him to remember that people who have land for sale are apt to praise it more highly than it deserves, and the tone of her letter is evidently in favor of his staying in North Carolina. Among the family news she says of me, "Kemp is well and looks as much like a Scotchman as ever." What her idea of the personal appearance of a Scotchman was she does not disclose but may be gathered from the fact that I was unusually lean and bony, with big blue eyes. A rattle-brained seamstress who often sewed for Mother sometimes addressed me, "You, Kemp, you taut-eyed Molly!" Taut-eyed is not in the dictionary, but the Molly, equivalent to Molly Hare or rabbit, shows that she meant having projecting eyes.

This seamstress served Father an evil turn once. He was in attendance on Nash court when she told a man on his way to Nashville (N.C.) that Kemp was very sick. He told my father this unpleasant news, whereupon Father hastened home. Mother met him. "How is Kemp?" "He's very well." "Where is he?" "Down in the field playing." "Hasn't he been sick?" "Not in the least." Either the lying seamstress dreamed the story or she was deceived by my cadaverous appearance. There could not have been a more false deduction. Although then and long afterwards I had not an ounce of fat, in fact was so lean that the children after some years nicknamed me Skeleton or, reversing the word, Noteleks, I was always among the healthiest. The infantile diseases, whooping-cough and the rest, I had more lightly than the other children. Mumps I could not catch even when I rubbed my cheek on my brother's swollen jaw in the vain effort to get a few days' absence from recitations.

I have some vivid recollections of my life in Louisburg where I lived for six years. The town had many bad boys in it. When drinking whiskey and brandy and rum, gambling, and cockfighting were common among men, the moral tone of boys was naturally low and we were not allowed to play with them. Until at seven years of age I was sent to school, three or four acquaintances were all I had.

Up to this time I was taught by my mother. My memory goes back to the time when I could repeat the Lord's Prayer, except the words "We forgive those." These I pronounced "eephanose." Then the other children would laugh, and I was forced to begin over again. It required Mother's authority to cause the laughter to cease and then I was able to finish. I must have been only three or four years old.

Mother had the power of carrying on her knitting, rapidly too, and at the same time telling stories about her young days. I recall her hearing my lesson in Webster's Elementary Spelling Book when I was so young that I could not pronounce words like sphere. I called it "suf-fere." It was this home instruction that placed me in classes with boys two years older.

The only fight of cocks with gyves that I ever witnessed I came across accidentally. I was accompanying the nurse who had charge of the younger children able to run about. We suddenly in a sequestered place near the river found ourselves in the company of about twenty men in a ring around two other men, one of whom held a gray and the other a red cock facing one another. The cocks were turned loose and the red fell dead the first flutter. I saw one of the men pull out his pocketbook and hand a bill to the backer of the gray. As my attendance on this bout was accidental, Mother took no notice of it, if it came to her ears. This is doubtful, as the nurse was probably afraid to tell of having been at a cockfight.

Mother gave me permission once to attend what was called a General Muster of the militia of the county. With dinner in my pocket I walked proudly by the soldiers as, armed with rifles, shot-guns,

MRS. WILLIAM HORN BATTLE

From a portrait of Kemp Plummer Battle's mother, painted by William Garle Browne about 1860. Now in the possession of Mrs. John M. Booker, of Chapel Hill.

Upper left, William Horn Battle, father of Kemp Plummer Battle, Professor of Law in the University, Judge of State Supreme Court. From engraving after portrait by William Garle Browne about 1860. *Upper right,* James S. Battle, father of Mrs. Kemp P. Battle, planter, cotton manufacturer. From engraving after portrait by Thomas Sully. *Lower left,* William S. Battle, brother of Mrs. Kemp P. Battle, planter and cotton manufacturer. From engraving after photograph of about 1900. *Lower right,* Richard H. Battle, brother of K.P.B., Raleigh lawyer, member of General Assembly, trustee of the University. (Engravings from Van Noppen's *Biographical History of North Carolina.*)

My Childhood at Louisburg

and some with walking sticks, they marched to an old field about a mile from Louisburg and went through the more simple military evolutions. The marching was accompanied by a drum and ear-piercing fife and the tune was "Yankee Doodle" or "Three Little Pigs and a Bobtailed Sow." I was struck with the spectacle of my father, who was a small man, and a companion over six feet high joining the procession to save their fines or possibly to retain their popularity, and walking ten steps behind the other soldiers. The enthusiasm of the muster, which was very manifest soon after the Revolution and was renewed after the War of 1812, was fast dying out. The higher officers, majors and brigadier generals and colonels, were proud of their distinctions. Dressed in picturesque uniforms and mounted on spirited chargers, they attracted general admiration. The contrast between these cavaliers in gay regimentals, swords, and epaulets shining in the sunlight, and the homespun clothes and slouchy walk of the common soldiers was most striking. The evolutions and the simultaneous firing of the ancient flint and steel rifles were impressive to the youthful mind.

I must record a story about a timid young militia man that was considered funny in the old days. His mother, a stout woman afraid of nothing, was proud of her only son preparing for war. But his nervelessness made him afraid to fire his gun. He loaded his piece with powder when the order was given to load but when "Fire!" was shouted, he shut his eyes and did not pull the trigger. Six times the powder was poured in and six times he failed to fire. When he returned home his mother inquired, "Did you shoot like the rest?" "No, ma'am, I was afraid." She jerked the gun from his hand, "I'll show you how to shoot!" As she pulled back the cock, he darted under the bed. The explosion was terrific. The recoil kicked her against the wall. Her son poked his head from beneath the bed and cried, "Hold on to her, Mammy, there are five more to come!"

There were traditions that when enmities sprang up in different parts of the county, by common consent it was agreed to fight the quarrels out at court week or musters, but I saw no conflicts that day though I anxiously watched for them. Notwithstanding my disappointment I thoroughly enjoyed my outing and especially the cold snack Mother placed in my pocket.

After our removal to Raleigh I neither saw nor heard of any militia gatherings. They were probably kept up at some points in the several townships but if any were held in Raleigh, they attracted no attention. Interest in them ceased as the wars and their excitements faded away. No militia were called to fight in the Mexican War. It was won by the regulars and volunteers.

I remember an oyster supper given by my father, the bivalves being eaten raw or roasted in their shells. Uncle William Plummer offered me one raw, but it was offensive to my taste. He endeavored to induce me to swallow it by the offer of a nine-pence (12½ cents). I made faithful efforts but failed. I then had a settled belief that I could not eat oysters, but eighteen years later, I was detained in court until after the dinner-hour. The only food left at the hotel table was oyster-pie. Urged by extreme hunger, I was tempted to eat some. I never tasted anything so exquisite. Ever since then I find oysters in any shape palatable.

It was about the time of our removal to Raleigh that I saw an immense drove of wild pigeons flying toward the west. Their formation was rectangular, probably a half-mile in breadth and several hundred feet in the direction of flight. It was remarkable that the flying birds formed an almost perfect parallelogram, without any visible leader. They were three or four hundred feet above the ground. The time was about three o'clock in the afternoon. The flight was quite as rapid as is attained by our turtle doves when doing their best. They did not roost near our town but we heard wonderful stories of trees broken elsewhere by the roosting masses. The neighbors gathered by night intent on slaughter and loud were the boasts of the numbers of their victims, often fed to hogs. I was six or seven years old and never consulted any grown person as to his observations, but I think that my account is accurate. I grieve that wild pigeons are now classed with the extinct. Certainly there are no more such swarms.

The wonderful flights of wild pigeons bring to mind that modern farmers cannot realize the devastation of crops, fowls, and pigs caused by wild animals, particularly squirrels, hares, foxes, raccoons, opossums, blackbirds, crows, and some species of hawks. My father once stationed himself near a mulberry tree whose fruit was just ripe, and killed twenty-seven squirrels in a few hours. Constant war was waged also against the birds mentioned. Every field freshly sown with grain was defended by an uncouth figure which came to be called scarecrow. I heard Mr. Oates, senator from Sampson, plead for a law offering head money for crows. He humorously stated that he was unable to erect scarecrows because neighbors mistook them for him and plodded over the field to talk to him.

My Childhood at Louisburg

I recall also flights of blackbirds and crows blackening the quarter of the skies where they flew. Whatever sentiment may exist in modern times that their destruction of worms and other pests overbalances the evil they do, certainly in old times the contrary was true. The opinion of farmers embodied in doggerel and chanted as a song was undoubtedly founded on experience.

> Said the blackbird to the crow,
> "What makes white folks hate us so?"
>
> "Ever since old Adam was born
> It's been our trade to pull up corn."

There is also a shorter poem:

> Old Jim Crow,
> The biggest thief I know,
> Every time he steals a corn,
> Says "Caw! Caw!! Caw!!!"

Farmers also had constant warfare by traps and otherwise with the enemies of their poultry. The hunting of foxes was a neighborhood frolic, wound up by such generous potations of old John Barleycorn, that the more rigid Methodist preachers banned fox-hunting along with dancing as anti-Christian. Polecats, raccoons, and opossums were dreaded visitants of the poultry yard. And the little weasel too, which would cut the throats and drink the blood of a score of chickens in one night and was so cunning that a domestic bard imagines a trial of wits between him and the crow, bird against beast. I recall the poem.

> The crow he peeped at the weasel,
> The crow he peeped at the weasel,
> The crow he peeped at the weasel,
> *And* the weasel he peeped at the crow.

I am inclined to think that the poet means for us to conclude that the weasel with superior cunning pounced upon the unwary bird whose watchfulness was not followed by speedy flight.

Somehow the early settlers did not hate the timid hare, although it too was destructive to early vegetables. An early song, the tune of which was played on the fiddle for dancing and marching, seems to regard it as a familiar acquaintance.

> Old Molly hare,
> What you doin' there
> Sitting in a corner
> Smoking a se-gare?

I was taken to the Presbyterian Church at night once when about six years old. I recall only that I fell into a sleep so profound that when the service was over I walked many yards from the door before recovering my senses. I went also to the Methodist Church and heard Rev. Mr. Langston, who was noted for the wildness of his gestures. It was told that once he leaped so high that his boot heels were seen above the pulpit. I did not witness this feat but I distinctly remember the frantic swinging of his arms and the loudness of his shouting.

I never attended a revival. My mother did not approve of revivals although she did not openly condemn them. She had too much respect for any efforts to promote religion. I remember, however, seeing and hearing one of our women filling the air with loud shouting as she walked along a public street towards home, and was told that she was under conviction for her sins. I was afterwards informed that she had "come through," i.e., was converted. Passing a negro church in Raleigh afterwards, I saw through the door men and women in a circle around an object on the floor. On examination I saw a woman prostrate, apparently in a stupor. Her sins had "struck her down" and the church members were "bringing her to."

We raised enough corn on our place to have annual corn-shuckings. Negroes were invited to assist in removing the shucks from the ears. Apple-brandy or corn-whiskey was provided and dealt out in tin cups. Sometimes the workers were divided into two gangs and to each was assigned a stack of corn for rivalry. Songs were sung under the leadership of an elderly yellow man named Silas, who had a rough leg of wood. We were all afraid of him because of his monstrous limb and reputation for uncommon mental gifts, although we could have outrun him if he had pursued us. This fear was mere fancy because he was a good, orderly man. I regret that I did not get someone to write down the words of the songs they sang. I recall the chorus of one, "Round the corn, Sally!" It is probable that old Silas improvised the words of the ballad, as the other negroes only joined in the chorus, emphasizing the last word and pronouncing it "Sallee-ee," the last syllable loudly. The scene was a wild one. The half-dressed negroes, the quick-moving arms, the white ears of corn flashing in the blaze of the lightwood fire, Silas like a prophet of old shouting the verses and two-score lusty throats bawling out, "Round the corn, Sallee-ee," left an ineffaceable impression on my mind.

My father was beyond the garden fence, hoping to see the fun unobserved. But one of the negroes espied him. He was a modest man and very dignified, he had been in the General Assembly, and was one of the leaders of the county; yet he was quickly surrounded, his protestations disregarded. He was hoisted to the shoulders of one of the stoutest Africans and carried around the house, a tumultuous crowd following and singing at the tops of their voices, "Round the corn, Sallee-ee!" My venerated sire looked very miserable, but as he furnished the liquor and his elevation was caused by gratitude, he did not get angry. Do not blame him. In that day no festive gathering was held without whiskey or brandy. It was as commonly drunk by many as water. It was on account of the drinking that preachers taught that fox-hunting, dancing, and the like were sinful. The negroes made the distinction that dancing was innocent if the legs were not crossed, because the devil crossed his legs when he danced. Their name for him was Satan.

The mention of His Satanic Majesty reminds me that the negroes taught us that the fires of hell were maintained by jay birds who every Friday flew to the infernal regions with twigs in their mouths. As the birds of all the world supplied this fuel, it did not sound unreasonable. We were also told that at twelve o'clock at night witches were allowed to torment bad children. Their favorite sport was riding the naughty ones like horses and we were told that the red mud could be seen under the finger nails. The child would awake worn out with fatigue even to sickness. The witch could be balked by hanging a sifter over the bed. She could not reach the sleeper without going through each hole in the sifter. This would occupy so much time that daylight would come and witches can't do mischief except at night, beginning at midnight.

One day a circus came to town! It is impossible now to realize the frantic excitement aroused in those humdrum days by such an event. The riding of men and women, the gay dresses, the witticisms of the clown, the little dramatic plays, the bears, lions, camels, elephants, were talked of weeks before and weeks afterwards. The crowds of people, many rough and some half-drunk, made it unsafe for ladies and children to attend without a discreet masculine escort. It so happened that this time my father was absent at one of his courts and no man could be found to whose care Mother was willing to entrust us. We were utterly miserable. The shouts of applause and the music were heard by us and smote upon our hearts as with knotted whips. Mother pitied us as only a tender mother could. She devised a home-made circus and menagerie. One of us under a table was a bear in his den; another was a horse and another rode him; another with black robe and paper tusks was an elephant; and so on. The experiment served to kill time but did not heal the heart-wounds. We afterwards felt like fighting anyone who told about the grand spectacle.

The circus in those pre-railroad days, when the public schools had scant educational influence, was of advantage to the community. It also introduced new words, especially slang. A half-witted woman, struck by an English farce in which a boy covered with brass buttons and called Buttons rode behind the fashionable carriages and waited on the inmates, called my brother William, Billy Button. The name stuck to him until at the age of eighteen he showed resentment and prevailed on his friends to drop it.

As a boy I attended circus performances once at Louisburg and again in 1842 in Raleigh and remember well the fascination, the wild delight. They were not allowed at Chapel Hill and therefore I did not attend another until after I settled in Raleigh as a lawyer. I was completely disillusioned. The faces bedaubed with paint, the slow canter of the horses, the flat saddles, the sorry, often coarse jokes, and the spiritless performances of the athletes, were a grievous disappointment. And the caged animals looked jaded and unhappy, so that the pictures of them in the book at home were more pleasing to look at and quite as instructive.

When I was seven years old, I saw a mad dog hunt. The news that hydrophobia was in the neighborhood caused terrified excitement. While we children were playing under some trees, we heard the noise of yelping, shouting, shooting. About fifty men with guns, sticks, and stones were pursuing a fleeing dog. With open mouth, yelping as he ran, he passed in a few yards of us. We were in no danger as he was too much frightened to stop for an attack on us. Soon the hunt passed out of hearing but I heard that it was a success.

Afterwards, as I was returning from school, I saw a number of men stoning a small dog said to be mad. Naturally I joined in what I considered to be a good work. The dog's tenacity of life was amazing. I went home boasting of my exploit, but Mother, who

My Childhood at Louisburg

had seen from afar the execution of the criminal, in order to impress me with antipathy to cruelty to animals decreed that I should not leave our place during the three weeks' vacation. This was the only punishment by her that I recall which I considered too severe. For the three weeks I felt as unhappy as a prisoner. The offence was really venial because I was following the example of grown men and thought I was doing good service in ridding the town of a dangerous enemy. In Mother's justification it should be remembered that she did not like for us to associate with the town boys and that our place contained sixty acres and ran for some distance along Tar River. Confinement to it did not seem to her an excessive deprivation of liberty. She had an uncommon sympathy with pain and suffering in man and beast, a sympathy which on this occasion warped her judgment. But this mistake, if it was one, is immeasurably overbalanced by the thousand instances in which she was wise and just.

The comparative isolation in which my early years were spent threw me much with our negro children. This had by no means an uplifting effect. Although our negroes were well treated and attended church, the children were sadly devoid of modesty and decency when they were young and no fit associates for the children of the white family. As we grew up the companionship gradually ceased. Moreover the slave children improved in manners and in many cases in morals.

Mother's conversation, her anecdotes and descriptions of the old-time life of Warren County, her stories from the Bible and other books she had read, were very instructive. The tale of Washington and the cherry tree was real to us, and once when I threw a stone at a flock of guinea-chickens and killed one, no grass grew under my feet as I imitated the Father of His Country and by a rapid confession procured a like gracious pardon.

2. My Father, William Horn Battle

MY FATHER, WHO HAD THE NAME OF WILliam from his grandfather and Horn from his grandmother, Charity, did not inherit a taste for business and adopted the profession of the law, He graduated at the University in 1820 next to the highest in the class and spoke the valedictory oration. He then studied law under Judge Henderson in Williamsborough, Granville County, and practiced law in Louisburg, Franklin County.

At Christmas, 1839, he removed to Raleigh and in June, 1843, changed his residence to Chapel Hill. He was a member of the General Assembly and was one of the committee who prepared the Revised Statutes of 1836. To him was entrusted the reading of the proof of the book and he spent some time in Boston for the purpose. He was Reporter of the Supreme Court in conjunction with Thomas P. Devereux, becoming sole Reporter in 1839. He was a judge of the Superior Court from 1840 to 1852 except for a half year in 1848 when he served on the Supreme Court by appointment of the Governor. In 1852 he was elected associate justice of the Supreme Court and served till 1868 when he lost his seat under the Reconstruction Acts. He then practiced law in Raleigh till 1876 when he moved back to Chapel Hill. For a year he was President of the Raleigh National Bank. From 1845 to 1868 in addition to his duties as a judge he was Professor of Law in the University and again from 1876 to his death in 1879. He reprinted some volumes of the old Reports of our state, and revised the Code of North Carolina, this work being adopted by the General Assembly under the name of Battle's Revisal. He also prepared a Digest of the decisions of the Supreme Court in three volumes which he issued at his own charges, called Battle's Digest.

In his religious relations he adopted the church to which his wife was attached, the Protestant Episcopal, and attended both Diocesan and General Conventions with regularity for many years. He was probably the only deputy who was member of the highest church legislative body before, during, and after the Civil War.

Father was well known for using neither tobacco nor alcohol. This came from an experiment that he made with whiskey and tobacco at the age of five. He had noticed that grown people were fond of these two articles. He therefore took a glass where a little whiskey had been left, mixed it with some tobacco, and drank it. Shortly afterwards he was found limp and senseless. This was enough for him. He never touched tobacco afterwards in any shape, and whiskey only as a medicine prescribed by the family physician.

Father's duties as judge took him from home nearly half the time for many years, and when he was at home he was busy with his law students, or with his Reports, Digests, and Revisal. Besides this, for years he had business anxieties arising from part ownership of the cotton factory at the Falls of Tar River built by his father. As a favor to his sisters he purchased their shares; and as a favor to his brother, Benjamin Dossey Battle, who also owned a share in the factory, he employed him as superintendent. Uncle Dossey proved to be an unskilful manager and Father for years saw that ruin was impending which he had no power to avert. At last about 1845 Uncle Dossey became insolvent and Father lost all his investment and paid considerable sums as surety for his brother. As he now knew the worst, his spirit regained its elasticity, and he became happy in his household.

He was never morose, however. We all loved and admired him to the utmost. But his professional cares prevented much association with his children. He had unlimited confidence in my mother's management, and his confidence was never misplaced. We did not fear him except when we dreaded his disapproval. He seldom gave orders. When he did, they were implicitly obeyed. I think he did not have by nature an aptitude for associating with children although his heart was kind and loving. Occasionally he would find time to read a comic sketch aloud as we sat by the fireside. I recall rolling on the floor amid gusts of laughter at his rendering of "The Georgia Breakfast" by Longstreet. Mother occasionally would threaten us with his wrath, but she never carried the threat into action. We knew she would not. She saw with delight our natural loving greetings and our rejoicings over the gifts he brought us after his long absences, and we did our best to second the care she took to make his time at home comfortable and pleasant.

Father made a mistake in settling on a farm. He did it on account of his wish to employ some inherited negroes. The result was that, though all his ambitions and sympathies lay in the practice of the law, his neighbors regarded him rather as a farmer. During his five years' stay in the country his practice was small. Brooding over this impaired his health. According to the medical science of that day his physician prescribed a toddy before breakfast. After taking the prescription for a few mornings, he paused while dressing and said, "Old woman," which was always his pet name for Mother, "I'll not take another toddy!" She said, "Why? I thought it was doing you good." "Well, I rather think it helped me, but I found myself dressing fast in order to get to it!"

It is a remarkable instance of the return of bodily ailments in old age that when Father was deprived of his position of Supreme Court justice in 1868 by the Republicans, the total change of his life thereby necessitated brought on an attack of sleeplessness which lasted many days. It was cured by a prescription of a very able physician, Dr. Johnston B. Jones, then of Chapel Hill, afterwards of Charlotte: a wineglass of raw whiskey on going to bed. No evil habit resulted. I have often wondered whether Maecenas, the Prime Minister of Augustus Caesar, who died after three months of insomnia, might not have been cured by Dr. Jones's single glass of whiskey.

Finding that living three miles from his law office was bad policy, Father bought sixty acres adjoining Louisburg from a man named Howze, whose son Ben became a lawyer and occasionally a member of the General Assembly. With the purchase is associated an anecdote which was a favorite in the family. A little white boy brought in some article for the table for sale. Mr. Howze asked him to dinner, helped him to food, and then addressed himself to supplying his own wants. After a while he noticed that the boy looked unhappy and was not eating. He said, "My son, why don't you eat? Are you sick?" With a whining voice the boy wailed, "My vittles is gin out."

The change from country to town was most fortunate. My father became known as a lawyer. His learning, integrity, and reliability, combined with pleasant manners, procured him clients. He was soon on one side or the other of every case on the docket.

3. My Mother, Lucy Martin (Plummer) Battle

I DO NOT EXAGGERATE WHEN I SAY THAT FOR wisdom, conscientiousness, piety, kindliness, in fact every Christian virtue, my mother had no superior. She had a most checkered life. In youth she was a lively, happy belle, fond of dancing, conversation parties, horse-races, concerts, and theatricals, but always circumspect in her conduct. She loved music and played well on the piano without notes. She knew the words and tunes of the songs of the day and could croon them to her children, although nature denied her control of the high notes. At the age of twenty she was stricken with fever of such violence that it left her with hair permanently gray. She bore well the pains and trials of the births and training of ten children. She reared to maturity six boys and two girls with loving and judicious care, checking disobedience and misbehavior with a firm hand. But she was so tender and kind that they almost never disputed her judgment. Being well educated, she aided them in their studies and encouraged them to avoid idleness. Living much of her married life at a distance from the family physician, she was skilled in remedies for most of the ordinary diseases. My father, especially in early married life when his practise was limited, was liable to fits of despondency. Her natural gaiety was then of inestimable benefit to him. For many years, though her health was not robust, her home was the centre of large hospitality. And always she managed servants judiciously in sickness and health, and raised her children in Christian paths.

My mother was a firm believer in the old truth which was a heading on a page in our copybooks: "Evil communications corrupt good manners." Drinking alcoholic liquors, gambling, swearing, betting on horse-races, cock-fighting, and other vices were common in Louisburg. She strove therefore to make her children contented and happy at home. She gave us entertaining word pictures of happenings as early as 1815. I remember a vivid account of a horse-race. Members of the best circles, male and female, attended. It was fashionable for the ladies to bet gloves, but not money, on the result. The great patron of the race-track was William R. Johnson, the owner and runner of Fashion against Eclipse, the South against the North, in which the North was triumphant, a race which attracted the enthusiastic attention of both sections. In the Warren

County race Col. Johnson's horse won. He was ridden by a slave jockey. The rider held in his mount until the home stretch was reached. Then he loosened his reins and shot ahead, courteously raising his hat and bowing to the ladies, as they clapped their hands with enthusiasm. That colored boy was the most popular person on the ground.

My mother had a strong aversion to the almost universal custom of using spirituous liquors. She abolished the making of eggnog at Christmas because she heard the children boasting of its excellence.

She had a good memory and made her children love home. She inculcated good habits and stirred up their ambition. No shirking of duty was tolerated and we were exhorted never to let anyone beat us in our tasks. She constantly assisted us at home in order that we might compete successfully at school.

A popular source of entertainment in her youth was the subscription ball. A committee settled on the persons to be invited and made all arrangements needed, including a good supply of eatables and drinkables. Each gentleman selected paid a sum, generally five dollars, for expenses. The committee, after procuring leave from the ladies, introduced the gentlemen to be partners in the dances. At one of these festivals a well-behaved young blacksmith was one of the guests. A committeeman applied to several ladies for leave to introduce him, but found them unwilling to accept one not in their circle. My mother, who was very popular, whispered to the officer, "Ask me, I will dance with him." The young man behaved with all proper decorum and never obtruded himself afterwards. Mother's conduct met with general approval. Her status in society, being the daughter of the leader of the bar, could not be affected by such democratic conduct, and the kind heart which prompted the act increased her popularity.

Mother gained fame as a horsewoman. She was a good rider and one of her beaux invited her to mount a favorite fast mare of his. As they neared home, going in a canter along the main street of the town, suddenly the girth of my mother's saddle broke. With rare presence of mind she disengaged her foot from the stirrup, and in sight of some friends who were alarmed at her situation, slid to the ground without falling.

Her mother's health was not strong and her father, Kemp Plummer, fond of company and hospitable beyond reasonable limits, overtaxed his wife's strength by entertaining all respectable visitors to Warrenton, then on a main route of travel between the North and the South. Mr. Plummer retained during life the hospitable and convivial habits of his race and paid the penalty that often fell to their lot—long continued gout. He was not intemperate, but drank wine at meals, ate highly seasoned food, invited to his table all strangers who came to the village, including as a matter of course judges and lawyers when court week came, and members of Congress on their way to and from the Capital. He was an excellent raconteur and of sparkling vivacity. His *facetiae*, often expressed in rhyme, were quoted in the counties of his circuit long after his death. His witticisms were entirely without stings. For example, riding once with a friend, an elderly, grave, sardonic lawyer of Scotch birth, Falkener by name, whose mount was a thick-set pony, known far and near as Shandy, Mr. Plummer sang out.

>Yankee doodle, doodle, doodle,
>Yankee doodle dandy,
>Little men ride little nags,
>And Falkener he rides Shandy.

He had not learnt from the Reverend Sidney Smith that it takes a surgical operation to get a joke into a Scotchman's head. The irascible Falkener leaped from his pony and challenged the surprised improvisateur to a combat. Mr. Plummer gently replied, "Why, Falkener!" The dark cloud of anger passed away as rapidly as it gathered. "Say no more about it, Plummer! Say no more about it," and they rode on as good friends as ever.

He was a good singer and was often called on to aid in the village amateur concerts. He was especially strong at the patriotic songs in vogue after the Revolution and the War of 1812. Once while, with blackened face, he was giving "The Constitution and the Guerrière," in the enthusiasm inspired by the recital of the glorious victory he doffed his sailor's cap and waved it vigorously, forgetting that his bald head was as white as nature had originally made it. The contrast of shining scalp and smutty countenance intensified the enjoyment of his audience. Even in childhood his musical gift was in demand. The family tradition is that when he attended church for the first time and the hymn was sung, he thought it his duty to add his contribution, and to the horror of the devout struck up the rollicking "Old King Cole" with all the energy of his boyish treble.

Grandpa opened his doors not only to the great but to the small, in fact to all who applied. In his day hospitality was more prevalent and unquestioned than at present. There was a little, harmless, half-witted man, called Jimmie Dickson. He would go through the country, sometimes working a little, but idling a great deal. His talk, without intention of wit, was often amusing. Grandpa had a small room which was always open to him without charge for board or lodging. I give specimens of his conversation and conduct. He called Grandpa "honorable Cousin Kemp" and Mother "Honorable Cousin Lucy." Once when he came after an absence of several months, Mother said, "Well, Jimmie, what have you been doing all this time?" "Well, Honorable Cousin Lucy, I will tell you the truth. I set in to help Cousin Susan Fain in her farm work. I stayed with her two or three months. She had no whiskey, nor brandy, and I had to stay sober. After a while she said, 'Jimmie, you've been sober so long, don't you think you could take a horse and cart and go to Williamsborough and bring me a barrel of molasses?' I said, 'Of course I can. I won't even look in a grog-shop.' So I hitched up and when I got by the shop I turned my head away from it and kept it turned until I passed it good. I got the molasses and coming back I turned my head away from the shop just like I did going. I hadn't gone far when I met a man driving a cart with a barrel in it. I stopped him and said, 'This is mighty funny. I've got a horse and cyart, and you've got a horse and cyart. I've got a barrel and you've got a barrel. If you'll tell me what is in your barrel I will tell you what is in mine.' 'Well,' said the man, 'I've got whiskey in mine.' Then I said, 'It is one of the curiousest things in the world, I've got molasses in mine. Now I'll make you a proposition. A quart of molasses for a quart of whiskey.' 'Good,' said the man, and he measured the quart of whiskey and I drawed for him a quart of molasses. Now, Honorable Cousin Lucy, I will not tell you a lie. When I got to Cousin Susan Fain's, I was real drunk, and that was not the worst of it. I forgot to put in the spigot and the 'lasses had all run out. But, Honorable Cousin Lucy, it would have done your heart good to see the little niggers soppin the cyart."

At another time Jimmie made his appearance after several months and was met with the usual question, "Where have you been all this time, Jimmie?" "I will tell you, Honorable Cousin Lucy. I went down to Nash County to work on the farm for old Mr. Sills. He was mighty good to me and I was to have twelve and a half cents a day and my feed. We would start out in the morning and he would say, 'Jimmie, we've got a long hot day before us. Don't you think that a drink of apple brandy would do you good?' You know I never could refuse, so I took it. And when we quit off at night he would say, 'Jimmie, you have had a hard day's work. Don't you think that a glass of brandy would liven you up?' and I would say, 'Oh, yes, sir!' I worked three months and then I said, 'I want to go to Warrenton to see my Honorable Cousin Kemp, so let us settle.' He took out his notebook and calculated eighty days at twelve and a half cents, $10.00. I held out my hand for the money but he said, 'Stop, Jimmie, there is something on the other side.' Then I heard him talking to himself, 'Credit by one glass of brandy six and a fourth cents, ditto, ditto, six and a fourth cents, ditto, ditto, six and a fourth, ditto, ditto, six and a fourth. I got tired of that and said, 'Mr. Sills, stop all that and tell me what is coming to me.' 'Well, Jimmie, after taking what you owe me from what I owe you there is due you just six and a fourth cents.' 'Well, by dad,' I said, 'Give me another ditto and let's be even.' And so I came away without one cent to show for my a'most three months work. But the liquor was good." *

It might be supposed that such a good-natured simpleton as Jimmie Dickson would meet with invariable kindness but such was not always the case. Two half-drunken fox-hunters once seized him by the feet and rode across Shocco Creek, dragging his head through the water, shouting their enjoyment of the sport. He was near being drowned.

Bishop Cheshire was so much amused by the story of the swapping of molasses for whiskey and the little negroes sopping the cart, that in riding through Granville County he inquired about Jimmie Dickson. He was shown the copse between Williamsborough and Warrenton which contained the little fellow's grave. It was near the farm where I stopped for water over twenty years after Grandpa died. An old man came to talk to me. He inquired, "Might you tell me your name?" I said, "Kemp Battle." Then he said, "I know all about you now. Your mother is a daughter of Kemp Plummer. Everybody called him the Honest Lawyer."

After her oldest sister married Alfred Alston, Grandma being an invalid, Mother was the virtual head of the household. She became well acquainted with the judges, lawyers, members of Congress, preachers, and others who were invited to dine at Mr. Plummer's.

She was always ready to help the needy and afflicted. I remember

---

* Bishop Cheshire tells these two stories of Jimmie Dickson in his *Nonnulla*. He obtained them from my father.—W. J. B.

distinctly that we children were often indignant at the impositions on her benevolence by country people not nearly as poor as they pretended. The long absences from home of my father while attending to judicial duties devolved on her the cares of the household. It is a great comfort to me that for seven or eight years of this period, after my older brother Joel graduated from the University, I acted as her prime minister. And after the Reconstruction laws turned my father out of his judgeship, first my brother Richard and then I received her and Father into our houses as beloved members of our families. She breathed her last in a room I had built especially for them, a part of our Raleigh home.

It would be a source of infinite pleasure if I could record that after doing good to so many all the first three-quarters of her life she spent the remainder in happiness. But it pleased Providence that she should mourn the death of seven children. Two she lost in infancy. The next to go was my older brother Joel in 1858, his bright mind clouded by disease and the remedies for it. Then Junius, after a most painful wound in battle at South Mountain, died in Maryland among strangers in 1863. He was followed by her youngest child Lewis, a few days after he was wounded at Gettysburg, likewise with no relative at his deathbed. Then in 1865, when she was expecting a visit from her youngest daughter, Mary, wife of William Van Wyck, came the telegraphic announcement of her sudden death in child-birth. Two years later her oldest daughter, Susan, an invalid for years, was taken to her reward. My mother was seldom seen to smile afterwards. She claimed the privilege of caring for Mary's daughter, Mary Van Wyck. It was noticed that she bestowed on the little girl far more anxious attention than on her own children. It was natural but it made her too watchful and unhappy. Father survived her five years.

THE CAPITOL AT RALEIGH, BURNED IN 1831

From a rare print of a drawing by W. Goodacre, Jr., New York. Engraved and printed by Fenner Sears & Co. Published in London August 15, 1831, by I. T. Hinton and Simkin & Marshall.

FACULTY OF THE UNIVERSITY OF NORTH CAROLINA IN 1878

President Battle is in the center. The Faculty, beginning bottom left and reading clockwise, are: A. R. Ledoux, State Chemist; F. W. Simonds, Geology, Zoology, and Botany; R. H. Graves, Engineering and Physics; A. W. Mangum, Moral Philosophy, History, and English; Charles Phillips, Mathematics; William H. Battle, Law; J. deB. Hooper, Greek and French; A. F. Redd, Chemistry; George T. Winston, Latin and German; C. D. Grandy, Chemistry, Mineralogy, and Latin; W. C. Kerr, State Geologist. From a photograph by C. P. Wharton now in the North Carolina Room of the University Library.

4. My Uncles and Aunts

MY UNCLE RICHARD HENRY BATTLE WAS A man of superior natural talent. He was named for his uncle, Richard Johnston, of whom I know nothing except that he was attentive to his duties as a farmer but ruined his health by taking as a companion to his labors a full quart of apple brandy daily, and that his method of killing hawks was to outwit them by donning a woman's cloak and hiding his flint-lock gun under its folds. Uncle Richard entered the University insufficiently prepared. By hard study without exercise he reached the first rank, but so impaired his health as to cut him off from the eminence which his talents would otherwise have enabled him to reach. An attack of hip-joint disease attended by acute suffering left him extremely lame. Notwithstanding his physical ailments it was evident that his judgment was always sound, his mind quick and strong. His voice was sonorous and he was master of a language pungent, deep in meaning, and often humorous. Few men were more agreeable in conversation. He was often elected a commissioner (alderman) of the city of Raleigh, was one of the commissioners to decide what obligations of the State incurred during the war were not in aid of the war, and was secretary of the North Carolina Life Insurance Company. He was distinguished for his diligence and accuracy in the performance of official duties.

Two anecdotes told by him deserve to be recorded. While he was a Raleigh commissioner, he was walking up the street and espied two negro boys fighting. With his stentorian voice he ordered them to stop. They ran off instinctively a short distance and turned to see who gave the order. One said derisively, "Shuh, he can't ketch nobody!" But the fight was not resumed.

Being of a punctual nature he went to his commissioners' meetings early so as not to be jostled by the others as they went up to the mayor's office. One day the mayor was obviously under the control of John Barleycorn as to both brain and tongue. His ravings making it impossible to transact business, one man after another of the commissioners quietly left the hall. Finally nobody remained except my uncle and the drunken mayor. As the last commissioner made his exit, the mayor exultingly exclaimed, "Battle, didn't I make 'em scoot?"

My uncle for a short while had a store at Rocky Mount. One day before sunrise he was awakened by a loud knocking. He arose from his slumbers to wait on his customer. It was a woman. She wanted an egg's worth of snuff!

After residing in Edgecombe for some years he settled in Raleigh and lived there until he died in 1878. He occasionally, however, visited his native county, sometimes by the public stage which passed through Nashville. Once, after an interval of twenty years, he walked about Nashville while the driver was changing horses. The place had a desolate look. A little boy was leaning lazily against a dilapidated gate. My uncle said, "Boy, your town seems to have grown since I was here twenty years ago." "Yes, *sir*," said the boy, "Mrs. Blount has got a new fence!"

Soon after leaving the University he endeavored to regain his health in the tranquil shades of my father's country place. He was never tired of speaking admiringly of the fortitude and equanimity which my mother displayed in the trials of those days—an uncongenial neighborhood in place of the gaieties of Warrenton, a husband low-spirited from half-sickness and want of success, the anxieties of motherhood, and the affliction of the death of her eldest born. He said there were few such women in the round world as Sister Lucy.

While he was visiting at Oakendale, an unusual and amusing incident occurred. My Uncle Dossey and Cousin Whit Horn were boarding with us and going to school. One Saturday they borrowed a plantation mule in order to visit their home twenty-two miles off. On their starting to return, the mule became dead lame after going two miles. They were forced to walk nineteen long miles, angrily urging on the afflicted beast. But when the hypocritical scoundrel smelled the savor of home, his lameness disappeared and he trotted the last mile merrily, amid the execrations of the beguiled and tired boys.

For years before his death Uncle Richard occupied an office on my lot in Raleigh. After some laxity of living in earlier days he became a consistent member of the Presbyterian Church. Owing to his bodily affliction his circle of friends was not large, but he had their unqualified admiration for his gifts of head and heart.

Amos Johnston, an elder brother of my father, devoted himself to the Christian ministry, being a Missionary Baptist. He was distinguished for the number of times he changed his home. He was at one time pastor in Raleigh and lost his property by too lavish assistance in the building of a new church. At another time he was principal of the Murfreesborough Female College. I remember him as a man of talent, a good preacher, extremely serious in manner. His wife, Margaret Parker, after many years inherited some property, which she invested partly in a home in Wilson. She then refused to move her residence again, whereupon Uncle Amos became an itinerant preacher in eastern North Carolina. On some dispute, the nature of which I do not understand, he changed his church relationship to that of the denomination known as Christians, or Disciples. The last days of his life were marked by rare heroism. A horrible cancer destroyed a part of his face and one eye. Determined not to be offensive, he shut himself up in solitary confinement in a secluded room and communicated with his family only through a window. His youngest son, Jesse Mercer Battle, starting life as an employee of a lightning-rod wagoner, by energy and talent in the pharmacy business in St. Louis became a man of wealth, generous, intelligent, and kindly.

Another uncle, Christopher Columbus, usually called Lum, was often an inmate of our household. He was a man of sprightly talent but inclined to dissipation, exceedingly kind-hearted and especially fascinating to children. He graduated at the University, then became private secretary to Governor Dudley, held a subordinate rank in the Mexican War, and practiced law, but failed of success by reason of unsteady habits. As a specimen of his conversation with children I give one of his descriptions of Mexican table manners. "They are very fond of frogs and red pepper. Their way of eating them is peculiar. They place the frog on the plate in front, the mouth of the frog pointing to the mouth of the eater. Then a pinch of red pepper is sprinkled on the frog's tail. The pain makes him jump. When he jumps, the eater opens his mouth and the frog goes down his throat. It is a favorite food but I could never try it. I was afraid the frog would miss my mouth and land in my eye." Baron Munchausen stories were popular in those days.

Once at a large dining Uncle Lum said, "When I was in Florida, I caught a catfish, eighteen inches between the eyes." His mother measured off eighteen inches on the table and said, "Lum, do you mean to say that catfish had eyes as wide apart as this?" Amid a general laugh he admitted that the fish was a trifle smaller. Being unsuccessful in an early courtship of a popular belle, he never married. He removed to Tennessee and died there.

There were other brothers and sisters of my father. Benjamin Dossey, already mentioned as unfortunate in the management of the cotton factory, was the father of Judge Dossey Battle. Isaac, who settled in Florida, was a member of the legislature. He died by his own hand, a tragedy which was concealed from his mother, although she lived about thirty years afterwards. Catherine married Dr. John W. Lewis, a popular physician in Raleigh, and was mother of General William Gaston Lewis, pronounced by General Lee to be one of his best brigadiers. Susan was the wife of Dr. William H. McKee, also a prominent physician of Raleigh, and the mother of Dr. James McKee, the excellent Superintendent of the State Hospital for the Insane. Youngest of all was Laura Caroline, who was a pupil in the famous school at Bordentown, New Jersey, conducted by the wife of Lucien Charles, son of Joachim Murat, King of Naples. She was a favorite with her teachers and has a beautiful handkerchief given her by the princess as well as several photographs of members of the Murat family. She was often a member of my father's household and was married at his house to Charles Phillips, then a tutor in mathematics in the University, a Presbyterian minister whose denomination she joined after marriage. Dr. Phillips was successively Professor of Engineering and Mathematics in the University, Professor of Mathematics in Davidson College, then, on the revival of the University in 1875, Professor of Mathematics there again for four years and Chairman of the Faculty for one. His health breaking down, he resigned his chair in 1879. In 1889 while on his way to Birmingham to make his home with his son William, he died at Columbia in the house of his son-in-law John S. Verner. My aunt nursed him tenderly through many years of sickness and now lives with me in fair health at the age of 91. Her son William Battle Phillips, a chemist and mining expert, was for two years Professor of Metallurgy in the University, later Director of the Bureau of Economic Geology in the University of Texas, then President of the Colorado School of Mines. He has published many monographs on geological subjects.

Another son, Alexander Lacy Phillips, was a Doctor of Divinity in the Presbyterian Church, in charge of its Sunday School interests in the South. He was noted for his energy and ability.

Aunt Laura, notwithstanding her many years and bodily infirmities, retains her interest in all public and private matters within her cognizance, and her friends, old and young, are legion. She is one of the best women in the world.

My Uncles and Aunts

The brothers of my mother lived quiet lives. William Plummer was a man of ability and was a successful lawyer in Louisburg for a few years but was forced to give up his profession on account of asthma, which ultimately caused his death. He was of dark complexion and was fond of telling on himself that he overheard a mulatto mother say to her child, "Hush, child, hush! That's not your father."

Being a Plummer he was fond of his joke. Once a lawyer friend said to him, "A client of mine is in a quandary. Billy Person (pronounced Parson) is suing him on a note. If judgment is had at this term, he will be ruined. If it can be delayed until next term, he can settle it." Uncle William knew that Person was innocent of legal knowledge, so he suggested to his friend, "Tell him that if he insists on taking judgment at once you will be obliged to apply for a writ of *supersedeas*." When the case came up, his friend made the threat suggested, adding: "For gracious sake, gentlemen, don't let us have the disgrace of such a writ as that! Anything is preferable to that. Person, give him his three months' continuance. Don't let so unheard-of a writ he brought in this court! Between friends, too, your client is able to wait. I know the defendant. He is perfectly solvent." Person was so intimidated at the idea of a *supersedeas*, of which he knew nothing (*omne ignotum pro magnifico*) that he agreed to the continuance and things turned out happily.

Uncle William Plummer married Eliza Armistead, a bright, handsome woman of considerable property. Forced by asthma to quit the bar he was able nevertheless to act as chairman of the County Court, and during his life, this tribunal was presided over as ably as the Superior Courts with their judges. He was a most pleasant raconteur in the intervals of his disease. I recall that, as he was walking in his garden which had a high close fence, he overheard two men on horseback talking about a fight. One said, "Was that Tom Smith?" The answer was, "*Same* man—only lost two ribs and a collar bone in the rabuse." When playing whist he created a merry laugh on one of his sons by quoting from Charles Lamb, "If dirt were trumps, you would have an excellent hand."

Uncle William had many earthly blessings—a congenial loving wife, promising children, a beautiful home, a taste for reading good books, abundance of this world's goods, the respect and admiration of his neighbors, prosperous and amiable brothers and sisters, but the grip of his asthma was a grievous drawback. In the last few years of his life he was forced to spend his nights in a reclining chair. During the Civil War he became fearful that Warren might be overrun by hostile troops. He came to my home in Raleigh on his way to Morganton with the intention of having a duplicate home in a safer region. Feeling his bodily weakness, he had prepared three supplies of money sufficient for his needs, one in a belt around his waist, one in an inner pocket, and the third in an outer pocket. But during the night his disease seized him and next morning he took the train back home. Even in these adverse circumstances his humor did not forsake him. The carriage which was to take him to the railroad station was delayed. He turned to an old negro who had long waited on him, "Ben, go down to the station and hold the locomotive by the hind leg until I get there." In a short while afterwards he was found in his reclining chair fast asleep in the Land of the Hereafter.

An incident in Uncle William's career at the University in 1815 should be recorded. The president of the University, Robert Hett Chapman, was not tactful in his intercourse with students. His task was more difficult because of his being a Federalist while the students generally were Republicans, ardently in favor of the war with Great Britain. Student William B. Shepherd was an able young man and a keen politician. Contrary to the orders of the faculty his senior speech was a strong political harangue. Prompting was allowed in those days and William Plummer acted in that capacity for Shepherd. President Chapman ordered Shepherd to stop speaking. The students shouted, "Go on!" Disregarding the President's orders, he continued to the end amid boisterous applause and Plummer was steadfast in his duty of prompter. Shepherd was dismissed by the faculty and Plummer was suspended for four months. His father thought the punishment unjust and refused to allow him to rejoin his class. His father's displeasure was doubtless directed against President Chapman, not the University, as he became a trustee after Dr. Caldwell became president the second time.

Uncle Alfred Plummer was a cadet of the United States Military Academy at West Point, but lost his place because he refused to give evidence against a fellow cadet. His conduct had the approval of his parents and of the community generally. He then became a country physician, winning a large practise and wide popularity. For years his home was in Warren but a large part of his farm lay in Virginia. He said that it was irksome to pay taxes in two states, and it was his wish to change to a farm in the interior of Warren County. After a while his desire was gratified, but lo, when the new county of Vance was cut from Warren and Granville, the line was between his front door and his medical office!

He was an exceedingly agreeable companion, an excellent mimic. He would repeat with most amusing faithfulness the distortions of the English language by his illiterate patients and other neighbors. The narrative of a possum hunt and the disastrous result of tying a young opossum to the tail of a year old dog lives in my memory. "Lord a' mercy, Dr. Plummer! You might as well a tried to stop a harry-cane with a broomstraw. The last time I seed him he was headin' for Mrs. Green's millpond. And that is the reason why I advise you, if you have a dog which you have any respect for, never tie no possum to his tail."

He played the banjo well and to its accompaniment sang the interesting and amusing folk-songs then popular. I recall one about the sad fate of the negro general who about 1800 endeavored to raise an insurrection in Richmond, Virginia, and was for a short while a terror to its people. I remember most of the song as follows:

> Now, my boys, I'm gwine to tell you,
> Wait a while and then I'll tell you,
> Tell you 'bout my Uncle Gabriel,
> Him they call the Nigger General.
>
> A thousand pounds they 'vertised for him,
> Him would 'tray the Nigger General.
> A little boy portrayed the General;
> 'Trayed him down at Norfolk Landing,
> Said, "How d'ye do, my Uncle Gabriel?"
> "I am not your Uncle Gabriel!"
> "Yes, you is my Uncle Gabriel,
> For I knows you, Uncle Gabriel."
> Tried to ruin old Virginny,
> Made hard times for old Virginny:
> So catch and tie the Nigger General.
> Den dey ca-ied him to city of Richmond,
> Ca-ied him up before de mayor.
> Mayor sent him to de justice,
> Justice sent him to de dungeon.
> Sad-day week come on de trial.
> All the county come to see him.
> Some dey called him Archy Muller.
> My true name is John Luculler,
> Here today and gone tomorrow,
> Never come to stay forever.

De judge, he sent him to de gallows,
Price's Ben he druv the wagon,
Wagon pulled by two gray horses.
And there dey hung him
And dey swung him.
And dat's de last of de Nigger General.

So, mammy, what you got for supper?
Taters, roast and peas a-bilin':
Good enough for hired niggers.
And now, my boys, I'm clean done!

Often in the narrative the banjoist paused with the words, "Now, my boys, I'm 'most done." I may omit a line or two but I give enough to show an admirable sample of negro verse.

Uncle Alfred Plummer was a vigorous specimen of good health, able at the age of eighty to ride horseback fifteen miles to Warrenton and back home the same day. At the age of eighty-two he went to the upper world by the happiest of all possible deaths. Asleep in his bed, without a pain or a struggle, he awoke no more. I recall vividly the loving tone with which Mother spoke of "Brother Alfred." I recall also the delightful conversation I had with him on our front porch in Raleigh, while our little girl Neppie played on the grass. That night she began her struggle with the sickness which ended her life.

Uncle Kemp Plummer never married. He was in love with a Scotland Neck belle, Betty Smith, and journeyed to that scattered village to learn his fate. When he returned, Mother said, "Brother Kemp, what luck did you have?" "Bad, bad! It was those cherries that caused it!" "How was that?" "Why before Miss Betty came in they handed me a basket of cherries. My mind was so full of Miss Betty that I ate a great quantity—more than I ought. They disagreed with me and, just as I made my pretty speech, my stomach gave a great growl and disgusted her. Those cherries missed my chances." And he remained a bachelor to his death.

He owned and lived on a plantation adjoining Warrenton, a prime favorite with a small circle of friends. He was peculiarly kind to his slaves. This trait is illustrated by the following. One of them, a boy of about ten years of age, waited on him as a valet. One day he was later than usual in returning home. The boy said, "Marster, where you been?" "Been to town." "What you been there for?"

My Uncles and Aunts

"To get married." The valet was indignant. "Marster, what make you tell so big of a lie?"

I remember well the large oak in his front yard which was surrounded with a short growth of green grass. As the sun moved, the chairs were pushed towards the east so that there was a regular path cutting through the grass like a quadrant.

In hunting in his fields I found in a rocky place near the dwelling a peculiar stone. I took it to Chapel Hill and showed it to Dr. Mitchell, our Professor of Mineralogy and Geology. "Doctor, what is this mineral?" "Lead ore from Davidson County." "But, Doctor, I found it in a field near Warrenton." "I don't care if you did. No lead in Warren County. It came from Davidson County." This conversation was about the year 1850. Afterwards, when the Colonial Records were printed, I discovered that a committee of the State Congress in the early period of the Revolution was appointed to investigate a lead deposit in the upper part of Halifax County. They reported that lead ores were apparent but not in sufficient quantities for economical working. My uncle for some years was in charge of a country store at Ransom's Bridge in the neighborhood of this deposit and it is evident that he carried some of the ore to his plantation in Warren. Dr. Mitchell for once was wrong.

While Uncle Kemp was a clerk in a country store a corpulent lady came on horseback for some purchases. When she started to go away, it became his duty to assist her to the saddle. This it was the custom to do by letting the lady step into folded hands. When my uncle essayed to perform this duty, his strength was unable to hold up the fair one's two hundred pounds. He hesitated a moment and then gallantly applied his shoulder and shoved her to the saddle.

His mercantile business at Ransom's Bridge was very successful and in addition he gained a handsome sum by the purchase, working, and resale of the Portis gold mine in this neighborhood.

My Uncle Henry Lyne Plummer, the oldest of the family, graduated at the University in 1815, in the class of Rev. Dr. F. L. Hawks and Willie P. Mangum, and became a physician of great local repute. His wife died early, leaving five children. As his health declined, he retired to his farm near Ridgeway and became one of the most successful planters in the county. He was distinguished as a most accomplished and loveable man and as the exemplar of the perfect gentleman. In his later years he always rode horseback over his farm. Once he finished his rounds near the public road leading by his dwelling. He alighted and let down the rails of the fence for the passage of his horse, then laboriously built it up again. His strength was well nigh gone when to his consternation he found that he had left his horse on the farm side of the fence.

My mother's sisters were exceedingly kindhearted and loving. Mary (called Polly) married Alfred Alston, a planter and militia major. Their home was a seat of boundless hospitality. I can see Aunt Polly now anxiously inspecting my plate and saying, knife and fork in hand, "Honey, *do* have some more pie!" In front of the house was a forest of many acres, oak and hickory, in which sported numerous squirrels. Their younger son and I killed twenty-three in one day. The dog that tracked them for us was perfect in his work. He would bark up the tree where the squirrel was hiding. When we shot, whether the squirrel was killed or not, it was apt to jump to the ground and then the dog never failed to capture it. As soon as we bagged the game, he would be off and sometimes have another squirrel treed before we could reload.

Uncle Alfred Alston had a negro boy noted for extreme ugliness. One day he and another boy got into a fight. They were called up for correction. "What were you fighting for?" demanded my uncle. Big Ugly was quick to answer, "Marster, he say he could pin his ears back and jump down my throat 'thout techin.'" Switches were placed in the hands of each and they were told to fight it out. Big Ugly was so enraged that he wore out his antagonist, who cried for mercy. It was soon granted.

When two other boys were found fighting, one of them said Epps, his antagonist, had been mocking him. "Marster, every time I say 'umph' (sniffling), Epps he say 'umph.'" He likewise was victor in the contest that ensued under the master's eye.

The eldest son, Kemp Plummer Alston, while a student at the University gave us a glimpse into the code of morals among the boys of that day. Fred Hill was had before the faculty for what was considered a dismissable offense, going to Pittsborough without permission. This town, by the bye, had very muddy streets, and Fred, who always dressed in the pink of fashion, hired a negro to take him on his back to the ball. When charged with absenting himself from town without permission, Kemp Plummer Alston testified falsely in Fred's favor. When charged with the falsehood, he pleaded that he thought it was his duty to tell an untruth to save a friend. When we recall that in his time the discipline was such as to make the relations between faculty and students much like a state of war, in which deception of the enemy is a virtue, Plummer's position was not as absurd as appears to us at the present day.

Kemp Plummer Alston had the humor of his grandfather. He had a family of three sons and one daughter. A neighbor who had several females and no male inquired, "Plummer, how many children have you?" "Oh, I have three children and a girl!"

My mother's youngest sister, Susan, was captured by a bright young man from St. Louis named Louis Cabanné, then a civil engineer engaged in the preliminary survey of the Raleigh and Gaston Railroad. Bishop Ravenscroft was to perform the ceremony. A day or two before this event Susan was rattling on with her bridesmaids, and declared that she would not promise to obey. This reached the ears of the bishop. When he pronounced the promise enjoined by the Prayer Book for the bride, and reached the words "to love, cherish," he lowered his book, paused, looked sternly into the face of the bride and in almost terrifying tones said, "AND TO OBEY." The promise was promptly given. Indeed my aunt was not in earnest when she avowed her intention to claim equality in the matrimonial relation. It was notably contrary to her real character. She had only one child, a boy named Shepard. He became a fine-looking man of courtly manners but was careless in business. Inheriting a large landed estate within and adjoining the city of St. Louis, he recklessly covered it with mortgages and, hard times coming on, he eventually lost it all, or nearly all.

5. School Days at Louisburg, Raleigh, and Chapel Hill

I WAS SENT TO SCHOOL AT SEVEN YEARS OF AGE—to get me out of mischief, my grandmother said, because I had played with and scattered some wheat which had been spread out to dry. On the west side of the road from Louisburg to Warrenton was the classical school, where boys could be prepared for the University. The principal was John B. Bobbitt, a graduate of the University in 1809. On the east side in the midst of a fine cedar grove was the school for girls and younger boys, presided over by his wife, a tall, spectacled lady whose parents were from New England. They had no children but Mrs. Bobbitt supplied the vacancy with two fice dogs which trotted always ahead of her and waited contentedly when she rested.

I spent a tolerably happy year under Mrs. Bobbitt's care. The only teaching was hearing lessons, and a moderate memory could ensure accurate answers. There was no instance of severity according to my recollection. The only troubles I had came from the older pupils teasing me because I was foolishly sensitive and verdant and because I was the smallest boy in school. For example, I was playing knucks with a boy several years older. I thought I won the game and had the right to shoot his knucks. He declared the contrary and being stronger than I held my arm and inflicted the penalty by force. I felt no pain but, strongly realizing the injustice, shed tears. Of course I was ridiculed for want of manliness. I defended myself by saying, "I'm not crying because he hurt my knucks but because he hurt my feelings." The bystanders could not understand that I was moved by a sense of injustice, of oppression by the strong hand. The story went over the town and almost everyone I met asked, "Kemp, how are your feelings now?" My life was made miserable and I welcomed the removal of our home to Raleigh because I got rid of this ridicule. People do not realize how much sensitive children suffer from such teasing. It may, however, tend to toughen them so as to be able to meet the rough wrestlings of life.

Another way of hazing the little boys was to provoke them to engage in friendly or unfriendly boxing or wrestling. I remember an absurd contest of this sort. Tom Fuller, a boy of about my age but twenty pounds heavier, entered the school. The big boys decreed that we must "rastle." He excelled in weight, I in agility. For many minutes he would throw me down by his weight and I would turn him over and get on his back. His strength enabled him to rise and then the throwing and turning would be repeated. At last I straddled his prostrate form and beat him on the neck with my fists. The crowd was pleased by this unexpected change and declared that I had gained the victory. About forty years after this I tried to revive the memory of my antagonist, then a distinguished lawyer and judge, but he was looking forward to greater honors and was not inclined to admit that he was a contemporary of the President of the University. He turned me off with the answer of D. E. Young to a question about the date of his birth, "I am not seeking people to tell my age to, this morning."

Although I was a lawyer twenty-two years, I never witnessed a trial which impressed me more than one which took place at the Bobbitt school. One of the older boys had a four-bladed knife, the only fine one among us. A classmate whom I will call Benjamin, though that was not his name, borrowed the knife and returned it with a broken blade, denying that he broke it. Jane Strother, a member of an upper class on the verge of womanhood, red-haired and self-confident, stepped out and said, "I can tell whether Benjamin broke it or not. Give me the knife. Benjamin, look me in the eyes!" Then holding the knife before him, she gave a stern gaze into his eyes and said, "Benjamin! tell the truth now. Did you not break that blade?" Down went his glance in confusion and the judge decided him guilty. There was no denial. As his means were limited, he was not made to replace the knife. We had not read Shakespeare but we felt in our hearts, "O righteous judge!"

One day the teacher announced to us that the trustees who employed the teachers were coming to make an inspection. To my amazement Mrs. Bobbitt told each pupil the answers to the questions she would ask. The examinations were therefore eminently satisfactory. I can point out in Webster's Spelling Book the one word whose spelling fell to my lot. I saw plainly the dishonesty of this, but it was not for me to expose the teacher. A story is told in more modern times on this subject. The boy who was at the head of his Sunday School class, instructed to answer the question, "Who made you?" was taken with internal trouble and left the room. Then No. 2 was asked, "Who made you?" His reply was, "Dust of the Earth." "Oh no, God made you." "No, ma'am, the little fellow God made caught the bellyache and went home." This anecdote confirms the suspicion that in old times the hood-winking of visitors was not uncommon. Do we not even now hear at closing exercises boys and girls make so-called original speeches evidently beyond their powers?

Mrs. Bobbitt after the death of her husband moved to Raleigh, then my home. I thought that she would like to talk of the old Louisburg times, fifteen years back. At the door was a duplicate of one of his fice dogs. She came out stiff and angular, with freezing spectacles. She was frigid as an icicle, asked no questions about my parents or other acquaintances. I said goodbye and left. Afterwards on account of old memories and in pity for my first teacher I paid twenty-five dollars for some useless books of her husband but never saw her again.

Here I wish to controvert assertions frequently made that the old-time teachers were commonly cruel. My experience is that they were just in treatment of pupils and inflicted punishment only when deserved. I had eight teachers from 1838 to 1845 when I entered the University. They were Mrs. Harriet Bobbitt, John A. Backhouse, Edwin Geer, Silas Bigelow, John Y. Hicks, Jefferson M. Lovejoy, R. Don Wilson, and Ashbel G. Brown. I think that the only punishment Mrs. Bobbitt employed was keeping in after school hours until the missed lesson was made up. At his school in Raleigh Mr. Backhouse was said to be severe, but to me he appeared to be just. For example, while the boys were going home by an unfrequented path they espied the deserted cabin of a colored man who had the reputation of being a spy on their conduct. Throwing their bags and books on the ground, they tried to pull down the cabin but failed, only tearing off some boards. I did not participate; I was only eight years old and small. Mr. Backhouse discovered the perpetrators and taking them upstairs in the rockhouse at St. Mary's whipped them well, one by one. I was below weeping over the beating which I expected. When the last blow fell he came down and said, "Kemp, I will not whip you as you did nothing but stay by the bags, but you must remember that the man who stands by the bags is as guilty as those who commit the crime."

Backhouse stood high at the University, was then studying for the ministry in the Episcopal Church. He was ordained but got into trouble and soon died. Such was the fate of a man of great natural gifts. His punishment of the boys above described and his strictness in requiring accurate recitations got him the reputation of undue severity which I think is undeserved.

Edwin Geer taught in Backhouse's school in the afternoon. He was likewise a candidate for the ministry. He was one of the best and kindest of men, and no one ever accused him of severity. He was over six feet high and large and strong in proportion, which may be the reason why the boys stood in awe of him. Here is an example of his kind manner. As a writing lesson he told me to copy the line, "Remember thy Creator," in capitals. I carried him my work in triumph. It read, "REMEMMEMBER." He arched up his brows and said, "It scares me. Try again." He also showed himself a good trader. The school-house had not been swept for weeks. He said, "Boys, if you will sweep out the school, you may have holiday the rest of the evening." We accepted the offer with alacrity. We rushed to the woods for bundles of twigs. Soon the dust was stifling, so thick as almost to hide the workers from view. We paid a heavy price for an hour or two of holiday. Mr. Geer became a popular Episcopal minister at Washington, North Carolina, and Norfolk, Virginia.

It was at Backhouse's school that I had my first experience of the artfulness of man. On account of the distance from home and the short intermission for dinner Mother put up dinner for my brother Joel and me in a bucket and we took it with us. The dessert one day was a small bottle of molasses with a saucer for one half and the bucket top for the other. As my brother was four years my elder, I cheerfully consented that he should put on style and take the saucer. Jack Guion, one of the oldest boys, preparing for the University, said to me in a persuasive tone, "Kemp, won't you give me one sop?" I felt proud to share with so prominent a student and eagerly gave permission. He produced a large slice of loaf-bread and with his one sop absorbed all my supply.

My desk mate, Carson Murray, took a fancy to the little eight-year-old stranger. He would tease me some on his own account but protected me from others. One day I was being imposed on by a much older boy named Bryan, afterwards a judge of the Court of Appeals in Maryland, who like Guion was preparing for the University. Carson miscalculated his strength, attacked Bryan, and soon got the worst of it. It agonized me greatly. Bryan did not worry me as much afterwards, however.

On the whole, considering that it was my first school with men teachers, I should have been satisfied if Backhouse, of whom I was mortally afraid, had not adopted a new spelling book, Townes, in place of Webster. Instead of applying his intellect to the word he was to spell, the mind of the boy was divided. He had to give a definition of the word. These definitions were sometimes portentous to a boy. Actually this wiseacre had D-r-u-g-g-i-s-t—pharmacopolist. By the aid of Mother and Sister I recited well enough to escape censure, though I was often anxious.

We had in the school a half-witted boy who was not expected to learn anything but was sent to school to keep him out of mischief. In his journeys to and from the school-house he pushed before him the wheel of a wheelbarrow. One day he undertook to declaim a very easy piece, Bonner, the largest boy in the school, with open book before him, being prompter. He made a brave attempt, asking after every line, "What next, Bonner?" Finally he rested one foot in his hands and in that attitude was prompted through the piece. It was inexpressibly ludicrous.

The first vacation after we moved to Raleigh came at last in June, 1840, but the period was full of woe to me. My father caused to be torn down an old house on the lot he had purchased. There was a pile of shingles which had not been removed. Of course, regardless of rusty nails, the children walked up and ran down it. I was the only victim. A nail went nearly through my foot. It healed in time for me to enter school next session but I missed all the hunting, swimming, and fishing, and the baseball and bandy indulged in by my associates. I was especially mortified because, as soon as I entered school again, the big boys arranged a race between me and another boy larger than I was. I protested that my foot and muscles were not in good racing condition. They would take no excuse and I was beaten by four or five feet. Happily, Henry Giles, my antagonist, was a good fellow and did not crow over me.

The teacher of my school for eighteen months in the Academy on Burke Square, now the Governor's Mansion lot, was Silas Bigelow of Danville, Virginia. He had been unfortunate in business but was a man of good talent and kindly heart and, so far as a boy could judge, sufficiently learned to prepare boys for college. I recall only one whipping of a student and there was no doubt of the punishment being deserved. I was surprised that the boy, really of stronger body than the teacher, stood the licking without a murmur, and then darted out of the back door. His father refused to make him return and it was not surprising that after a while he

MRS. KEMP PLUMMER BATTLE
From a daguerreotype taken about 1865

KEMP PLUMMER BATTLE
From a daguerreotype taken about 1865

was living in the country with a woman without marriage. Very strangely he was faithful to her. Eventually the County Solicitor threatened the twain with prosecution under the Fornication and Adultery Law and for fear of that they were married.

There was a similar case in Pennsylvania. A judge who was a friend to both parties came to spend the night. After supper, when they were having a social chat, the judge said, "You ought to get married. Your example is hurting you and hurts the neighborhood." "Well," said the man, "we do not think it necessary. There was no ceremony between Adam and Eve." "Well," said the judge, "don't you regard this woman as your wife?" "Certainly I do." Then to the woman, "Don't you regard this man as your husband?" "Certainly I do." Then the judge arose in his dignity and said, "By virtue of the powers vested in me by the Legislature of Pennsylvania, I pronounce you man and wife. You are married." It is said that this vagary about marriage had its origin in opposition to certain Colonial laws requiring that the ceremony should be performed by a priest of the Established Church.

My teasing by larger boys continued, probably because I was the most diminutive in stature although not in proficiency. My mother's counsel and aid out of school-hours kept me ahead of boys of my age. It was strange that those who treated me roughly were friendly to me. I remember how Clinton Thompson seemed to like me but sometimes gave me pain by pulling my hair. Once the pain was so acute that I lost my temper and bit his finger. He threatened to whip me but my big brother stepped up and prevented the attack. It is singular that this act of self-defence on my part caused a general better treatment of the little lad.

Let me tell of another case that throws light on the unhappiness of sensitive little boys. Two of the school-boys, Tom and Henry Cobb, were about to emigrate to Alabama. One had a desk in the school-house and Bryan, the boy about to enter the University, pretended to sell it at auction. I entered into the joke and it was knocked off to me at seventy-five cents. After that, whenever Bryan met me he dunned me for the money. Although I knew that Bryan had no right to sell the desk, his constant persecution made me unhappy. The possibility of my incurring a debt without permission from my parents was appalling and he was apparently so much in earnest that I feared I had incurred a legal obligation. The last time I saw him before he left for Chapel Hill, he shouted, "Kemp, have you got that seventy-five cents ready?" We became good friends afterwards and I associate him with one of the pleasantest incidents in my memory. As I was on my way to the chapel when I was a freshman in the University, he shouted an invitation to help eat a watermelon. Of course I accepted with enthusiasm.

It was in the Raleigh Academy before my time that Leonidas Polk, later bishop and general, met his first defeat. He was one of the big boys about to graduate from the school. The teacher was a Presbyterian clergyman, Dr. William McPheeters, an excellent man but stern and impartial in enforcing his laws. Leonidas was full of life and fond of adventure. The Polk mansion was a short distance from the school-house. He said, "Boys, I'm going to show you some fun. I have put up the back fence so high that the old doctor can't jump it. I can. I've tried it. I am going to make him mad and when he runs for me, I will clear the fence and leave him on the other side. I will not return, as I am going to Chapel Hill in a day or two. Father (Col. William Polk) is in Tennessee and there is no one to send me back to school." Beautifully planned, but see the result. He had underrated the agility of Dr. McPheeters, who cleared the fence at a single leap and gave him a good trouncing. Years afterwards, when he returned to Raleigh on a visit, he thanked the good doctor for this trouncing and said that it was a most valuable lesson to him. He did not turn his attention to religion until about the middle of his course at West Point.

Another ludicrous incident will illustrate school manners. Several years before my day a boy named Philemon Haywood yearned for a fishing holiday and took it without permission. To avoid punishment he must carry to the teacher a written excuse. He had a sister named Sally, who was head of the household. In his desperation he forged a certificate thus, "Philemon are contained at home by disposition. Sally Haywood." Dr. McPheeters said severely, "Your sister did not write this." Much scared, Phil blurted out, "Sister Sally never could write good no how." History veils her face over the tragedy of the next few minutes. Philemon became a useful and honorable man.

My next teacher was John Y. Hicks, an able, dignified, reserved man but a good scholar and of large experience. He was strict but just. Indeed the force of his manners prevented breaches of discipline. He had as assistant a younger brother William who was very popular. We all grieved when after the five months' term they settled beyond the Blue Ridge on land bought by the State from the Cherokee Indians and resold on easy terms. The elder Hicks was a member of the General Assembly, 1846-1848. The younger became a preacher.

Then came a man of formidable reputation for severity, Jefferson Madison Lovejoy. He was an uncommonly good teacher according to the methods of that time, which meant hearing lessons out of a book with corrections of wrong answers. I studied under him Virgil's *Aeneid* and Mitchell's *Ancient Geography* and he seemed thoroughly familiar with them. He was dreaded for his severity, but I thought his punishment, striking with a short stick in the palm of the hand, in extreme cases on the back thereof, was deserved. Most of my class avoided every duty possible. For example, one of the required exercises was writing off a translation in our own language of seventy-five lines of the *Aeneid*. I always performed this duty. The translations were read aloud in class. It occurred to my class-mates to cheat by slipping my paper from one to another. Of course the artifice was discovered. The teacher suddenly stopped the last reader and called on me to read. It was necessary to pass my paper to me. The punishment of the delinquents was severe. Because of the attempted fraud the blows were on the back of the hand and given with unusual force. To my surprise he did not blame me for lending my paper.

I had the inglorious opportunity of ascertaining the painfulness of this blow by personal experience. We were reciting Mitchell's *Ancient Geography*. The lesson contained a long string of names of no interest or importance, the memorizing of which ought not to have been required. I missed one of these but my class-mates hardly answered correctly at all. Mr. Lovejoy was angry. He said, "I'm going to give a lick for every word missed. James, how many?" And so on. The answers were honestly given. When he got to me I answered "One" and held out my hand. He hesitated a moment. He saw I did not deserve it but felt bound to keep his promise. As I went to my seat I heard in exultant tone, "The favorite is licked. The favorite is licked!" All this sounds egotistical but really I am entitled to no credit. I prepared my lessons first because I had a nervous fear of the disgrace and pain of punishment and, second, because of the fear of the disapprobation of my superiors. Moreover, my mother coached me. My ambition to excel for my own sake came later.

The passion for hazing is an inborn propensity of man and beast. We see lions, tigers, dogs, cats playing with weaker animals before devouring them. We see dignified men sporting with the new members of fraternities, unions, guilds, etc. It is especially strong in children, both boys and girls. One form of it when I was at school was, when we went in swimming, to tie our clothes into hard knots so as to make dressing difficult. Another was to throw mud at one another. At school a big fat boy would sit on me, nearly to suffocation, until I would say I was humble. It was only when in despair that I could be induced to admit my humility. Tripping up a boy, especially in a muddy place, was fine fun. An excruciatingly ludicrous form of hazing was "running for a knife." The greenhorn whom it was plotted to fool was shown a very good knife and advised that a number of boys would run for it as the prize of the winner. The knife was pretended to be buried in the sight of all. A quantity of slimy mud or other offensive matter had already been concealed at the place selected. By easy sleight of hand the knife was slipped into the pocket of the master of ceremonies. Then the race would be called, all knowing the state of things except the greenhorn. They would allow him to come in ahead and the fun consisted in his intense disappointment and shame at being made a laughing-stock.

While hazing is natural, it is undoubtedly contrary to good morals. Its enjoyment depends on the annoyance if not suffering of its victim. It is a direct violation of the Golden Rule and its eradication is essential to the progress of civilization and refinement. It is a direct violation also of gentlemanly courtesy. The habit of caring for the rights of others should be cultivated and is totally inconsistent with boisterous and unfeeling conduct towards another. The hazer is really more injured than the hazee. Some contend that there is benefit in hazing to the hazee. Where he is tricked, he will become wary; where the work is rough, he becomes more enduring. But surely better ways can be found to secure these results than those which brutalize the perpetrator and accustom him to be a law-breaker in secret. The element of danger, even loss of life, enters also into the question. Independently of mere accidents, the general possession of modern weapons and the ease with which they can be used with deadly effect prompt bold and reckless temperaments to desperate resistance. There are such instances in the history of all institutions.

After our removal to Chapel Hill, for one term our teacher was Richard Don Wilson, who needed money in order to study law. He was a plain, unconventional man of real ability. As he had only seven pupils, there were no incidents worthy of commemoration.

School Days

He became a soldier in the war. Afterwards, embittered by want of success, he took his own life.

For the year and a half prior to my entry into the University in June, 1845, I was under a recent graduate, Ashbel Green Brown, one of the best of teachers. He was strict but just and had a strong mind, but was inclined to a melancholy which developed after eight or ten years into occasional fits of high temper amounting to insanity. His teaching was of the old style, i.e., hearing lessons, reading the classics, parsing the sentences, and giving the declensions and conjugations. He was the only teacher who practised me in translating English into Latin, but when he became a tutor in the University he did not continue the practise. It would have been too laborious to correct the bad Latin of forty or fifty students.

While Mr. Brown was a stern, strict man, he was impartial and just. He once punished severely a very unruly boy named Jim, the only son of a widowed mother. The punishment was by stripes on the legs, which were covered only by linen or cotton pantaloons. As soon as the whipping was over, Jim darted for home. Soon he returned led by his mother, the angriest woman I ever saw. She was large and strong, weighing probably two hundred pounds. We watched the encounter with thrilling interest. But there was no back out in Mr. Brown. She upbraided him for his cruelty and made Jim pull up his pants and show his injuries. Sure enough his legs had numerous black and blue bands across them which had an ugly look. Mr. Brown quietly said, "Madam, I never whipped any one before, and I did not understand the effects. I punished more severely than I intended and I am sorry for it." Awed by his self-possession and quieted by his apology she took Jim off and never sent him back. After a wild life he became a captain in the Civil War and his body, yellow from the disease which carried him off, was brought from Wilmington for interment in the Chapel Hill cemetery.

The schools of the State must have been on an average about the same as those I attended. I repeat what I have already said in substance. If there were Dotheboys Halls, or other academies presided over by Squeerses or other similar ruffians, I never heard of them. In the nature of things they could not have flourished. Parents and older brothers would have avenged a boy's wrongs. I am glad to give my testimony in behalf of a much maligned profession.

Some stories told me by my father about the schools he attended may be interesting. His first was what was called an Old Field

School. It was on a gentle hill from which the pines had been cut. To keep out hogs and cattle, then allowed to run at large, a rail fence enclosed about an acre around the log school-house. My father and his brother Richard were continual playmates and Richard claimed the privilege of going with him to school and waiting outside until school-hours expired and they could go home together. He began to hunt up and down the fence to see what of interest he could find. Soon he came across a brown lizard and in his excitement loudly shouted, "Here's a lizard!" Father forgot where he was and darted out of the room, giving the answering shout, "Where?" The teacher ran in pursuit and haled him back to his spelling lesson. The incident was fun equal to a circus.

At another school the teacher ended his morning duties by spelling the school, that is, placing the children in a line and giving out a word to each to spell. If a word was missed, it was passed on to the next and so on, he who spelt accurately going above the delinquent. Father seldom missed. Once, after spelling his word, he asked for leave to go to the pail for water. Leave was granted and having had his drink he hurried rapidly to his place. The teacher remarked, "You are in a terrible hurry." Father thought a new word was given him, so he shouted, "t-e-r-r-i-b-l-e, terrible." The children were almost bursting with amusement but were afraid to laugh because it was a rule of the school that there should be no laughter until permission was given. So when the class was ended, the teacher gave the order, "Now you may laugh!" and the pent-up cachinnation shook the walls.

6. Phases of My Life as a Boy in Raleigh

MY FATHER WAS A WARM HENRY CLAY MAN. He attended the convention at Harrisburg which nominated Harrison and returned politically heartbroken, though he always voted the Whig ticket. His regrets however were not shared by his children. I strutted about proudly with a motto on my cap, "Tippecanoe and Tyler Too." In a vacant lot on Fayetteville Street was erected a log cabin in which was kept for a while a barrel of cider. To show my loyalty to my party I quaffed a gourd full. Although labelled "Hard Cider" it was of the sweet variety. Doubtless this was a prelude to the Grand Celebration. Before describing this I must tell of the fight between Dr. William G. Hill and the candidate for the House of Commons on the Democratic ticket, D. B. Massey. Massey in his speech ridiculed the Whigs for building this log cabin, "A piece of low-down demagoguery, gentlemen! Built by the rich aristocrats of Raleigh." Dr. Hill, an ardent Whig, interrupted, "Mr. Massey, you are mistaken. I helped build the cabin and know that aristocrats had nothing to do with it." But Massey was insistent, "I repeat it, fellow citizens. Built by rich aristocrats to fool the people." Hill struck him and they clinched. Down they went in hostile embrace, both powerful men. John Manly, one of the strongest men in the county, a warm friend of Hill and a Whig, surveyed the struggle. He noticed that Hill had seized a handful of Massey's hair. He shouted, "Part these men," and jerked Hill away with all his might while Massey was pulled off by a Democratic friend. The result was as Manly foresaw. A huge bunch of Massey's hair remained in Hill's grasp. This lock was hung up in the log cabin and labelled "Massey's scalp."

The Whigs made a gallant fight for the county but in vain, the Democracy of Wake having as compact ranks as in any county in the State. It shows the mutability of earthly things that twenty years afterwards the little eight-year-old boy who wore "Tippecanoe and Tyler Too" on his cap-brim should be one of the candidates to break the solid phalanx of the Wake Democracy.

A state mass-meeting of the Whigs was held in 1840 at Raleigh. I never witnessed such enthusiasm. Many counties were represented not only by leading citizens but by agricultural and other products. For example, New Hanover and Craven had real schooners with sails, masts, and cordage, manned by boys dressed like sailors, hanging in the rigging. Franklin County had a real log cabin, with a man painted and dressed like an Indian and brandishing a tomahawk seated on top. I was much impressed with the Stanly County exhibit. It seems that a Democratic editor named Chapman once had false news of a Democratic victory and presented in his newspaper sundry cocks splitting their throats with triumphant crows. Then came the news that the Whigs were victorious. The derisive phrase, "Crow, Chapman, crow!" passed through the land. An expert chicken-fancier trained a handsome black rooster to crow when he was patted on the back and the exhortation to editor Chapman repeated. This is not an exaggerated tradition. I myself walked a mile to the Stanly camp and repeatedly coaxed a lusty response from the well-trained fowl.

When I remember the slowness of travelling before the advent of railroads and steamboats, the bad roads, the want of bridges, the tardy pace of horses and mules, when a man living two hundred miles from his journey's end counted on a week's absence from home, leaving out of the question the sickness of horses, breaking of vehicles, and other accidents, I am amazed at the number of those attending notable celebrations. The crowds that swarmed on the streets of Raleigh during the Log Cabin and Hard Cider gathering were really phenomenal.

There was a celebration the same year of a different character. The news that the first locomotive engine was about to enter Raleigh drew all the population from the country for many miles around. Her name was "Tornado," locomotives being regarded as feminine. Her sisters were "Tempest," "Volcano," "Whirlwind," "Spitfire." The railroad irons were flat strips, three-fourths of an inch in thickness, spiked on wooden stringers. The locomotive had no spark arrester, and as dry pine was burnt in the furnace, the sparks, although beautiful at night, kindled fires among the dry leaves near the road bed and often burnt holes in the clothes of passengers. On my first trip on a train I had a hole burnt in the sleeve of my jacket and in the skin below it. But all defects were overlooked in the unbounded joy at the novelty. People felt that it was the beginning of great things. A journey in coaches rolling smoothly through hills and high over deep ravines seemed like magic. Although the beginnings were rude and inefficient, people were right in their prophetic boastings.

There was boundless enthusiasm as "Tornado" puffed in. Many felt like the old lady in Goldsborough who said on her first sight of a locomotive, "Verily the power of God is great but the ingenuity of man is greater."

Defects of construction and management led to the ruin of the railroad as first projected. The stringers, on which the strap-iron was laid, decayed in sappy places and of course the superimposed rails were broken. Fragments called "snake-heads" sometimes burst through the car. Rev. Dr. Thomas E. Skinner told me that one day, when he and a lady were sitting together, a snake-head shot up between them and pinned a part of her dress to the roof of the car. Transportation became difficult and irregular. The chief management fell into the hands of non-experts. One president showed the state of his knowledge by saying, "So many of the roadmasters are calling on me for spikes that I am going to Petersburg and buy a whole keg full."

A Virginia fox-hunter was said to have been so much amazed at the wild jumps of the locomotive that he offered to purchase it for a fox-chase. A story of an elderly man, limping along in the same direction as the locomotive, being offered a ride and declining, "No, I thank you. I am in a hurry today," was often told and thought not incredible. I myself in 1850 at 6 o'clock A.M. took the train drawn by the "Volcano." Approaching Franklinton, twenty miles from Raleigh, we assisted in hauling the "Whirlwind" to that town. At Henderson, ten miles further, we passed the "Tempest" lying in the ditch. Ten miles further our locomotive left the track and a long delay ensued, so that we missed connection at Gaston at 4 P.M. and had to spend nearly twenty-four hours at a hotel on the hot river bank. We had ten hours to cover only eighty-six miles and failed.

But no fears of failure were heard at the first railroad gathering in Raleigh. Read two of the toasts given at the banquet in honor of the completion of the road. By Governor Edward B. Dudley, the president of the banquet:

The Raleigh and Gaston Railroad

Its structure will accelerate with the velocity of a Tornado the train of public opinion in its favor.

By Weston Raleigh Gales, editor of the *Raleigh Register*, who was toast-master:

The City of Raleigh

It has exceeded in gallantry even its renowned namesake, Sir Walter. He but laid down his cloak for one lady to walk over. Its citizens have helped to lay down eighty-six miles of railroad for the whole sex to ride over.

One of the most regrettable things in my memory at this period was the exactions of Sunday school and church service. Until he was near forty years old my father connected himself with no church. His parents were Baptists but he showed no preference for that denomination. My mother's forebears were Episcopalian, Church of England people in Colonial days. Although her sympathies were with them, she did not present herself for confirmation until her husband had made up his mind to go with her.

She had very strong views of sincerity and keeping promises and she therefore required her children to obey the mandates of the rector. The Sunday school was very tiresome, keeping the children together in the church from nine o'clock A.M. until a quarter of eleven. During this time we recited a lesson from Hobart's Catechism, third volume. The rest of the time we sat quiet and miserable. The Catechism answered most of the questions in biblical language, giving references to chapter and verse. The teacher had no better sense than to require us to answer not only in the exact words of the Bible but to give the references. This was not only a hard burden on the memory but useless and tiresome. What made it worse for us was the fact that Mother was so conscientious that we had to memorize the lesson before going to our fishing or hunting or play Saturday morning.

After a quarter of an hour's interval we attended church service. Rev. Dr. Richard S. Mason, our rector, was a good and learned man but his mode of reading and speaking was monotonous and uninteresting, especially to children. For over an hour and a half the luckless urchins sat in the gallery of the old church, their only diversion being to watch the girls in the congregation in hope of a sly glance upwards. The sermons were what was common in that day in the Episcopal Church, orthodox essays written with the approbation of the writer but not fitted to arouse the attention of the hearer. After dinner we were forced to undergo another hour and a half of affliction and then we could enjoy recreation until supper.

What was this recreation? Our mother had the tenderest love

for her children and great capacity to enter into their feelings but also a most acute sense of duty to church and society. How was she to reconcile the happiness of her children and her duties under the Fourth Commandment? She made a compromise. She allowed them to shoot at marbles, to pitch and catch a ball, but on no account have another to share in the fun. Nothing like a game could be played. And so we could walk along the streams and in the forests provided we had no companions, that is, we could make up no walking party. Her rules in other matters were analogous to these. I never saw one disobeyed. We understood her distinction and such was our love for her and respect for her wisdom that we were silent if not convinced.

Even with these relaxations my recollections of Sundays in my boyhood are gloomy. When my wife and I had children, we allowed them to leave the church before the sermon began and dispensed with their attendance in the afternoons. And the walks we took together were a pleasure to me as to them. I am glad to say that the practise of requiring not only the answers to questions to be memorized but the chapter and verse sustaining such answers has been abandoned in recent years. The Morning Service too has been considerably shortened. In my day Morning Prayer, the Litany, the Epistle and Gospel and the Ten Commandments, even when the Communion was not administered, were invariably recited and the sermon was at least thirty or forty minutes long. As a result of the irksomeness of Sunday school and church service, they became so distasteful to me that for years I found no pleasure in them. My body was punctually in attendance but my mind was somewhere else and the final Amen was a joyful sound.

The church had the usual reading desk and elevated pulpit. At the former the rector officiated in his surplice until the time for the sermon. He then retired into the vestryroom, donned a black gown and entered the pulpit. A cousin of mine, when a small boy, gave a ludicrous description of the change. "The preacher talked a long time with nothing on but his shirt. Then he went up into the sulky [pulpit] with a black shirt on and talked a long time again."

7. My Brothers and Sisters

I NOW PROCEED TO DESCRIBE MY BROTHERS AND sisters. Julian, the oldest, died in infancy. Then came Joel Dossey, named after his grandfather and uncle. My uncle was named Dossey after a Baptist preacher honored in the eastern part of the State. Although not notably talented, my brother Joel had a strong influence over others. When he began the study of Latin, the village boys would swing on the limbs of a tall cedar near our premises and shout in a monotone, "Jo-él! Jo-él! Hic hoc!" in celebration of his advancement. He was endowed with great physical strength in proportion to his size. The great distance to which he knocked a ball in a game of baseball was known as Joel Battle's Knock long after he left the Raleigh Academy. He graduated with distinction at the University in 1847 in the famous class of Generals Pettigrew and Ransom and then entered on the study of medicine under our uncle, Henry L. Plummer. He then obtained his diploma at the University of Pennsylvania. He had fair prospects of success until he was seized with a combined attack of dysentery and rheumatism which left him with an impaired constitution. Born March 12, 1827 at the old home near Louisburg, he died November 22, 1858, leaving a childless widow, who afterwards married William H. Crow.

The next child was Susan Catharine. She had an extraordinary mind, uncommon tact, and pleasing ways. She was not beautiful but she had a perfect, petite figure. She was fond of poetry and was able to quote appositely on almost any subject. She never married, although she had many eligible suitors. She said that it was not right for her to impose her shattered constitution on any man. She said she was afraid of nothing in the world except an angry man and this fearlessness was the cause of her bodily affliction. When she was fifteen years old one of her beaux came by on a horse disposed to be wild. She asked for a ride and he heedlessly allowed her to mount on a man's saddle. The horse ran away and making a sudden swerve threw her violently to the ground, her head striking a stone. For the rest of her life she was a nervous invalid, sometimes for many days in extreme pain from neuralgia, sometimes almost frantic from nervousness, but usually able to perform domestic duties and take part in the entertainment of company, and to sing sweetly in the church choir. She was a favorite with all classes, but had especial powers of being agreeable to the students of the University. Her kindness of heart and unexcelled tact led her to encourage the bashful and those neglected by other ladies. Once she was entertaining a rather awkward youth with such success that others came up to enjoy the fun. He looked around the smiling faces and remarked, "Miss Sue, we have increast-ed our family." Another from a distant State, after a painful silence said, "Miss Sue, don't you want to buy a puppy?" She replied, "No, sir. Why do you ask?" "Oh, I just meant to make talk."

My sister and I were intimate friends. When separated we constantly exchanged letters. But when my wife was elevated in my heart above her, she was never jealous. Her notions of right conduct were so stedfast and accurate that she was always a wise counsellor. In my memory she lives as one of the noblest of God's creatures. Without being pedantic she had a quiet way very remarkable of turning her associates from evil thoughts and ways. Colonel Robert Bingham, a close observer of the faults and virtues of others, in a two-column tribute in the State Presbyterian journal after her death bore strong testimony to her good influence.

Her kindness of heart overflowed to all creatures, however unprepossessing. I remember once in a hotel, when a showman brought in a dwarf whom he was exhibiting for money, she made friends with the manikin, inviting him to the fire and endeavoring to make him feel at home. Her efforts were not appreciated by the showman, who sought to keep the poor little man unobserved until the exhibition began. She was born February 14, 1830 and died September 20, 1867. She always positively declined to have her picture taken, so that she lives only in the memories of a few octogenarians.

Now begin the December births in our family: Kemp Plummer, December 19, 1831; William Horn, December 14, 1833; and Richard Henry, December 3, 1835. These outlived all the others.

William Horn was named after my father. There is a Welsh strain in our blood, my paternal grandmother's mother being Dorcas, daughter of John Williams of Pitt County, whose father came from Wales. As the Irish and Welsh are of the same blood, it is not surprising that William in his thick-set person and his words and ways should have showed some Irish characteristics. He had greater fondness for sport and less for books than his brothers, he had greater self-confidence and was more amusing, he was perhaps more generally popular. I give some of his sayings which made people laugh in the old days.

When Bishop Ives made his visitation to Louisburg, he was entertained at my father's. He was most distinguished looking and on this account and on account of the grand dignity of his office the children generally were afraid to enter his presence. Not so William. Rushing into the parlor from the kitchen, smutty from baking a piece of dough on the coals, he jumped on the great man's knees and shouted, "How do you do, Uncle Bushup?" The bishop was greatly amused.

Once he was lucky enough to catch a sparrow in a trap. He ran to the house swinging the bird triumphantly and shouting, "Oh, Mother, Mother, I sot a trap, and cotched a bird and fotched him to the house!"

He was boon companion with his younger brother, Dick. He said once in triumph, "Dick, I've written a novel: let me read it to you." "Go ahead!" said Dick. Here is his novel. "Frenchman, Frenchman, why art thou so tender, melancholy, and sad? Is thy wife, thy dead Maria, dead?" "Go on," said Dick. "That's all, that is the end of it." There are many novels which ought to be as short as William's was.

When a little boy he saw Uncle Kemp coming up the lane and hastened to meet him, all excited at the news he could tell. "Uncle Kemp, Mother's sick! Uncle Kemp, Mother's got a baby! Uncle Kemp, *every* time Mother gets sick, she has a baby!" This was almost true. Mother's health for a long while was unusually good.

Someone gave me when in Louisburg a kitten which grew into a stalwart mouser and was very beautiful. "Kemp's cat" was known among all our near neighbors. When we removed to Raleigh, the instinctive love of felines for localities rather than persons was respected and she did not accompany us. One day Uncle Lum took William on his knee. "What are you studying, Button?" "Geography, sir!" "Can you tell me where Kamchatka is?" "Yes, sir, left her in Louisburg to catch rats" (Kemp's cat).

There was an excellent school in Raleigh of which Mrs. Eliza D. Taylor, widow of Solicitor General James Fauntleroy Taylor, was principal. William was placed under her charge and was asked on his return home how he liked the school. His reply was, "I would have liked it fine, but there was an old woman there hollering 'Silas' [silence] all the time." He distinguished himself as a declaimer. The speech was:

> One honest John Tompkins, a hedger and ditcher,
> Altho' he was poor, didn't want to be richer.

And so on. Reciting the words with a kind of musical tone, he accompanied them with a rhythmical motion of his right arm as regular as the motion of a crank. About the middle of the poem the author brought in as emblematic of Tompkins' industry the bees flying round and round among the flowers. Here William rapidly revolved his arm in imitation of a circular saw. It was very comical.

Mrs. Taylor had in her backyard a wild Canadian goose. William was attacked by him, thrown to the ground, and beaten by his wings. His bruises were only slight but he was mercilessly ridiculed for being whipped by a goose.

His oddities followed him until he entered on the serious business of life. He paid an attractive young lady some attention and thought it incumbent on him to propose matrimony. When he returned from his expedition, I asked, "What luck?" "The worst in the world. She refused me. I expected that. But I disgraced myself by making such poor remarks. I thought up a beautiful speech but forgot every word of it. I made the poorest speech I ever made in my life. I have only one comfort. She did no better than I. She said merely, 'I don't love you.'" He was as gay as a lark in describing his adventure.

Shortly afterwards he followed a bright young lady to Tennessee. When he came back, I asked the usual question, "What luck this time?" He exultingly replied, "The best in the world." "You are engaged then?" "No, I didn't want her to have me. I didn't like the looks of things. But I felt bound to go through with it. And I made a glorious speech. I wish you had heard it. You would have been proud of your brother."

As he grew older, he settled down into an excellent physician and became a brigade surgeon in General Lee's army. After the war, though impeded by bodily infirmities, he continued his practise and the management of his farm until his death. He had many strange experiences in his practise. For example, he told me of being called to a woman of forty years who, angry because her father ordered her to prepare dinner for some threshing machine operatives, cut herself open with a razor. In the work of sewing together the severed parts he actually had her beating heart in his hand. It was impossible to save her. She refused to aid the surgeon.

William died in 1893. As he lay dying, his thoughts went back to his youthful days when he and Dick were inseparable companions, and his words were chiefly to him, committing the charge of his family mainly to him. Dick although two years younger had much influence over him. Once William, from association with a wild companion, thoughtlessly used the word damn. Dick ridiculed him mercilessly. "Oh yes, got to be a big man, imitating John Clements, dirty niggers, lousy white rascals, lowest-down scamps. Joined their society, trying to get first honor as a cusser!" He never offended again. Although never what is called a pious man, he abounded in kindness and generosity. He was not successful as a financier. But he was a noble man and we loved him dearly.

Richard Henry Battle my next brother, born December 3, 1835, was a boy of remarkable gifts. He had a very independent mind, formed his own opinions, and adhered to them with a tenacity which approached obstinacy. When he was three or four years old he considered himself aggrieved by something in the hands of his brother William. Seizing it, he threw it on the hearth whence it rolled near the fire. Our mother, who, though kindness personified, was firm as a rock in exacting obedience, told him to pick it up. Thinking himself in the right, he refused. She gave him a mild whipping but he again refused. Six more whippings, gradually increasing in severity, were necessary to make him yield. Seventy years afterwards I heard him laughingly say that he had always regretted that he gave up. I do not remember whether he was right or not but I do know from an intimate observation of seventy years that his views on all moral questions were eminently sound and that nothing could prevent his conduct from conforming to his views. I never knew him to do anything he thought wrong. While he was agreeable in conversation, he was a hard student and a thorough investigator, whether engaged in his tasks at the University or cases in law. His pluck and constancy were clearly shown in his freshman and sophomore years. During nearly all of these two years he was afflicted with chills every alternate day. Mother advised him to give up and take a rest. But he had set his head to win first honors in his class and to be read out at Commencement as perfect in punctuality. He succeeded in both these aspirations, an achievement all the more remarkable because he was forced to reach the chapel for morning prayers at sunrise over half a mile from our house and one of the three daily recitations was before breakfast.

After graduating with first distinction he was tutor in Greek for three years, and then practised law first at Wadesborough and then at Raleigh, reaching the eminence of the Father of the Bar.

ALLEN BATTLE

For many years, as slave and free man, overseer of Mrs. Kemp Plummer Battle's plantation "Walnut Creek" in Edgecombe County. Photograph taken about 1870.

EASTER SNIPES

Senlac cook for some thirty years. Photograph taken in 1917.

THE CHAPEL OF THE CROSS, CHAPEL HILL

From a photograph by Bayard Wootten, taken before the new church, with its connecting cloister, was built. Kemp Plummer Battle attended this church for many years.

He never went out of his way to obtain public office but was occasionally called out of his private life. He was elected to the General Assembly, was State Auditor, President of the State Agricultural Society, and Chairman of the State Democratic Committee. He was appointed Superior Court judge but declined the honor, as his income from his practise was much larger than the salary of a judge.

He was an active member of the Protestant Episcopal Church, a deputy to the General and Diocesan Conventions, Senior Warden and one of the founders of the Church of the Good Shepherd. He was active in all church and city charities, especially in the organization and support of Rex Hospital. He spent hours each week in talking to and encouraging the patients. For years he was Superintendent of the Sunday school of his church. He was an active trustee of the University, a member of its Executive Committee and Secretary and Treasurer of the Board. He was my successor as President of the Oakwood Cemetery Association. It was a joke between us that we were apt to be chosen to fill offices which gave work but no pay.

The next son of the family died in infancy. He was named Thomas Devereux from gratitude to Thomas Pollock Devereux, who associated my father with him as co-Reporter of the Supreme Court.

My sister Mary Johnston, named after my father's mother, was a sweet, amiable, bright woman, a great favorite with all her acquaintances. Her devotion to her husband during a protracted sickness was worthy of all praise. Her death was tragic in the extreme. She died in June, 1865, leaving a girl a day old. The child was called Mary Battle Van Wyck and was for several years under the charge of my mother. She was very bright and attractive. Many years later her father married again. When her step-mother died, she took charge of her half-brother and sister until they reached maturity. It is a proof of her lovable character that her step-mother left her a handsome legacy. Her care of these children is doubtless the reason that she never married, though a handsome and attractive woman.

My parents' next child was a son, born in Raleigh, Junius Cullen Battle. The Junius was in honor of my mother's brother, who got the name from Lucius Junius Brutus the tyrannicide, greatly admired in America and France at the time of the French Revolution. The middle name honored Dr. Cullen Battle, first cousin and friend of my grandfather Joel Battle. It came from our Sumner kin. Junius was a first honor graduate of the University, and was a teacher at Oxford when the war began. Being a stranger in the county he was elected to no higher office than corporal, though he had not only an unusual mentality but remarkable physical strength and activity. One of his ankles was shattered by a Minié ball at South Mountain and he was taken to a hospital at Middletown, Maryland. My wife was sick at the time so that I could not leave home and my brother Richard, Private Secretary to Governor Vance, volunteered to go and nurse our brother, while I looked after his work during his absence. The Richmond authorities gave him a permit to go by way of Norfolk, but there the Federals refused further passage. So we had many days of painful suspense.

At last news came to us in an unexpected way. One night about dark a Confederate officer came to my home in Raleigh. Said he, "I am a relative of yours, General Cullen Battle, of General Lee's army. I am taking to his home in Alabama a wounded officer, Captain Webb. Our train missed connection and the hotel is so crowded that we cannot procure a room. It occurred to me that possibly you could accommodate us." I was delighted to do so. During our conversation Captain Webb remarked, "When I was in the hospital at Middletown, Maryland, on the cot next mine was a young soldier named Battle. He was well cared for by some ladies of the town. He read the Bible to near-by soldiers and was so patient and agreeable that he was a general favorite. It was said that he was a son of a judge and I thought that was one reason why so much attention was given to him." Anxiously we inquired, "Is he living?" "No, he died about a week ago, peacefully and resignedly."

My youngest brother was named after Dr. John Wesley Lewis, husband of my father's sister Catharine. My mother insisted on names for her children which had no unpleasant associations. Wishing to compliment her sister-in-law, one of her nearest friends, she rejected the name John because a distant relative who bore it committed suicide. She settled with Father's concurrence on Wesley Lewis for her infant. He was called Wesley until he reached the age of sixteen. When I hung out my shingle in Raleigh in 1854, I found that there were some Wesleys in the county of opposite politics to mine, who were not agreeable to me. Besides, the name misleadingly suggested that we were of a Methodist family. With the consent of our parents, I offered to give him a new rifle, if he would induce people to call him Lewis. He agreed to the proposal, all his companions eagerly helped him and in two weeks the rifle was won. He became very expert and many a hawk that counted on his distance from the marksman for security gave up his chicken-stealing life. My brother was thenceforward W. Lewis Battle.

Lewis was a very bright boy. My brother Richard, who, when he was Tutor in Greek at the University, was much thrown with him, thought that in natural gifts he was superior to all his brothers. He entered the University in the summer of 1859, was a freshman declaimer at the Commencement of 1860, volunteered for the war in 1862, and was soon made a lieutenant. He fought in several of the great battles in Virginia, notably in that of the Wilderness, and was in the famous Pickett's charge at Gettysburg. Lt. Col. W. G. Morris then in charge of his regiment afterwards wrote:

We drove the enemy in front of us from his position in the road, then from behind the stone fence, and held this position at least half an hour. Right here, between the road and stone fence (the enemy having disappeared from our front), we became engaged with a flanking party on our left and were soon surrounded and captured. Six officers on the right of my regiment were wounded in the enemy's works and captured. Among the number was the lamented Lieutenant Battle whose wound proved fatal.... Pettigrew's and Archer's brigades remained longest on our right. Pickett's division did not go further than our command.

We soon learned that Lewis had died but it was not until communications between the North and South had been restored that we learned that he was tenderly nursed by ladies from Philadelphia and a chaplain of the Episcopal Church. They sent us a lock of his hair and some things from his haversack—a small Prayer Book, a parting gift from his mother, and forty dollars in Confederate notes. He was a very lovable boy of twenty, full of humor and of most agreeable manners. The surgeon resected his arm, that is, he sawed off the ends of the bones, and endeavored to make them reunite, but his constitution was not strong enough to stand the strain.

I visited Gettysburg in the fall of 1865 and was deeply gratified at the care taken to identify the bodies of the fallen soldiers by neat tablets and inscriptions and well-kept graves.

On the 16th of April, 1866, the relics of the two brothers were brought home to be buried in the Chapel Hill cemetery. The ode composed by Mrs. Cornelia Phillips Spencer on the occasion has been printed but should find a place here.

Come, southern flowers, and twine above their graves;
  Let all our rathe spring blossoms bear a part.
Let lilies of the vale and snowdrops wave,
  And come thou too, fit emblem, bleeding heart.

Bring all our evergreens, the laurel and the bay,
  From the deep forests which around us stand;
They know them well, for in a happier day
  They roamed these hills and valleys hand in hand.

Ye winds of heaven, o'er them gently sigh,
  And April showers fall in kindliest rain,
And let the golden sunbeams softly lie
  Upon the sod for which they died in vain.

8. *Amusements of My Boyhood and College Days*

OUR FAVORITE GAME AT SCHOOL WAS BASEball. It differed from the modern game in several particulars. The players were selected by lot. A flat paddle was marked on one side with a cross and on the other with several straight lines called "piles," said to be derived from *pila* (javelins). One of the large boys would throw this up and another would guess which side would fall uppermost. If he guessed aright, he would have the first choice of players; if wrongly, the other boy had first choice. Then each would choose alternately until there were two equal teams or sides, as they were called. The next difference was that the pitcher was bound to pitch a good ball, that is, fast or slow, right or left, high or low, as requested. I do not remember that anyone was accused of acting contrary to the wishes of the striker. The pitcher had one privilege only. If a striker attempted to steal from one base to another, he had the right but was not bound to hit him with the ball and put him out. A third difference was that the striker running could be hit with the ball, which was wrapped with yarn so as not to hurt too severely. If the ball after being struck was caught in the air or on first bounce, or if the striker missed three times and the catcher similarly caught it, or if the runner was hit by the ball between bases, he was out. In fact in this game if one was put out, the side was out.

There was a variation of baseball known as old hundred or townball. The putting out of one player did not put out the whole side and when by successive losses the side was reduced to one, presumably a skillful player, the one left had the privilege of knocking in any of his choice. This was possible by his knocking the ball so far that he could run through all the bases without being outed. He thus had the power of reinstating one of his side and so continuing the game.

Roly boly was played with a ball of rubber, sometimes wrapped with yarn threads to make it softer. Each player had a hole, all being in a row. If the player succeeded in rolling the ball into his own hole, he was privileged to throw it as violently as possible at any of the others. It was simple but very exciting. As the boys grew larger there was reluctance to play: the pain of being struck became too great.

As our Academy building at Raleigh was in a public grove with no fence around it, we were able to engage in a game of extraordinary interest and intense excitement. It was called "Hee over, here she goes." A player having the ball in hand was on one side of the building and the remainder of the boys on the other. The boy with the ball threw it over the building shouting, "Hee over, here she goes!" As it came over, there was great competition to grasp it, and he who succeeded had the right to hit anyone he chose. Of course there was a rapid scampering to get out of his way.

Another rough amusement was pelting one another with acorns. A hit with a big white oak acorn was very stinging and left a black or blue mark on the skin, as I remember well from sad experience.

A most exciting but dangerous game was bandy or shinny, much like the Indian lacrosse. The two sides were chosen as for baseball. Two poles were erected at both ends of the playground and the competition was to drive the ball between these posts, using sticks with one end curved. When the ball was underneath a player, it was his duty to get out of the way. If he declined or neglected to do so, his adversary had the strict right to strike his feet or ankles, but I never saw such a blow intentionally inflicted. Skill was shown, however, in what was called "scuffling," that is, entangling the ball between the adversary's feet or stealing it away from him. By rule the stick was not to be raised in striking higher than the shoulder but in the excitement this rule was often violated and those near-by were in serious danger. When a strong arm had a good lick at the ball, which was heavy and round, it sped its way with fearful velocity. This too was a source of real danger. Once at the University my brother William was struck on his left jaw by one of these projectiles and his right jaw was slightly fractured, so that he was forced to subsist on soup and milk for weeks. My mother said, "You ought to thank your stars that you were not struck on the temple. You would have been killed!" He was in too much pain to appreciate the comfort. He profanely blurted out, "I think I ought to abuse my stars for letting me get hit at all!" When I entered the University, I was so small that my mother expressed the wish that I would not play this dangerous game and I refrained from doing so but in avoiding Scylla I fell on Charybdis. I took to cutting wood for exercise and made a horrid gash in my left foot which kept me confined for three weeks.

Bandy had this advantage over any game in these days, that all the students could engage in it, and with more or less exertion as was agreeable. And although there was peril of bruises, there were not as many deaths as occur now from football and baseball. I see from a picture in an old penny magazine that we played bandy as did the Highlanders of Scotland. The other games were brought from England.

The indoor games among girls and boys were usually such as are described in children's books. One which was popular in Raleigh was new to me when I came from Louisburg. A girl would take a pillow and deliver it to a boy with a kiss, then the favored youth handed the pillow and kiss to a girl, and so on. I remember to this day the gratitude I felt at my first Raleigh party to the belle of the evening, who noticed how forlorn a stranger I was and honored me with an osculation. The girl who was so kind to the eight-year-old stranger was the prettiest of all. Her name was Lucy Williams. She married Dr. Burke Haywood.

We also played prisoner's base. We divided the players into two equal companies. We gave dares, that is, one would leave base and tempt the others to a run. He would be quickly pursued by one of his antagonists, and then the latter would be pursued, and so on. If the pursuer could catch number one before being himself caught, he was safe and carried the captive home in triumph. But he was under two dangers. The dare-giver might reach his base before being touched. If so, he could turn and chase his pursuer. The other danger was that an ally might come out to the rescue of the dare-giver and chase his pursuer. Honestly played, prisoner's base cultivates swiftness in running and sound, quick judgment. It is chronicled that Napoleon and Josephine and their guests often engaged in it at Malmaison.

The games with marbles were either for fun or for "winance," i.e., gaining other marbles. If for fun, a ring was traced on a level place and small marbles called "chaplins" placed in the middle and on the circumference. The game began from a line called "taw," fifteen or twenty feet distant. Each player had a larger marble called "alley taw," of agate if procurable. The player was entitled to count all the marbles he could shoot out of the ring. If his taw remained in the ring he was called "fat" and was out of the game. If one could hit the taw of another, the latter was "killed" and his victor could take a marble out of the ring. We did not play this dilettante game often. We preferred playing for winance. It had the excitement of gain.

In the game for winance each player placed a marble in the

circumference or in the interior of the ring, and the adversary was entitled to any marble he could knock out. If he could hit the adversary's taw, the latter forfeited his marble and could play no more. There was opportunity both for skill and for strategy. One who was not able to hit at a long distance could by moving his taw from place to place get near enough to the ring or to another's taw to make available his peculiar skill.

Playing for winance has been denounced as gambling. It has that appearance but really is a game of skill. There is no chance about it. It is a copy of the strivings of mature people for success in business. I never heard of its forming the gambling spirit. Richard Hines accumulated about a thousand marbles; he became a preacher. My brother Richard was such an accurate shooter that he was ruled out of the game; he abhorred gambling.

Some of the boys occasionally inaugurated lotteries for chinquapins or hickory nuts. It was only for amusement. Each boy put up five or ten nuts. Bits of paper, some blank, others with numbers on them, were placed in a hat and each player drew out a blank or a prize.

Another favorite marble game was knucks. It won the devotion even of students in the higher classes of the University and was satirized by S. F. Phillips in his poem on Chapel Hill.

> 'Tis the land where the junior,
> Sworn foeman to books,
> Beats college all hollow
> At playing for knucks,
> From supper till sundown
> Still kneels at his taw.

Holes in the ground were made about a yard apart in a straight line. Each player endeavored to roll his marble consecutively into these holes. His antagonist had a right to drive his taw away by hitting it with his own taw. The player who was last in securing an entrance into the holes was bound to hold the knuckles of one hand on the ground and allow them to be shot at. Sometimes considerable pain was the result.

The surprising skill obtained by some of the marble players was a precursor of that of the modern baseball pitcher. I recall that at the University Bartholomew Fuller (nicknamed Tholly) won the palm in the early fifties. But when my brother Dick entered the University, he triumphed so easily over the champion that he quit playing. Dick had similar skill in throwing stones. Few could hit the mark with a pistol-ball as often as he could with a rock, which was our name for a stone. Once he came boasting, "I killed a bullbat, one throw." Father said, "What did you kill my bullbat for? You must quit it!"

Dick was a much better marble-player than I. He could beat me at long distances, but at moderate distances I had the skill usual in our family. I employed strategy with success, i.e., I would locate my taw at such points, adjacent to the ring or my adversary's taw, as suited my skill. I was thus often a winner though not a brilliant one, and my marble bag was never entirely empty of captured chaplins.

Before we went to Chapel Hill our Saturdays and vacations were spent partly in games, mainly in fishing and hunting. The hunting was somewhat of a farce. We had a single-barrelled shotgun but no bird-dog. We hoped for and sometimes obtained a dove or robin or yellow-hammer or lark. Brother Joel carried the gun and it was my privilege to walk behind and carry any birds which might be the victims of his prowess. As a reward I was allowed to shoot a sparrow or snowbird towards the close of the hunt. Such was my devotion to him that I was proud of this companionship. If the game had been more plentiful, I should have had more frequent chances. He was afraid to trust me to shoot a large bird and besides it would have detracted from his glory.

The fishing at Raleigh was more entertaining. The fish were small, mere minnows, and we easily caught twenty or so by dinnertime. The sparkling brook and the lovely trees, casting a grateful shade, added to the pleasure. To enhance our pleasure our cook, a good-natured creature, fried the minnows brown so that they could be eaten bones and all—as pleasant a dish to a hungry boy as is conceivable. Years afterwards I walked out to our old fishing stream, carrying letters from my loved ones to enjoy reading them amid such pleasant associations.

The hunting at Chapel Hill was good provided the hunter had a reliable setter or pointer. There was a famous setter belonging to Dr. Moore that was excellent alike at finding, pointing, and fetching. She was prolific too. In fact she was so valuable that her name, Nell, should be recorded. The culture of cotton had not then extended to this neighborhood and there was an abundance of partridges, never called quails or bobwhites. The landowners were very kind. There was only one posted farm, i.e., one on which there was a prohibition against hunting, and the owner of this based his action on pity for the birds.

Hunters usually enjoyed the sport in pairs, but as only two or three dogs were available, few could enjoy the sport at the same time. A pair of skilful hunters usually brought in forty or fifty birds, which afforded a luscious supper. As for me, I was a poor shot, being so nervous that I fired away at the first whirr of the bird, not waiting to take aim. I am ashamed of my deficiency even now.

A good story is told of Lawrence Smith. He was of a solitary disposition, a good member of the church. To him an oath was unknown. He seemed to take little interest in anything except hunting partridges. One lovely Saturday he borrowed a dog and went out on his favorite sport. His dog found a covey and down came two birds. The remainder lit in an ideal place for a sportsman. Smith rapidly reloaded his piece while the dog was on a point. When he felt for the caps, to his horror he found he had left them at home. He slammed the butt of his gun on the ground and exclaimed, "I've a good mind to cuss!"

The chief hunter of my time was George Valerius Young, known among the students as Val, son of a wealthy Mississippi planter. He had been fond of field sports all his life. I admired him so much that I named my dog Val in his honor. I gave this dog to my brother William, who taught a while in Bertie County, and he acquired a wide reputation, not only as a setter but as a snake-killer. His method was to jump from a distance of five or six feet on the snake, usually a water-moccasin, give him one bite back of the neck, then leap back out of harm, then watch his chance and jump and bite again until his adversary expired. He was skilful in finding the serpent by his scent. It really seemed that he could distinguish a venomous from a non-venomous snake, but this was probably our fancy. I grieve to write that at first I ignorantly took the advice of one supposed to be a dog expert and tried to teach Val by punishments. It was a mistake. It made him unfriendly to me.

Our removal to Chapel Hill somewhat changed our sports. We had ponds convenient for skating and there was a considerable number of skaters so skilful that they could cut didos, as it was called, that is, trace names or circles or pictures on the ice as they whirled. The most accomplished of all was the favorite bootmaker, Wash Davis.

The climate of Chapel Hill is probably equal for pleasantness to any in the world but the skaters found that in some winters their skates were useless. There would be a freeze occasionally but the ice would be too thin for sport. Several years might elapse before real skating cold would come. I remember well one of these hard freezes. In the brook through Battle Park running water, as well as pools, became solid ice. Then the warmer currents that exuded from under the banks ran beneath the ice. Afterwards a rain came and its muddy stream ran over the frozen water so that we had three streams at the same time in one brook-bed.

I too learned to skate and regarded the exercise as highly agreeable. There was a sheet of water in the eastern part of town called Hatch's Pond after the nearest resident. It owed its existence to a ledge of rock that kept back the rain-water. Prof. B. S. Hedrick, who built a home east of it, the house occupied later by President Winston and then by Prof. Horace Williams, blasted away the obstruction and the pond disappeared. I have seen most of the students and the young people of the village disporting themselves on this pond at the same time—some skating, others pushing the girls about in sleds and chairs, others sliding and chasing one another with frequent merry falls.

The mention of Hatch's Pond recalls another sport popular among us boys—shooting bullfrogs by the use of hickory bows and sourwood arrows. We found the most frogs in the pond above King's Mill, afterwards called the Valley Mill, on the Hillsborough road. There were some also in Hatch's Pond and in the Graveyard Pond, like Hatch's long since drained. The frogs when hit would jump into the water but would come to the top again and be detected by the arrow piercing them. The arrows were of sourwood because there were no reeds nearer than three miles. The hind legs of the frogs made excellent food; the rest of the body was thrown away.

Swimming was a favorite sport with me. I learned the art in a brickyard hole near Raleigh where the water was only waist deep. From this modest sheet I struggled with the currents of Crabtree Creek and acquired a skill creditable to a mere boy.

While I confess that I was a failure as a hunter, I was at the head in swimming and diving. I had faith in the statement that the human body has about the same specific gravity as water and so had confidence that there can be no danger in still water and with presence of mind very little in running water. The skill I acquired greatly enhanced the pleasure of bathing in the ocean.

Once I made a miscalculation while sporting with some boys in the French Broad River. I saw a cave on the opposite bank in front of which was a rapid current. I swam to the margin of this current and attempted to dash across. As the water ran three or four times as fast as I could swim, I was forced down stream. But there was really no danger. After going with the current thirty yards or so, I struggled to the bank again.

The old-time grist-mills have been ruined by modern inventions. They cannot compete with steam-mills. When I was a boy, the neighbors brought their grain to the mill and gave generally one-tenth of it to have the rest ground. The miller ground what he received as toll and what he had by purchase or production on his own farm and sold it at home or sent it off by wagon, mainly to eastern counties. Merritt's flour was widely known and prized. Now the dams are in ruins, the ponds have disappeared, and the swimming, fishing, and skating of the old days survive mainly in tradition. I grieve that the University now lacks the facilities for outdoor water-sports, so full of delight and improvement to mind and body, whether in winter or summer. The excitements of football, baseball, and basketball cannot compensate for boating, swimming, and skating. I add that no miller ever prohibited us from fishing in his pond, but infinite patience was rewarded with only a small catch.

When Father moved to Chapel Hill, we boys did not know a soul on the Hill and until we made acquaintances amused ourselves roaming the forest near our house, fighting the bluebirds and catbirds that stole our blackheart cherries, and exterminating the wasps and yellow jackets that infested the place. Our home had been occupied by a couple with three or four small children. They were impoverished and had allowed the fences to rot down and things generally to go to wreck and ruin. It was eight months before the erection of a new house and general repairs put the premises in comfortable condition. Axe had never touched the grove belonging to the University in front of our dwelling and the water-boughs reached nearly to the ground, so that our place seemed to be in the country although really only a very moderate distance from stores and post office.

The wasps, here as always partial to decaying houses, were aggressive. We fought them for fear of their stings and for another reason peculiar to our situation. They took possession of our boxes set up on a high pole for the summer visits of the purple martins whose twittering and graceful evolutions were a delight to old and young. They were too high to be reached by brushes. With courage born of wrath and pride I stormed the stronghold. Placing a ladder against the pole, with a blazing torch in my left hand and a bunch of switches in my right I ascended the ladder and killed or drove away the enemy—the first fight in the air within my knowledge. I was really in no danger, however, as the insects feared the fire.

As soon as the wasps were defeated a new enemy of the martins took possession of their house, the bluebirds. These although smaller than the martins entrenched themselves, as it were, in the nest-holes and fiercely pecked at other birds that attempted to enter. Seeing that our favorites were averse to warfare, we invoked the aid of a shotgun, shelled the trenches, and triumphed. For many years we had annual visits from our delightful friends but since the Civil War they have ceased to come. I attribute this to want of food. Formerly the farmers in this neighborhood raised principally wheat, corn, and oats. Those who had no farms generally bought what they needed and stored it in loosely built barns. Winged insects, particularly weevils, had abundant breeding places. On these the martins and bullbats fed. About a half-century ago cotton fields began to replace grain fields and towns-people now find it more convenient to buy what they need from merchants who deal in home necessaries. The supply of winged insects is cut off and the birds who eat them go elsewhere. I have seen in the old days multitudes of weevils flying upwards from a barn stored with grain, and swarms of bullbats, leather winged bats, martins, and swallows circling round and round enjoying the feast.

Another of our amusements was fighting bumblebees in their nest in the wall of a near-by kitchen. They were plucky little creatures and would follow an enemy a considerable distance with stings ready to plunge into his body. The best way to avoid this was to fall suddenly to the ground, when the bee in perplexity would return to his nest. Yellow jackets also would fight in defence of their homes. Wasps would attack for a short distance but would not follow so fast nor so far as the others. Yellow jackets had a habit of making their home in a hole in the ground near our places of resort and attacking us, if accidentally or by design we ran near them. We soon learned how to exterminate them. We threw over the nest armfuls of dry leaves, then applied a torch, and the insects were burned as they flew out. I learned afterwards that they die when winter approaches but their queen survives and when spring comes raises a new colony. They are harmless if unmolested, but pugnacious if attacked. Once my brother William and I were walking in the woods with his children, girls and boys. Our dogs stirred up a nest and yellow jackets attacked us. Our rapid running through the woods was a ludicrous sight. Six or seven got into the hair of one of the girls and she had as many wounds. They do not leave their stings in the wounds as bees do.

Quite recently, after getting some lilies out of a lily pond I once had but drained because people dreaded mosquitoes, I hid in a clump of bushes the pole I got the lilies with. Unwittingly I stirred up some wasps and was saved from stings only by a rapid retreat. In running I invaded a hornets' nest and out came a number of hornets in pursuit of me. I threw myself on the ground and so outwitted them. That night I had my revenge. After they settled in their nests, I blew them to pieces with a shotgun.

At one time we had two or three hives of bees of the ancient fashion. When the bees swarmed, i.e., when a colony left their old hive, it was believed that they would migrate to parts unknown unless induced to settle on a limb of a near-by tree by the clanging of bells and pans, tongs, and whatever else would make a noise. I participated in these exercises and can testify that the bees did not journey to a far country. I noticed that although we all beat on our instruments with the bees humming around us, they did not offer to sting or show any signs of displeasure. In modern days it is affirmed that our tintinnabulations did not cause the stoppage of the swarm, that the habit of bees is to choose their home near the hive from which they flee.

When the time came to take the honey, we invited a party of girls and boys to join us. There was not an expert in the company. When we found that the little animals intended to fight for their property, after some daring attempts and screaming flights on the part of us youngsters we called on our old cook, Aunt Jinny, to help us. With a courage and indifference to pain that excited our admiration, repeatedly crying out, "One has got me," "Another got me," she procured us a feast of the coveted comb, dripping with the sweetest honey. We then carried our prize to the dining-room and had a delightful frolic, eating and playing Clap in and Clap out. There was some adverse criticism in village circles of the boys' inducing the girls to sop up the precious liquid with their fingers and transfer it to the tongues of their beaux. But from my standpoint of fourscore years I pronounce it excusable. I never heard of any hostile bacilli leaping from the fair digits of our girls.

Children's dances were sometimes held at Chapel Hill, the piano and an amateur performer furnishing the music. I engaged in one with sad consequences. Being fond of music and having no fat on my bones, I went through the saltatory motions with too much vivacity. As I returned to my seat a pretty but satirical girl called me Limber Jack. Being very sensitive to ridicule, the remark so stung me that I have passed through a long life with that one performance in dancing to my credit. There was no dancing-master in Chapel Hill and I was unwilling to risk another jibe on my uncouth amateur motions. I have missed much innocent fun but I comfort myself with the thought that, if I had been a dancer, I would have wasted much time.

We had the impression of angels usual among children. Our mother had such reverential feeling towards the Bible that we never confounded angels with fairies. Angels were sacred and not to be joked about. Our notions about fairies, ancient giants, and witches were not restrained by religious feeling. Santa Claus (Saint Nicholas) was in the class of fairies and we had many jokes about him and his Christmas gifts. We called him Old Sandy. For several years it was thought indispensable to hang up stockings as receptacles for presents, but because we threw the loaded stockings at one another and finally one fell into the fire, Mother decreed that waiters and plates should be substituted. Old Sandy made no objection to the change.

Although the Santa Claus legend existed long before my infancy, I cannot remember that I ever considered it true. Descending the chimney with a load of eatables and playthings seemed incredible even to my infantile mind.

We played a trick once on my brother William which gave us boundless merriment. The elder children slept upstairs, William among them. He placed his waiter on one of the steps in order that he might get to it sooner in the morning. He had the habit of talking to himself when much interested. After he went to sleep we removed the candy, cakes, and nuts from his waiter and substituted a piece of cold egg-bread and other articles unpleasant to the taste. While it was still dark he crept down the cold stairs. We could hear his words, "I wonder what Old Sandy has brought me! Here it is! A big slice of cake! I'm going to take a bite!" Then his voice changed to anger. "Nothing but cold egg-bread! Dog take

Old Sandy! I don't want any of his old egg-bread! I wonder if he thinks we haven't got egg-bread!" Here the explosions of laughter in the beds upstairs informed the wrathful boy that he had been sold.

After we knew that Santa Claus was mythical, we delighted to keep him alive for the little ones. And when we grew up to reading history, we were interested in the half mythical story of the excellent Saint Nicholas: how when living at Myra in Cilicia he became the guardian of sailors; how he brought to life two boys slaughtered by an innkeeper on their way to the University at Athens; how he overheard a maiden lamenting that she lacked the money necessary for her marriage and threw a purse of gold into her chamber; and how he thus became the guardian saint of boys and girls, caring for them and dispensing presents.

The Christmas tree comes from the legend that when in Egypt the Virgin Mary was nearly exhausted from heat and hunger, her divine son ordered a cherry tree full of ripe fruit to bow down to her hand.

When Holland became a great maritime state, her sailors borrowed St. Nicholas from the Mediterranean, and by rapid pronunciation St. Nicholas became Sant-Nicklaus, Santa-Claus. The Dutch carried him to Manhattan, New York, and thence his cult has spread through the land.

We were undoubting believers in Satan, as the devil was usually called among us. We derived our notions of him and his abode from the negroes. We felt sure that his abode was a vast fire-plain. All bad people were thrown in it, the worst in the central flames. The fuel was heaped on the coals by the devil and his angels. When the chief went on a marauding expedition over the earth, seeking whom he might devour, he left his imps in charge of his dominions. There were some offences for which there was only temporary punishment. I remember one distinctly. If any food was thrown into the fire, the offender would be obliged to pick it out of the everlasting fire with naked fingers.

I knew many members of the Baptist denomination in my youth. They did not press the doctrine that all unimmersed persons would go to the bad place, as hell was called, but years afterwards a professor in the University and a doctor of divinity enunciated the ghastly doctrine in Chapel Hill.

There was no dancing for grown-ups in Chapel Hill except at Commencement. But young people will get together for pleasant companionship. Taking walks together was more frequent than at present. Every pleasant afternoon saw young couples wending their way over some one of the beautiful walks around Chapel Hill. The favorites were to Mr. (afterwards Bishop) Green's plantation, now Tenney's, Roaring Fountain, Piney Prospect, Merritt's (now Purefoy's) Mill, and Glenburnie, above King's Millpond.

Frequent parties were given at which the amusement was conversational and musical. My recollection is that it was the fashion to talk and laugh all the while but it was not obligatory to answer intelligently. Music, instrumental or vocal, resounded with a minimum of listening. Punning was fashionable. President Swain set the example. His favorite butt was Professor Fetter because his name was easily played on and his answer was equally stereotyped, "I can stand that from a beardless Swain," the president's chin being smooth by nature.

An amusing entertainment, called the Rusk Pun celebration, is worthy of being recorded. Exum Lewis made an atrocious pun on the word rusk, whereupon the Rusk Pun Society was formed and he was made king. A chair, duly draped, was placed on a table in the parlor at our house to answer for a throne. A procession was formed, Exum at the head, which marched in from the porch, my mother playing a march tune on the piano. Exum was duly installed on the throne. Then a committee of three was chosen to decide a competition for the worst pun. Various members of the company competed. The puns were offered in writing and read to the company. The victor was to be King of Bad Puns for the succeeding year. Then came a burlesque oration filled with extravagant foolishness, pronounced by James Williams who called himself the Gentleman from Warren. The ridiculous performance gave great fun to the company, but could not be successfully reproduced at this time because puns have become unfashionable, unappreciated, and almost obsolete.

Perhaps I ought to chronicle the original Rusk Pun, as it was considered so uncommonly bad. Richard Hines was in love with a handsome lady, Miss Huske. For fun he called her Miss Ruske. In a jolly company Exum asked, "Why will Mr. Hines never die of hunger?" Answer: "Because he will always have his rusk to eat." Exum was good-natured and stood our laughter very amiably. But Exum never minded jokes on him. He would even tell them himself. For example, this. He said that once he was visiting his ladylove. She coyly said, pointing to the mirror, "That fly yonder looks like two flies." He replied, "Very similar to two flies, but that's not the question."

Bathos in poetry, i.e., the descent from the sublime to the ridiculous, was much liked when I was young. Here are some specimens. The quatrain form was very popular:

> She raised her melting eyes to mine:
> They were filled with drops of woe.
> With trembling lips she faintly said,
> "Now, darn you, let me go!"

Sometimes prose was employed:

She rushed from her bed like a raging catamount, and in her gigantic, tearing strength seized him by the collar and tore his shirt.

The following was considered the most absurd of all:

> His brawny arm beclasped her waist,
>   With love their eyes did burn.
> From his warm lips she snatched a taste
>   And then he tasted hern.

Sometimes there was a good deal of elaboration:

> This longing after beauty,
>   This sighing after curls,
> This chasing after fashion,
>   Wherever fashion whirls,
>   And all that sort of thing,
>
> May do for those who like it,
>   For those devoid of taste,
> For those who barter diamonds off
>   For diamonds made of paste,
>   And other blockheads.
>
> But to the wife who dearly loves,
>   Who'd be what she appears,
> Who'd spread a sunshine round the heart,
>   Who wipes away her tears,
>   And brings her taters home,
>
> We'd fix it in her memory,
>   We'd grave it on her heart,
> That knowing well to fry a steak
>   Beats sentiment and art
>   A dog-gone sight.

Amusements of My Boyhood

When my father removed from Raleigh to Chapel Hill in 1843, the village had few inhabitants. There was no dwelling west of Columbia Street except that of Mrs. Nunn, which had once been the most popular boarding-house in the place. This was at the northwest corner of Columbia and Franklin Streets. Beyond was forest. It was the policy of the University to confine the village to Franklin Street and Columbia Avenue. An exception was made of the lot on which I reside because of a spring on the northeast corner, there being then no wells in the village. As cattle were allowed to run at large, it became necessary to fence in a part of the University lands including the buildings, i.e., the campus. This was done under the superintendence of Dr. Mitchell, who being used to stone walls in Connecticut adopted them in Chapel Hill. As it was impracticable to carry the wall across the Raleigh road, the grove east of the campus between the campus and my father's place was not included. With the approval of all interested I spent most of my leisure time one winter about 1850 in trimming the trees. It was interesting work but in one instance dangerous. In order to reach a large dead limb on a white oak of uncommon size thirty or forty feet from the ground, I was forced to stand on the uprights of my ladder, holding with my left hand to a small live limb. When I had sawed the dead limb half through, it suddenly broke and knocked the ladder from under me. My left hand held firm, and climbing up by it I was safe. To reach the ground, however, I was forced to wait until a passer-by righted the ladder, the trunk of the oak being too large and smooth for me to climb down. My tenacious grasp of the small limb saved me from a broken leg or worse. While I praise my hand, justice requires that I should bestow a malediction on my head for overlooking the danger of cutting into the middle of a decayed limb.

The woodland back of our house is now called Battle Park because of my love for it and the paths I cut through it. What started me opening the paths through it was the circumstance that in getting ready to deliver the valedictory at my graduation in 1849, I resorted to the vicinity of a lofty poplar in the middle of the woods as a retired place for the rehearsal of my oration. A projecting rock was "Venerated President," a clump of bushes "Respected Faculty," a larger clump "Fellow Students," and a smaller group "Beloved Classmates." Prompting of speakers was not allowed in those days and forgetfulness of the speech would have disgraced me, so I resorted to my sylvan stage so often that it was impossible for my memory to fail. When I returned to Chapel Hill as president I provided a seat under the poplar so that by reading an interesting book or journal in that secluded spot I might forget for a time my University cares. Then I cut a path to facilitate reaching the place. The exercise was agreeable and I concluded to cut another path to the brook and of course there had to be one along the brook. This led to others until I finished the park in a rough way. I induced Professor (afterwards President) Winston to see my work. He was enthusiastic. He said, "This is an important addition to the University. You must have some money to finish it. How much do you want?" I replied, "New York paid $7,000,000 for Central Park. Three dollars and a half will do for me. All I want is a darkey to clean out the paths. I do not like that work." No effort has been made to make the paths smooth and even. In truth I do not like the hard conventional paths of city parks. They resemble too much the sidewalks in the public streets.

After I gave up the presidency, I had more leisure and cut other paths—to the Meeting of the Waters, up Chapel Branch, to Judge's Spring, and other points of interest, including a lovely one along Bowlin's Creek on one side and the Fern Banks on the other. The latter has been ruined by the neighbors' habit of depositing dead animals at the northeast end. Another path which I opened through the forest opposite Piney Prospect hill on the south has been ruined by the erection of a wire fence.

9. Life as a Student and Tutor at the University

MY FATHER WAS ELECTED A SUPERIOR COURT judge in 1840. The duties of this office could be performed just as well if he lived at Chapel Hill as if he lived at Raleigh. Before long he concluded that as he then had five sons to be educated at the University, it was best for him to remove his residence to Chapel Hill. In June, 1843, with my brother William and me he came in advance of our mother and the younger children, bringing supplies for camping for a day or two. Soon after our arrival good Professor Green came over and offered to entertain us until we could go regularly to housekeeping. We proudly told him of the cooked hams and chickens and many scores of biscuits and pounds of butter our mother had put up for us and declined his offer with thanks. Commencement was going on but the novelty of our situation made us unwilling to leave home for its ceremonies.

My poor mother had a hard time until a new dwelling was erected. Her bedroom and usual sitting-room were in a cottage of three rooms with a storeroom upstairs. Her dining-room, used as a parlor, was fifty or sixty feet distant. Above this was the attic sleeping apartment of the larger boys, including me. A broad staircase led from this to the room below. Our bedroom had dormer windows besides two others, and it was hot in summer and cold in winter. Even after the new house was completed, it continued for some years to be our study and sleeping room. It then had another disadvantage. The female servants married and had children whose wailing was not only disagreeable but seriously interfered with study.

I think that having a room at home where I was not liable to be interrupted had one disadvantage. I had too much time for preparation of lessons. I was not forced to intensive exercise of brain. For example, when looking out for the dictionary meaning of classical words, I whistled, ate apples, or engaged in other amusement. My son-in-law, Richard H. Lewis, had a conspicuous room at college much frequented by student visitors, and in order to retain his high position in his classes he was forced to study very hard when his time was at his disposal. In order to cultivate the habit of intensive mental work, I consented that my own boys should occupy rooms in the college buildings. When a boy is so constituted that such interruptions are fatal to honest application, let him have quarters where he can command his time.

The advantage of freer mixing with other students is also to be considered. I do not, however, think that my isolation was a serious drawback to me and for several reasons. I thought myself welcomed by some classmates who roomed at college and frequently visited them. Friday nights and Saturday mornings I mingled freely with my fellow members of the Dialectic Society. My sister Susan was very popular and I saw many visitors at our home. Moreover there were frequent assemblies of young people at parties, where gay talking and foolish talking, as well as simple noisy games, were all the fashion because there was no dancing to check conversation.

The first two years of my college course were not happy. From childhood it had been instilled into me that I "must not let anyone get ahead of me." In my freshman year, although I succeeded in sharing first honors with three others, I was constantly uneasy about the result. As the sophomore year came on, we heard the news that two uncommonly good new scholars were coming and this was alarming. To make matters worse, I was attacked by colds in the head which were unnerving. But I plodded away and succeeded in sharing the first honor with two Fayetteville boys, Thomas J. Robinson and Peter M. Hale, my freshman associates falling to the second rank. I succeeded too in getting rid of my colds by taking the advice of a Dr. Warren of Boston, who wrote a book on health. He postulated that colds were inflammations caused by sudden changes of temperature when the body was unprepared. Sleep with windows up winter and summer, and sudden changes on an enfeebled body will be avoided. I tried this with entire success. I had no cold at all until after I was married and it was deemed unsafe to have the windows open when our baby was threatened with croup. The principle of the modern fad of sleeping in the open was thus promulgated by Dr. Warren as early as 1846. It certainly is useful when bedrooms are unventilated and warmed by hot air or hot water pipes and there is no current of air blowing through, no fire in a grate to carry the air up the chimney. But with rooms open to the sunlight, windows opposite one another, and the air continually renewed through open doors and windows, beds in piazzas seem unnecessary.

One thought especially troubled me. As the unwritten family decree required me to be a lawyer, my heart was heavy with the knowledge that I was a poor speaker. My ideal of declamation, conceived from watching the manner of fine speakers like William Henry Manly, was so high that a successful imitation of it was far beyond my reach. I consulted one of the most level-headed students I ever knew. His answer gave me great comfort and was of permanent value. He said, "You make the mistake of thinking too much of your manner and too little of your matter. Speak in a conversational way, with your hands in your pockets if you like. Prepare yourself on your subject and talk as if you were trying to persuade some one man of the truth of your views. Do not try to make gestures in imitation of the best speakers. You will get warmed up and the gestures will come naturally, when appropriate. Don't be frightened. A hundred men are not a hundred times as smart as one man. They have, as a rule, no more sense than the ablest one man among them. My Uncle Richard Smith of Halifax, who is a lawyer, talks to juries in a conversational way and wins as many verdicts as any man at the bar—in fact, I believe, more." I took his advice and soon felt perfectly easy in the Dialectic Society debates. As he predicted I soon unconsciously began to gesticulate, and was rewarded by the members with the dignity of being the second president from our class. The practise was to elect to this office monthly from the members of the senior class.

Some years afterwards, when I was a young lawyer in Raleigh, John W. Norwood, an able and experienced lawyer, came into my office. He said, "What are you copying out of that book?" I replied, "I am copying a covenant from this form-book. I have written many instruments but never before a covenant." "Oh!" said he, "throw away your book. I will give you a form which will do for all manner of writings. Think carefully what you wish to say and write it down as clearly and strongly as you can. You will form your own style. It will not be a labored imitation of the style of someone else." I adopted his suggestion and ever since then have given my attention to matter and have let the manner take care of itself.

A speaker should by all means cultivate clearness of utterance. The want of this is the main cause of failure to interest and to persuade. In Henry Ward Beecher's church in Brooklyn, which holds seven thousand people seated, I was one of the most distant from the great orator and heard every word of his sermon although he spoke in a conversational tone. I have often sat in a few feet of a loud, even screaming speaker and listened without profit because many of his words were lost.

We had once a spirited debate between two champions, Matt Howerton, a Democrat, and Victor C. Barringer, a Whig, on the query whether the United States was not in fault in bringing on the Mexican War. Barringer contended that as the territory between the Nueces and the Rio Grande was claimed by both nations, a peaceable mode of deciding the question of ownership should have been adopted, that President Polk in ordering General Taylor to take possession of the disputed lands committed an unjustifiable act of war. He said with emphasis, "Taylor and his army should have remained at Corpus Christi pending negotiations." Howerton adroitly induced him to repeat this statement several times. Barringer of course thought that the town was east of the Nueces. Then Howerton pulled out a map and showed that it is situated to the west. The mistake of geography was quite annoying to his adversary but his reputation as a debater was too high to be lost by his carelessness in this instance. The incident, however, shows the importance of careful preparation. The old advice, attributed by some to President Jackson by others to Davy Crockett, doubtless originated by a Greek or a Roman, "Be sure you are right, then go ahead," is excellent advice.

I witnessed another contest of giants in debate, the leaders being William K. Blake, then of Fayetteville, and James S. Amis, of Oxford. The question was whether Great Britain was entitled to run the southwest boundary line of Canada, our northwest line, as far south as the parallel of 49°. So much interest was felt on account of the question itself and its having got into politics and because of the reputation of the chief speakers, that even ex-members of the society came to hear the debate. A young lawyer of wide reading and uncommon talent, afterwards Solicitor General of the United States, S. F. Phillips, declared that this debate was equal to that in the Federal House of Representatives on this subject. I think that Blake had the affirmative. He was one of the most polished speakers I ever heard and one of the most superior men. Ill health deprived him of the loftiest heights but he was principal of several important female schools and a member of the South Carolina Legislature. Amis, though not as polished as Blake, was very forcible and became a good lawyer and state legislator. Of the two debaters heretofore named, Barringer was afterwards a judge of the International Court of Egypt; Howerton made a good beginning in politics and law but died early.

One of the greatest privileges and pleasures of the ante-bellum

SENLAC

The home of Kemp Plummer Battle in Chapel Hill. From a photograph taken about 1884.

A FAMILY GROUP AT SENLAC

Left to right, Thomas H. Battle, lawyer, banker, president of the Rocky Mount mills, trustee of the University; Kemp D. Battle, later lawyer in Rocky Mount, president of the State Bar Association, trustee of the University; Kemp P. Battle, Jr., physician in Raleigh, professor in the University Medical School; Richard H. Lewis, Jr., later cotton manufacturer in Oxford; Ivey F. Lewis, later Professor of Biology in the University of Virginia; Mrs. Kemp P. Battle; Kemp P. Battle; Kemp P. Lewis, later president of the Erwin Cotton Mills, Durham, trustee of the University; Mrs. Kemp P. Battle, Jr.; Pattie Battle Lewis, later Mrs. Isaac H. Manning. From a photograph taken about 1893.

Above, Senlac, view from the front walk toward the barn and woods (later Battle Park). Photograph taken about 1903.
Below, View from the front porch towards the campus. Mr. and Mrs. Battle are standing in the gateway. Photograph taken about 1903.

days was the acquaintance we made at Commencement with the great men of the State. There being no railroad to Chapel Hill, many visitors came in their own carriages. Franklin Street was at times almost covered with vehicles. Scant hotel accommodations made faculty hospitality imperative. My father being a public man naturally entertained prominent trustees, orators, and others and we found their conversation of the greatest interest. One of the most entertaining was Governor Charles Manly, Secretary and Treasurer of the University, and never absent from Commencement. I must perpetuate one of his stories, told in inimitable manner. He began, "Do you think it wrong on occasion to tell a lie to your wife? I don't and I will give you my experience. There was to be a great horse-race at Raleigh. I had just joined the church and at that time many church people thought it wrong to attend horse-racing. So to avoid fault-finding at home, I went early and mounted a pile of rocks. I had a good time. But when I came down, a rock crumbled and gave me an awful bruising. I reached home in agony. My wife Charity met me, 'Mr. Manly, what is the matter?' 'Rheumatiz, Charity, terrible rheumatiz! Send for Dr. Fab Haywood.' Fab came. 'Everybody leave the room but Fab.' Then I told him the truth and begged secrecy. For several days he doctored me for rheumatism. Now did I do wrong in saying, 'Rheumatiz, Charity, rheumatiz'?"

Another frequent visitor at our house was Governor William A. Graham of Hillsborough. Governor Graham was one of the most perfect specimens of the high-toned statesman I ever saw. He never stooped to sharp practises, never attacked the motives of opponents, never indulged in personalities. He was always dignified and no one ever dared to throw ridicule on him or his speeches. And yet the laugh was on him on one occasion. He was prosecuting a man for biting off a piece of his client's ear. The opposing lawyer brought a witness, old and half-deaf, who constantly answered, "It mout and then agin it moutn't." It was the object of the defendant's counsel to convince the jury that the mutilation might have been accidental. He asked, "Where was the fight?" "In an empty barn." "Didn't Governor Graham's client strike the first lick?" "Well, he mout and then agin he moutn't." "Did you see them fall?" "Yes, sir, I seed 'em drap." "Didn't Governor Graham's client fall on top?" "Well, he mout and then agin he moutn't." "Were the planks nailed down?" "No, sir, they were loose." "Could you put your finger in the cracks?" "Yes, sir, they were mighty loose." "Now I ask you if, while they were fighting on that floor among those loose planks, the prosecutor might not have had his ear pinched off in a crack of the floor?" "Well, he mout and then agin he moutn't." "Take the witness, Governor."

Governor Graham put on his severest manner, "Witness, you saw all the fight?" "Yes, sir." "You say the ear might have been pinched off between the cracks?" "I said it mout and then agin it moutn't." "Well, sir [sarcastically], might not my client have bitten off his own ear?" "Well, Governor, he mout and then agin he moutn't!" The court-room was convulsed with laughter. For the first and only time in his life the Governor's dignity was upset.

The visit of President James Knox Polk in 1847 was an event of which all University men without distinction of party were very proud. He was a first honor man of the class of 1818, a good speaker and writer. It was a rule in the Dialectic Society for the members, if they strongly approved an essay by a member, to file it in the archives for preservation. This honor was voted Polk several times. He had quiet, easy manners and was much liked. The society voted to have his portrait painted by an artist of reputation, Thomas Sully, and it is now hanging in the society hall.

I admired James Johnston Pettigrew, afterward a general in Lee's army, without stint. He was, it still seems to me, the brightest man I have known in all my life. His mind flashed through the hardest problems without effort. He was unexcelled in everything he attempted. He was superior to all the class in mathematics and not inferior to his strongest competitor, Matt W. Ransom, in the classics. In awarding honors President Swain announced, "The first distinction is awarded to Messrs. Pettigrew and Ransom in the order of their names," and the valedictory was assigned to Pettigrew. In manners he was friendly and by no means stuck up. In athletics he was among the best, and when his friend Burton was on the sick-bed from which he never rose, he was a watchful and skillful nurse. The University then had no hospital and trained nurses were unknown.

There were three first honor men in the graduating class of 1849, P. M. Hale, T. J. Robinson, and I. Although not so dignified by the faculty, the valedictory was generally considered the prize and we therefore drew lots for it. I was successful and bade farewell to the president, professors, fellow-students and classmates in such mournful tones as made a country lady remark to a friend of mine, "He must be a very pious young man."

Having in my course taken a few lessons in navigation and surveying, it occurred to me that before beginning the study of the law some practical work in the survey of the North Carolina Railroad would be useful. Accordingly I applied to ex-Governor Morehead, president of the company, for a situation as rodman and hoped that, as he was present as a trustee when my Commencement honors were won, I might gain the humble post. Before the answer came, I was offered a tutorship in Latin at the University with a much larger salary, $650 per annum. The answer to my application for railroad work came in the form of a letter from Chief Engineer Gwinn to report myself for work as chain-bearer at Morrisville on a day's notice. The letter was addressed to Mr. Rollins but President Morehead notified me that it was intended for me. I preferred to accept the tutorship, as thereby I could accumulate money which would be needed for the early days of law-practise. But the village caricaturist did not spare me, depicting me as dragging a heavy iron chain across ploughed fields.

Another reason influenced my decision. All animals were then allowed to roam in unfenced fields and numberless ticks attached themselves to cattle. After sucking their blood as long as nature designed, these parasites would drop off and give birth to numerous minute offspring called seed-ticks that climbed up the nearest blade of grass and attached themselves to the clothing of the passer-by, then made their way by the most convenient route to the body beneath. Burying their minute probosces into the flesh and infusing their poison into the system, they would each be the cause of acute itching and sometimes nauseous sores. I have seen white pants and ladies' skirts darkened by them. When boys and girls went chinquapin hunting, they often carried bunches of penny-royal, the only shrub which would make them turn loose. They were peculiarly injurious to me, causing great discomfort and nervousness. Those who live in times when cattle are not allowed to run at large can form no conception of the tick evil of old times. Being extremely fond of roaming in the forest, I suffered more than most people from this curse. One of my ambitions was to learn the plants around Chapel Hill. Each spring I made progress until about the first of May, but then the ticks began to be hatched and kept me out of the woods.

I am reminded here that for years after I came to Chapel Hill there were great numbers of chinquapin bushes around the village. Many have been cut down, the rest have died, and the old diversion of chinquapin hunting is gone forever. It is not an unmixed evil. In olden days it was the custom to carry the nuts about and eat them on all suitable occasions and many unsuitable. Often in grave assemblies the noise of crunching chinquapins was disagreeable and in some recitation rooms they were freely thrown about in order to tease nervous professors. Some years ago the chestnut trees in our piedmont and mountain country also died. I suppose that in the gradual disintegration of our surface rocks the food proper for this growth becomes exhausted and the soil more suited to another.

It was with many misgivings that I accepted my tutorship. The previous year, S. F. Phillips had taken the freshman Latin class to supply a temporary vacancy. He was a practising lawyer and while he was at his courts, I took his place. The pleasure of teasing nervous professors was then freely indulged in, and there was much disorder in some of the lecture rooms. As I was only seventeen years old and of very juvenile appearance, I was doubtful of my ability to keep order. By being always polite, even friendly, and refraining from sarcastic criticisms, I had no trouble. When afterwards Tutor in Mathematics, I adopted a novel expedient which worked admirably. I had thirteen blackboards in my recitation room. I would call up twelve men, one for each board. I kept the thirteenth vacant, telling the class that if any one not employed felt that he could not refrain from whispering or other irregularity, I would cheerfully give him a problem for the vacant board which would occupy him the rest of the hour. Whereupon two of those most unruly elsewhere moved their seats so near to me that I could see their orderly behavior.

The chief reason for the bad conduct of certain unruly boys in recitation rooms presided over by tactless professors was the hard and fast curriculum. All students, except a very few called "milish" (militia) who for special reasons were allowed to choose their studies but could not have University honors, were forced into the old curriculum of Latin, Greek, and mathematics, with a little philosophy and rhetoric. About one-third of the class, desiring either first, second, or third honors, studied well. But two-thirds felt little interest in their work, were satisfied with the unhonored grades of Respectable, Tolerable, Bad, and, rarely, Very Bad, and the hour of recitation was to them so irksome that they sought unlawful fun. When they were detected and brought before the faculty for punishment, that body, probably thinking that the offence was partly the teachers' fault, only administered admonition which was not regarded as painful.

Between my graduation in 1849 and the summer of 1854 I studied law as well as mathematics. As my father, the Professor of Law, did not have time to deviate from his curriculum, which covered at most two years and I was tutor for five, of course I read the same books several times. I knew the chief work, second Blackstone, by heart, that is, I could give every principle laid down in that volume in the order in which it occurs. But I was deficient in the application of the principles to the facts coming up in life. When I consulted my father as to the propriety of spending a year at the Harvard Law School, he advised, as my intention was to live in North Carolina, that I should study diligently North Carolina Reports of cases decided by our Supreme Court. I took this advice and gained some triumphs by being familiar with these Supreme Court decisions.

The law in that day required that after getting license to practise in the County Courts a year must elapse before obtaining license to practise in the Supreme and Superior Courts. I concluded not to attend the courts at all until in 1854 I was fully fledged.

As to my mathematics, I confess that I did not study with the diligence I ought, although I qualified myself to teach, as I was bound to do during my four years' tutorship, all the mathematics in the University curriculum—algebra, geometry, trigonometry, analytics, differential and integral calculus, astronomy. Although I kept ahead of my students, one of them, Alexander McIver, being an ex-school teacher nine years my senior, I did not dive deep into mathematical mysteries.

My want of severe work was stimulated by our having very agreeable social privileges. Among the ladies there were some excellent singers, mainly of ballads and negro melodies. Meetings of girls and boys full of fun and frivolity were of almost daily occurrence, and I could not have kept out of them if I had tried—which I did not. My mother (I mention her because my father was off at his courts half the year) was very hospitable, especially to those of even remotest kinship. The high reputation of students for gallantry attracted young ladies and we had much company. There were also living in the village sundry attractive young ladies. The streets being dark at night, ladies never made nocturnal visits without a male escort and I was often the only available beau. I have often acted as protector of ladies so robust that they could have pitched me over the fence, but custom required the presence of a male.

I give one example of the time-killing functions to which I necessarily belonged. We had some excellent singers, the best being Miss Mary W. Green, daughter of Professor W. M. Green, afterwards Bishop of Mississippi. She sang with a sweetness and feeling that approached that of stars on the operatic stage. John Manning, afterwards Professor of Law in the University, had an admirable bass, and Richard H. Whitfield had the talents needed as conductor of a choir. My sister Susan had a good alto. The first choir known in the Chapel of the Cross was formed, and although I was a very indifferent singer, I was obliged to join in order to escort my sister to and from the meetings, always at night. The leader, supported by no organ or melodeon or piano, used a tuning fork. Notwithstanding this drawback the choir achieved much fame.

I must describe a member of the choir of marked ability who was especially gifted as a wit. His name as a freshman was Johnson De Berniere Mallett, but his aunt, an elderly maid who adopted him, had it changed to Johnson Mallett De Berniere, to win the favor of a bachelor uncle of some wealth. He was totally lacking in reverence. As I sat by him once under a chandelier lighted by candles, the preacher read from a hymn the words, "unction from above." De Berniere gave such a comically alarmed look upwards to the flaring candles that I came near laughing out. Another time one of our boon companions, whom we called Buck Moore, had been telling some tales which taxed our credulity. The preacher gave out a hymn beginning something like, "Thy hand, O Lord, will tune the lyre." De Berniere whispered to me, "Isn't that awful on Buck Moore?"

Afterwards De Berniere and I went together to Pilot Mountain in my father's buggy, while he was holding court in Salisbury. We dined on the road at the hospitable home of Tyree Glenn. We asked him to direct us by the best route to the Mountain. His answer was, "There are two fords across the Yadkin, Sycamore and Shallow. Aim for Sycamore by the most travelled road. To save your lives you cannot tell which is the most travelled road. You will certainly get lost but inquire for Sycamore Ford. Reaching that you will be safe." Guided by the Mountain we lost our way only once and came to the edge of the broad and beautiful Yadkin. It flowed so majestically over its rocky bottom, and looked so deep that De Berniere declared he was afraid to risk it. I said, "I am a good swimmer. I will wade across and see how deep it is." I stripped off and cautiously sounded the depth and found that the water only came to my waist.

I learned on that trip something new about the nature of a horse. Ours was strong and healthy but very lazy. I had been driving and our pace was slow. Finding that we were in danger of being overtaken by night, De Berniere, who had taken a drink from a private tickler, asked me to let him have the reins. I gladly complied and he at once began a vigorous shouting, "Get over the high grass! Go long, you five-hundred-dollar nag and not half valued at that!" And such like. The lazy rascal cocked up his ears and tore along at a rapid trot, evidently thinking that the Old Boy was behind him. We reached the Lanier country inn in time for our supper.

We found three other student friends at the inn and had a delightful visit. I left De Berniere at a crossroad a mile or so from Chief Justice Pearson's law school and spent the night at the house of a man named Hutchings. He and his wife, an intelligent couple, received me kindly in their two-roomed house. The supper was good corn bread, milk, and fresh butter. I slept in the upper room with a pile of unshelled peas under the bed and no sheets, Mr. and Mrs. Hutchings and about half a dozen children in the room below. A ladder led to my loft. They told me that they had relatives in Indiana and in a few days, after gathering their crops, the entire family would journey in their two-horse wagon for a short visit to their western kin. For my breakfast the good lady had flour biscuits large as saucers, brown on the crust but damp and tough in the interior. Not knowing of their indigestibility, I stuffed one into my bread-basket and went on my way to Salisbury through Mocksville. It was a dismal ride. The mass of dough gave me a headache and dizziness so that I could hardly see the road. A few hours rest in Mocksville enabled me to reach Salisbury, and a night's rest and my good constitution restored me to my usual health.

In addition to the gatherings at Chapel Hill at Commencements there was at least one other during the year. This was when the sheriff came to collect taxes and the list-takers to perform their duties. The country people came from far and near and there were as a matter of course watermelons and the like, cider, hard and sweet, abundance of whiskey and, most important of all, speaking by candidates for the General Assembly and state and county offices and sometimes by would-be congressmen.

The speaking for some years was at the northwest corner of

Columbia and Franklin Streets from a large rock, flat on the top, in a beautiful grove. After this lot was sold to John W. Carr for a residence, the crowd met usually under some very large elms on Franklin Street. Some men merely announced themselves as candidates but often excellent speeches were made. I recall as particularly effective speakers S. F. Phillips, Henry K. Nash, Josiah Turner, Sidney Smith, John W. Kerr, Abram Venable.

As the day wore on, of course, some of the crowd would become acquainted with old John Barleycorn and fights would begin. There were traditions of numerous conflicts at these gatherings, but public opinion turned against the practise and court fines had a sobering effect. In my day the fights dwindled down to three or four and then became obsolete. The injuries suffered were usually slight but I remember seeing on the floor in a doctor's office a stalwart six-footer with a knife-blade hole in his breast. He recovered.

People as a rule listened respectfully and the speaker was not interrupted. I remember, however, there was a feud between two families and once, while a member of one was speaking, a member of the other gave a whoop. The speaker asked his hearers not to mind the 'jackassible brayings' of his adversary. The heckler was persuaded to be silent and that was the end of it.

In 1850 Dr. James Phillips was appointed a Visitor at West Point. His son Charles, then Tutor in Mathematics, proposed that he and I should accompany him and after his duties were over, we three would visit various cities of the North. From the letters written home I wrote an account of our experiences and will not repeat it. [Most of it was printed in *The New Yorker*, May 18, 1935.] The trip stands out in my memory because in Tripler Hall, New York, listening to the divine singing of Jenny Lind, my future wife and I were for the first time under the same roof together. We did not then know each other but shortly afterwards I met her at West Point, then walked with her from the train to the hotel at Troy, and visited her for a short while at Warrenton, North Carolina, on my way home. I admired her greatly but being only eighteen years old and still preparing for a profession, I had too much sense to fall in love with anyone. It was four years before I met her again.

I have described President Swain and the faculty and the college savants in my History of the University. Let me add here a few recollections of some villagers.

Dr. Johnston Blakely Jones, the leading physician, used to tell a ludicrous story of his courtship. Driving from Chapel Hill to

Raleigh he had a horse trained city fashion to trot on being pulled. Not knowing this, Dr. Jones found himself going faster and faster. Pulling to stop the horse only increased his speed. His tail was bobbed and Dr. Jones, thinking that the pressure by the spatter-board on the stump was the cause of the unruliness, managed to open his knife and cut a hole in the spatter-board to relieve the pressure. This had no effect. Finally he entered Raleigh nearly exhausted. To his consternation he passed by his sweetheart's house with her and a bevy of ladies on the porch. Fortunately his high-strung steed stopped from habit in front of his hotel.

Not long before the Civil War Mrs. Jones became possessed of a handsome sum of money. The doctor invested it partly in a new dwelling and partly in a plantation and negroes in the eastern part of the State, borrowing more money on mortgage. When the war ended all was gone. He then removed to Charlotte, where his undoubted skill gained him reputation and practise.

Dr. George Moore, the other prominent physician of the village, had a strange brother. This brother was perfectly upright but almost a hermit. He had only one love, his ducks. He doted on them, protected them from all harm. His nephew, William, commonly called Buck, planned to give a large party. He killed a great number of partridges for the feast. He prepared cakes and fruit and other dainties. Being a wag and having excellent command of voice and features, he went to his uncle and said, "Uncle Lloyd, I have everything ready for my party except one thing and you can help me to that." "What is it, Buck?" "Ducks' feet jelly; it is a great delicacy. Won't you let me cut off the feet of your ducks?" "Buck, you are a fool!" And that was all his answer.

Another odd character was Old Man Tenney (pronounced Tinny). He had a high repute for probity and industry but lost his sanity. The first indication of this was his continued promulgation of the doctrine that as the leaves of the trees fall every year, the earth must be growing bigger. According to him, the consequence of this would be that it would turn on its axis more slowly, the days would be longer, everything would be changed, and the world would be ruined. In season and out of season, to learned and unlearned, rich and poor, male and female, he harped on this subject until his mind became entirely distorted. One Sunday afternoon I heard in the forest cries of "Murder! Murder!" I hurried to the rescue only to find that his son and a friend were taking poor Mr. Tenney home after a temporary escape. He migrated to this place from Boston. I met a relative of his who was Professor of Geology at Williams College, Massachusetts. He was a man of ability but died early.

In an old house in the bushes north of the village or rather in the northern part of the village, for it was within the corporate limits, lived Peyton Clements, one of the last professional hunters of the old school. He brought in wild turkeys, squirrels, opossums, but I think he did not shoot partridges. I grieve to say that this was not his only mode of making a living. He made money also through several physically attractive daughters, not common to all comers but living as mistresses with chosen lovers. Once an uncle of mine was sitting by a student of whom it was demanded, "Why have you been absent so often from prayers?" Uncle William whispered as excuse, "Say inclemency of the weather." The youth answered, "Peyton Clements, sir!" Although he was really innocent, he seemed to imply more than was creditable. The youngest girl was pretty and modest and several good ladies endeavored to keep her straight but she finally fell. She had a nephew, John Clements, dissolute and conscienceless, who by a curious provision of nature wrote a good hand and was often employed as a copyist with the pen.

Once, when John Clements' wife was sick, he asked the aid of a physician whose skill was equalled by his carefulness in collecting his dues. "What have you to pay me with, John?" "I have two nice fat pigs. You can have them." Sure enough they were in a pen near the front gate. The doctor felt proud of his fee, but, while he was doctoring the wife, the pigs were spirited away. He was not rewarded with even the music of a squeal.

10. A Trip to the Mountains in 1848

IN THE SUMMER OF 1848 I HAD A GRAND TRIP with my father to the mountains. I was a rising senior in the University but only sixteen and a half years old, very thin and boyish looking.

Our stages to Asheville in 1848 before the advent of railroads were: first, Smith's, a pleasant country inn about eighteen miles from Chapel Hill; second, another pleasant inn in Davidson County, about ten miles from Salisbury; third, Lincolnton; fourth, a wayside inn; fifth, Harris's or Chimney Rock; sixth, Asheville.

Near Greensborough we met an old acquaintance of my father, a refined and educated Quaker named Richard Mendenhall. On parting he said courteously, "Come and see me, Kemp, and I will entertain thee for thy father's sake until I know thee and can entertain thee for thy own." I afterwards found this was a quotation from Swift's *Tale of a Tub*.

While Mr. Mendenhall did not keep a hotel, he was willing to furnish meals to travellers at his house in Jamestown (pronounced "Jimston"). My father and I had dinner with him. Some friends had told me that he was fond of testing their knowledge of history. I determined to put a bluff on him. He began by asking me what was a giaour, the title of one of Byron's poems. I happened to know that it was a name given by the Turks to disbelievers in Islamism. I answered his question and at once plied him with counter historical questions so fast that he refrained from catechising me further. It was in Jamestown that I saw a most wild-looking maniac, a woman, half-dressed, about sixty years old, with long gray disheveled hair falling over her neck and shoulders, with face distorted, singing at us in a shrieking voice:

> Chicken, my chicken, Crany Crow!
> What's o'clock, old witch?

It was a horrible sight.

That night our host, who lived in what was called the Jersey Settlements, gave a perfect description of a matrimonial quarrel. Father said, "I've heard that Mr. and Mrs. Crump have separated. What is the matter?" "Well,

> They jawed it awhile,
> Backward and forward,

> Between one another,
> And couldn't agree.
> And so they concluded
> To siparate."

The next day to avoid a heavy rain and to get dinner we stopped at the house of a thriving planter, James E. Kerr. As he was at the University shortly after my father graduated, the conversation was very pleasant. But I had an experience trying to a bashful youth. A coach and four was driven up in haste to avoid the downpour. The passengers were a German professor leaving the College of South Carolina on his way North, his wife, and one or two grown daughters. We sat in the parlor on chairs set against the wall. For some reason a solemn dumbness prevailed. This seemed to me so ill-bred that I formed a desperate resolution to break the silence. So I bashfully made to the wife who was near me the brilliant remark, "Quite a heavy rain!" With a most high-pitched voice she inquired, "What did you observe?" All eyes were now on me. With face burning red I repeated more loudly, "Quite a heavy rain!" In a most indifferent tone she cried, "I can't hear you!" And I retired into my shell like a highland terrapin. That was the last of the conversation. Gloomy silence settled on the room, broken only by the summons to dinner.

That night was spent in Lincolnton at the hotel of Benjamin Sumner. I was greatly interested in the conversation between him and my father about the University, their Alma Mater, and about the Sumner family. Both were descended from William Sumner of Sumner Manor in Isle of Wight County, Virginia. The ancestress of my father, Elizabeth Sumner, settled on Tar River with her husband Elisha Battle. The ancestor of our host settled in Camden County.

Asheville was a very small town when we were there. The hotel was an ancient wooden building, kept by Robert Smith, the first white child born west of the Blue Ridge. Apartments and food were plain but pleasing. I was invited to a reception and dance but I was unacquainted with the ladies and knew not how to dance. At the reception, which was at Mr. Nick Woodfin's, I met one of the most beautiful ladies I had ever seen, Mrs. William, usually called Bill, McKesson. She was a descendant of Gen. Charles McDowell of the Revolution. Her pleasant chat made me feel less lonely. I was prevented from falling in love by her mention of her husband. She did not have a long life. In extreme sickness she spent some weeks at a watering place, but was not benefited and returned home by railway to Charlotte. Thence her husband provided relays of men to take the stretcher on which she lay on their shoulders by easy journeys to her home at Morganton. I recall her and Misses Sallie Jones of Hillsborough, Minerva Haywood of Raleigh, and Bettie Davis of Wilson (my son Tom's wife) as known for their beautiful faces, graceful figures, and queenly bearing.

The monotony of the fortnight at Asheville was broken into by a two or three days' trip to Warm Springs, now called Hot Springs, near the French Broad River thirty-seven miles below Asheville, at the invitation of James Patton, a college mate whose Uncle John A. Patton was owner and manager. We had a charming time, everything being informal, rude according to later ideas. The bathing in the river, in some places forming pools almost still, in others tumbling over ledges of rocks, was delightful and the warm bath afterwards the perfection of luxury. The warm pool was divided by a wooden partition, one-half allotted to males, the other to females. The arrangement was rather primitive and there were traditions of peeping through knot-holes in former days!

Thirty-seven years later, after lecturing in Asheville I went to the modern Hot Springs and was much disappointed. Everything was fine, but in place of swimming in the waist-deep pool there were a number of small pools encased in marble, where the bathing was in solitary luxury, with a negro to wait on me and half a dollar to pay.

A story was told of a German who stopped at Warm Springs to get a drink of water. When the hot water touched his tongue, he shouted, "Hitch up the horses, Hans! Hell ish not two miles from this place!"

On the way back to Asheville we dined at the old Baird house, once the home of Zebulon Baird (pronounced Beard), Zeb Vance's grandfather, and of his father, David Vance, who married Margaret Myra Baird. We found there six or seven gentlemen of the neighborhood. I was amused at the solution offered by one of them to the problem: "How do you divide into two equal parts eight gallons of whiskey when you have only an eight gallon, five gallon, and three gallon measure?" "Guess at it and drink the difference."

I was sitting one moonlight night on some lumber that was to be a part of the new courthouse with Newton Coleman, President Swain's nephew, who, if he had cared for his health, would have been distinguished. A youth about my age passing by was called and introduced to me as Zeb Vance. I had never met a brighter or more agreeable young fellow. Amid frequent flashes of humor he showed glimpses of familiarity with the Bible, Shakespeare, and Scott's novels which surprised me. It seems that the library of his Uncle Robert, who was killed in a duel by Samuel P. Carson, had passed into the possession of his mother and he had made good use of it. It doubtless contributed much to the formation of his clear and vigorous style of writing and speaking. I told my friends at home that a great man was growing up beyond the Blue Ridge, a prediction verified when he became the greatest war governor of the South.

Nicholas W. Woodfin, at whose house was held the reception that I mentioned, was a remarkable man. The first time he came to Asheville, he was a barefooted country boy riding a mule without a saddle. He struggled upwards and became a most successful lawyer, attending the county courts of Buncombe and the Superior Courts of every county in the mountain district, following his cases to the Supreme Court whenever there were appeals. All business entrusted to him was transacted with the most untiring and intelligent care. And he found time to represent his senatorial district for five successive terms in the General Assembly and accumulated a handsome fortune, as fortunes were then estimated. He and General Clingman were then the most conspicuous men in the mountains. I grieve to say that he lost his property by undertaking a railroad contract of too great magnitude. He also made the error of buying negroes on credit a few years before their emancipation.

While he was successful as a jury lawyer, his delivery of speeches was singular, only relieved of grotesqueness by the intense earnestness of his features and the sound sense of his arguments. His pronunciation of many words was so odd as to require shrewd guesses as to his meaning. Why a man of his talents should have adopted a style of utterance so affected is puzzling. His brother John pronounced his words as other folks do but his gestures were as energetic as windmill sails in a storm.

Nick Woodfin was the counsel for Mrs. Silver, the only white woman ever hung in North Carolina. Not long before his death I asked him about the case. He replied earnestly in substance, "She was unjustly hung. Her story was reasonable and told with every evidence of sincerity. Her husband came home drunk and began to beat her with a stick; she struck back and killed him. She did not intend to kill him, but only to keep him from beating her. She tried to hide the body by cutting it up and burying it. She did not know the difference between murder and manslaughter or self-defence. The law at that time did not allow her to testify in court and she was convicted. If she could have told her story to the jury, the result would have been different. I rode through the mountains three weeks to get signatures to her plea for pardon. I got a goodly number but Governor Swain refused to interfere. It was a miscarriage of justice, sir."

The fourth of July was celebrated in grand style while we were in Asheville. Mr. Edney, the principal teacher of the town, was master of ceremonies. Robert B. Vance, afterwards a brigadier general and congressman, brother of Zeb, was the orator. He made a good speech but used one gesture which struck me as absurd. Describing the afflictions of war and the tears they caused, he traced with his finger the course of the drops as they ran down the cheeks. At night there was music by a brass band in the Presbyterian Church. The band filled nearly half the church and the noise totally destroyed the music. It was deafening.

Robert Vance lacked the genius of his brother but had a more religious temperament. Zeb said of him, "Bob is a Methodist and believes in falling from grace but never falls. I am a Presbyterian and disbelieve in falling from grace but am always falling."

From Asheville Father and I journeyed to Burnsville, crossing the same creek about twenty times, sometimes driving in its bed among the rocks for a hundred yards or so. John Woodfin followed us, starting an hour later, but as he was alone with a faster horse and a lighter buggy, he overtook us before we reached the end of the journey. He came up laughing, saying that he had asked a mountain boy if he had seen two gentlemen in a buggy pass by. The boy replied, "No, I hain't seen no gentlemen in a buggy but I seen a man in a waggin and a little boy a-drivin on him." Rather severe on a rising senior in the University! I received another cut at the hotel of Mr. Penland, whose wife was a niece of President Swain. Mrs. Penland was a pleasant, refined, handsome woman. I noticed her little daughter whispering to her, at the same time glancing at me. The mother afterwards told me what she said. "Mother, won't you give me the key to get some sugar for the judge's little boy?"

I saw at Burnsville a specimen of mountain canvassing for the General Assembly. The candidate, a man named Flemming, spoke from a goods-box in front of a grog-shop most animatedly and effectively for about an hour with a tin quart-pot in his right hand. Then he went into the shop inviting the crowd to follow him to partake of whiskey. He was elected.

Flemming was a man of rough tastes and temper, principally engaged in buying horses and selling them south. He got into a quarrel with a prominent lawyer, Waightstill W. Avery, and struck him with a horsewhip. They did not meet again until three weeks afterwards. Avery in the meantime brooded over the disgrace of being horsewhipped. He was sitting in the courtroom with a cloak around him, distracted by the recollection of this indignity, when Flemming came in to speak to his lawyer and ostentatiously passed in front of his adversary. Protruding a pistol from under his cloak Avery shot him dead.

My father was the judge on the bench and witnessed the tragedy. Avery was placed under arrest, in truth made no attempt to escape. The trial came on next day. As the solicitor was akin to Avery, John Woodfin was appointed to prosecute. The defence was emotional insanity and acquittal was prompt. My father told me that the jury would have found him and every member of the bar guilty before they convicted Avery. Public opinion in that day was clear that any man subjected to the ignominy of being horsewhipped would be *ipso facto* rendered insane and the death of the assailant would be righteous retribution. Avery's popularity was increased by his act. He was often elected to the General Assembly, Senate and House, presided over the Breckinridge wing of the Democratic party and was a Confederate States senator. During the Civil War a squad of Federals rode into Morganton, Avery's home. Avery headed a volunteer party to pursue them and was the only man killed.

I witnessed a hotly contested slander suit which throws light on the pitiable feuds which spring up in uneducated communities. A very respectable looking woman was at a social gathering passing near a group of neighbors when one of them remarked, "I'll make that tray of biscuits whistle under your apron." This was construed to affirm the truth of a charge that she had stolen some biscuits. The people of the neighborhood took sides in the controversy. The lawyers made heated speeches on the subject. I sympathized with the woman and rejoiced that she won. A young lawyer named Davis was allowed by courtesy to make the opening speech, the first he ever made. When I next saw him thirteen years later, he was a member of the lower house of the General Assembly. The question of secession was in the air. He was a Unionist and I was president of the Wake County Union Club. At my invitation he and six or seven other members of the General Assembly opposed to secession (I remember Cutlar and Dr. Arendell) met at my invitation and sang patriotic songs. It was the best amateur choir I ever listened to. One of the songs in honor of the South was written to the tune of Dixie. I recall a line or two.

> Shall traitors dim its glory?
> Never! Never!
> A gallant band around will stand
> To live or die for Dixie.

Nearly all of this band volunteered in the army, and Davis and Cutlar were among the earliest slain. Oh, the pity of it!

A word or two about Cutlar. The Dialectic and Philanthropic Societies in those days had a praiseworthy habit of paying all the expenses of one penniless student, the cost being about $500. These students were called Society Beneficiaries. Among them was Senator Matt W. Ransom. Cutlar had a high reputation in his native county for talent and the Dialectic Society elected him to receive its benefaction. After a few months' trial it was found that he took no interest in University studies and he returned home. He soon became a lawyer and politician and was a distinguished speaker. He was rapidly rising to the front rank of our public men when he was killed in battle.

My pleasure in Burnsville was shortened by recklessness. Seeing a mist on a near-by mountain top, I thought it would be a good thing to tell the children that I had washed my hands in the clouds. I accordingly went rapidly to the mist. I found it unpleasantly cool and instead of walking carefully down the mountain I ran and turned one of my ankles. Limping to the hotel, I was the victim of pain, swelling, and vinegar wrappings for several days.

My father and I returned to Chapel Hill through Turkey Cove, a fertile and lovely valley, then by Morganton and Greensborough. Stopping for dinner near Greensborough, instead of giving our horse his usual light dinner of meal in water, we allowed the hostler to put him in the stable and give him a full dinner of oats. The result was that he came out of the stable wet with perspiration and nearly broke down on the road. He could hardly get out of a walk all the way to Chapel Hill.

It is hard nowadays to realize the discomforts of travelling in old times. It was mostly in buggies without tops. If the weather was propitious, the horse gentle and spirited, a short trip was delightful, as there was abundant time for conversation and viewing the changing scenery. But often the roads were sticky with mud or too rocky for fast movement. Sometimes the sun was broiling hot, the air full of dust. Again, the feet ached with cold, the rain was dismal and required holding up an umbrella. Under such conditions pleasure gives place to pain or discomfort. Once I was obliged to drive all day alone, holding up an umbrella with one hand, driving with the other. To add to the bodily discomfort, the heat and monotony often brought on drowsiness which could not be indulged because I held the reins and because the loss of consciousness might have tumbled me to the ground. Nevertheless, for all the drawbacks of ten hours a day of misery, four miles an hour over roads rocky or sandy or rough with hardened mud, my recollections and the information I gained have been a lasting benefit.

When I was a student of the University, Chapel Hill had not reached the dignity of having horses and vehicles for hire. Once when my aunt was called on to journey to Raleigh to see her sick mother, we were forced to borrow from Professor Green a pair of mules and a driver, and a carriage from Mrs. Anne C. Hall. It took nine hours to go twenty-eight miles. When we reached Raleigh, the mules set up loud notes of rejoicing. My aunt doubled the veil over her face and begged that we should take a back street.

There was no Durham in those days and the trading of the Chapel Hill neighborhood was mainly with Raleigh. The heavy four-horse stages passed each way three times a week. The road overseer as a rule had no plan for repairing the roads other than filling the gulleys washed into them by the rains with the earth which was carried into the side ditches. The consequence was that in winter the mud became deep and sticky. It is said that once there were seven hacks mired in the Widow Atkins' lane. Actually the Raleigh road near the village became so impassable that a new road for a stretch of two miles was made ascending the hill on its southern side.

In 1854 a special passenger train over the North Carolina Railroad was run west from Raleigh out of courtesy to members of the General Assembly wishing to spend Christmas at home. On the invitation of S. F. Phillips, a member from Orange, I was one of the passengers. There was only one house at what was called Durham's Station, the residence of Dr. Bart Durham, after whom the place was named. He was a good hunter and had killed large numbers of partridges. These, with fried chickens and fresh butter, gave us a royal welcome to the future city. There were no conveyances available, so I walked to Chapel Hill—twelve miles in three hours.

The county of Durham was formed long afterwards and named after the town but it might claim a more dignified name than that of a country doctor. In the Middle Ages it was necessary to give to the counts, dukes, etc., of districts on frontiers extraordinary powers for defence against the neighboring enemy. So the Palatinate was ruled by the Count Palatine of the Rhine. Such powers were entrusted to the Duke of Lancaster for defence against the Welsh and to the Bishop of Durham for defence against the Scots.

When the Province of Carolina was granted to the eight Lords Proprietors, it was manifestly impossible to meet sudden attacks by enemies whether Spanish or Indians by forces sent from England: vessels were often three months crossing the ocean. The charter therefore expressly granted to the Lords Proprietors the powers of the Bishop of Durham, thus associating the name of the English city and county with the newly created colony. It would certainly be appropriate to transfer it to a subdivision of that colony, albeit the legislators of 1881 were not cognizant of the fact and intended to honor the rapidly growing city named after a local physician.

11. Eminent Men of My Youth

IN MY YOUTH NORTH CAROLINA WAS FORTUnate in having among its leaders men of unusual ability and character. My father was a Whig and I was brought up to honor and admire especially the Whig statesmen and jurists. My life was undoubtedly influenced by them. It seems appropriate therefore to give sketches of a few of the most eminent.

My mother told me when I was a boy that the greatest men in North Carolina were Chief Justice Ruffin, Senator Willie P. Mangum (the first name was pronounced Wi-ley), and William A. Graham. These men were probably more talked about in her circle, but forming an opinion after they had withdrawn from the public view I would certainly add to the list William Gaston and John M. Morehead. My mother formed her estimate prior to 1840. The fame of Mangum was much dimmed before he died in 1861. His death was most pathetic. He was in extremely bad health. His only son, a very promising young man, had gone from the University into the war. While seated on his porch into which he was carried when the weather allowed, the ex-Senator saw a company coming up the avenue. They brought the body of his son—killed in the First Battle of Manassas. The shock was too great for the strength of the father. He soon was carried to his grave.

About 1841, when I was ten years old, I was playing marbles in the street. A fine looking old gentleman came by and putting his hand on my head said, "What is your name?" I answered, "Kemp Battle." "Oh no! Not Battle, but Skirmish!" This was my only interview with the great jurist, William Gaston.

William Gaston attained his greatest reputation as a judge of the Supreme Court of North Carolina when he was a colleague of Thomas Ruffin and Joseph J. Daniel. I do not believe that either England or America ever had a stronger court. For many years Judge Gaston was one of the best loved and most admired men in the State. He had a high reputation as a lawyer, was distinguished for literary culture, and had a peculiar hold on our people by his urbanity, popular manners, and integrity.

He was a sincere Roman Catholic and it is remarkable that this was not in the way of his favor with the people, although in 1776 they were so imbued with feelings hostile to Roman Catholicism that they inserted in the State Constitution a provision prohibiting from holding office all who should deny the truths of the Protestant religion. Notwithstanding this Gaston was elected by the General Assembly a judge of the Supreme Court and accepted the office. He contended that he could not be said to deny the truths of the Protestant religion because he believed some articles of faith which Protestants do not. Moreover, the provision in the Constitution, if aimed at those of his faith, was contrary to the Declaration of Rights, that "all men have a natural and unalienable right to worship Almighty God according to the dictates of their own consciences." While some thought that his arguments were jesuitical, his acceptance of the judgeship was acquiesced in generally and all doubts were settled by a provision in the Constitution of 1835 repealing the former prohibition and substituting a ban on those "who shall deny the being of God, or the truth of the Christian religion, or the divine authority of the Old or New Testament." This, which was aimed at Jews, was repealed by the Convention of 1861, commonly called the Secession Convention. I had the honor of voting for this repeal. Another Romanist, Matthias E. Manly, was also a member of the Supreme Court.

Among the may able opinions filed by Judge Gaston the most prominent was that in the case of the *State vs. Will*, a slave of my wife's father, James S. Battle. While running Will was shot in the back by his overseer, but being immediately overtaken and assailed by him killed him with a knife. The Attorney General, J. R. J. Daniel, in an able speech contended that as the overseer was in the place of the master, the killing was murder, not manslaughter; that all killing of masters by slaves must be punished by death. Will's master employed for the defence B. F. Moore, who first came into public notice as a great lawyer by his argument for Will. Judge Gaston's opinion sustaining Moore's contention that the killing was manslaughter, not murder, gained him great repute. The negro was branded, however, and it was deemed best to sell him to a planter in Alabama. I have heard, but am not sure of my authority, that he was hung for murder in that state. While in jail in Nash County his mistress regularly sent him food from her table.

Gaston was a Federalist, a representative in Congress, 1813-1817. He gained high favor in the public eye by his course there, but the Republican, later called Democratic, party became so overpowering in North Carolina that he retired from the political field. He often represented New Bern in the General Assembly as Commoner, i.e., member of the House of Commons, and was Speaker of the

House in 1808, one of the few offices in his day which entitled the holder to be called Honorable.

His song "The Old North State" brought him much popular approval. He happened to write it in this wise. He lived, when in Raleigh, at the home of Mrs. James F. Taylor, widow of the Attorney General. Her daughter Louisa was a fine singer. One night she brought back from a concert given by a strolling dramatic company from Switzerland a tune which had been much applauded by the audience. She said, "Judge, can't you write some words for this tune?" "I will try," said the judge, and next day brought in "The Old North State." It is a favorite with our people, but some critics object to the admission that "scorners may sneer at and witlings defame us." Perhaps the poet had recently heard the humorous description of North Carolina as "a strip of land between South Carolina and Virginia." Certainly Daniel Webster's jibe at Vermont as "a splendid state to emigrate from" might apply to our State, as its sons and daughters are inhabitants of all southern and many western communities. They are numerous even in New York City.

When Judge Gaston was a practitioner at the bar, he was employed by the heirs of Earl Granville to recover the vast domain which he owned in Colonial times. Many sales to settlers were made prior to the Revolution; then the State of North Carolina claimed the residuum as her own. After Independence was declared the heirs of Earl Granville claimed that by the treaty of peace their title was restored. Gaston was their attorney; Duncan Cameron was his chief opponent. The case was tried before the Federal Court in Raleigh, Judge Potter presiding. Chief Justice Marshall declined to sit because he had before his appointment to the Supreme Court acted as attorney in a similar suit by the Fairfaxes in Virginia. The jury decided in favor of the defendants, William R. Davie and Josiah Collins, who had bought parts of the land in dispute. There was an appeal to the Supreme Court of the United States but it was not pressed to a hearing. The British government appropriated an indemnity to the claimants. It is remarkable that Gaston did not lose his popularity by acting as attorney for this odious claim. It was probably because the people had no fear of his gaining the suit.

His oratory was much admired both as to matter and manner. His language was clear, his manner graceful and winning. There was sincerity in his utterances. He evidently spoke his convictions and disdained sophistry. When he arose, he trembled with excitement but soon overcame it and then his speaking flowed like a majestic river.

Judge Gaston was an active trustee of the University. It was on his motion that the office of president was created and Joseph Caldwell elected in 1804. In his address before the Literary Societies in 1832 he had the nerve to pronounce slavery the worst evil that afflicted the South and expressed the hope that means would be found to eradicate it. In the same address he denounced all attempts to weaken love of the Union.

His death in 1844 was dramatic. While sitting in the Supreme Court he became faint and was carried to his room. After being laid on his bed his spirits rallied so as to talk freely with his friends. An avowed infidel's name having been mentioned, he emphatically announced that he could not trust such a man. Then raising his head from his pillow he said earnestly, "A belief in an overruling Providence who shapes our deeds is necessary. We must believe and feel that there is a God all-wise and almighty." There was a rush of blood to the head. He fell back and expired. Edward Everett, in looking at his tomb said, "This eminent man had few equals and no superiors."

Joseph John Daniel was a judge of the Supreme Court from 1832 to 1848. He was regarded by many as fully equal in ability to Ruffin and Gaston. His opinions were strong and clear, covering all the points necessary to the decision, but he made no effort to write treatises on the subject or to gain reputation by rhetorical effort.

He was a member of the Episcopal Church but in conversation was apt to use what are called cuss-words. Once when he saw the contribution plate approaching, he found that he had no coin less than a five dollar gold piece. He whispered to his companion, "Ruffin, lend me a quarter." Ruffin shook his head. "Lend me a half!" Again the response was in the negative. Then excitedly, "Lend me a dollar." Ruffin had none. By that time the plate was in front of him. He threw down the five dollars, with the exclamation, "Damn you, go!"

No man exceeded him in kindness of heart. He had a farm not far from the town of his residence, Halifax. His foreman, a favorite slave, came in his wagon one day with a load of produce for sale. On interviewing his master he showed signs of being under the influence of brandy. The judge spoke sternly to him and ordered him to go home at once. A very cold, bitter rain began to fall and it became evident that the man would encounter suffering, if not danger, on the road. The judge's fears became so strong that he called for his horse and buggy and rapidly pursued his slave, carrying him a protecting blanket. A grandson of his, George Gordon Battle, a prominent lawyer of New York City, inherits his talents and his amiability. John Rives Jones Daniel, the Attorney General who ably opposed B. F. Moore in the homicide case of *State vs. Will,* and who was afterwards a representative in Congress, was a cousin. He left our State and settled in Louisiana.

Chief Justice Thomas Ruffin was considered one of the most learned lawyers in the land. His opinions were quoted with praise by the highest courts in this country and even in England. He pursued the plan of Chief Justice Marshall, not only deciding the case before the court but writing as it were a treatise covering the whole question. Chief Justice Pearson compared him to a young dog of excellent qualities but not well trained. As a young dog would break from the pursuit of a fox to run down a rabbit which crossed his path and then resume tracking the fox, so Pearson said Ruffin would leave his argument on the main question, run off on a collateral inquiry, and after exhausting it come back to the case before the court. But Pearson was a bit prejudiced. When on the Superior Court bench he gave much study to a certain case and was sure that his decision was correct. On appeal the decision was reversed by the Supreme Court, Ruffin delivering the opinion. Pearson never forgave him and years afterwards, when he had himself attained the dignity of Chief Justice, he persuaded his colleagues to join with him in reversing the former decision.

I once witnessed a trial before Judge Ruffin as chairman of the County Court of Alamance. A well-dressed young man was being tried for stealing a five dollar bank-bill from the railroad office. The judge's son Thomas, who years afterwards himself became a Supreme Court judge, was the counsel for the prisoner. The testimony was so conclusive of guilt that all that young Tom could do was to take exceptions to the description of the five dollar bill in the indictment. He spoke long and earnestly, contending that the bill in evidence was not that which the jury had to pass on. The court was patient and did not interrupt his earnest pleading. But when he finished, the judge made no allusion to the points he brought up but said, "Gentlemen of the jury, if you believe the evidence, the prisoner is guilty." The jury brought in a verdict of guilty. Then the judge turned to the prisoner, "Young man, in con-

Eminent Men of My Youth

sideration of your youth and the fact that this is your first offence, so far as is known, the court will deal leniently with you in the hope that hereafter you will obey the laws of your country." "Sheriff, take the prisoner to the whipping post and give him thirty-nine lashes on the bare back." The mandate was carried out at once and we wondered at the judge's idea of leniency.

Chief Justice Ruffin was not a cruel man but he was strict in enforcing the law. He seemed to think that one who committed crime made the choice of the punishment. It was a wrong to him and to society not to give him his choice.

In the Convention of 1861 an ordinance was offered to abolish corporal punishment. Its advocate spoke feelingly of the atrocity of publicly whipping a free man. Judge Ruffin rose with indignant wrath. "Whip a free man? *No! Whip a rogue! Whip a rogue!*" The criminal law deprived the culprit of free privileges such as the right to vote. The convicted rogue was not a free man.

My father told me that when he was a student of the University, 1818-1820, the faculty allowed the students to attend the trial of one Sparrow for the murder of one Hunt on the edge of the campus. The future Chief Justice Ruffin defended him, in the vehemency of his oratory often beating on the floor with his knuckles. He did not, however, save his client from the gallows. The oratory of his son was as energetic as his father's.

I once had the good luck to travel in the stage drawn by four horses from Raleigh to Chapel Hill and beyond, carrying the mail, in company with the elder Ruffin. To my surprise he chose the front seat with his back to the horses. He sat bolt upright without touching the back of the seat. I learned afterwards that he would not allow his children to lounge in a chair but required them to sit rigidly erect. About eight miles from Chapel Hill we dined at a noted inn called Moring's (vulgarly Moreen's). After this he slept soundly in the same posture, his head, from the movement of the stage over the rough road, jerking back and forth and sideways as if it would snap the bones of his neck. He acquired this habit from riding day and night from court to court.

He was a man of wonderful energy and toughness. He studied law under Judge Archibald Murphey and afterwards his preceptor aided him in procuring clients. He therefore felt bound to become surety for him to large amounts. Murphey became insolvent and Ruffin not only lost his property but was heavily indebted. He determined to retrieve his fortunes. He actually for some years attended courts in three counties, often traveling all night, the lawyers kindly arranging the cases in which he was counsel to suit his convenience. To increase his hardships he suffered much from rheumatism, often being lifted from his buggy into the hotel by his driver. He succeeded in discharging his debts and accumulating a handsome fortune.

He had the reputation of wisdom in investments but few men are always wise. When the Civil War came on, his ardent pro-Southern temperament caused great losses through purchase of Confederate securities and receiving Confederate money for debts.

The chief justice of the Supreme Court until the adoption of the Constitution of 1868 was chosen from their own number by the judges of the court. The custom arose of giving this precedency to the judge longest in office. Ruffin attained it on the death of Chief Justice Leonard Henderson in 1833 and held it until his resignation in 1852. Six years afterwards, no other lawyer being able to secure a majority vote in the General Assembly, he was by way of compromise elected to fill the vacancy created by the death of Chief Justice Nash. Some surmised that the other judges, Pearson and Battle, would as a matter of comity tender him his old place as chief justice. But when the judges met, Pearson said, "According to precedent I am to preside. I call the court to order." There was no objection, and, so far as I know, there was no hostile criticism.

Judge Ruffin died at the age of eighty-two. B. F. Moore and I attended his burial in the Episcopal Cemetery at Hillsborough. I was asked to be a pall-bearer and assigned to the heavy end of the coffin to assist the old sheriff, George Laws. I record as a warning to the conductors of funerals that so much weight was thrown on me that I barely escaped serious injury.

Judge Thomas Ruffin, the younger, had probably the ability of his father. In his younger days he was not a hard student of legal principles, although he gave his whole mind to the trial of his cases. Indeed so eager was he for victory that there were accusations of sharp practice. But I personally had no evidence of this. On the contrary, when thrown intimately with him for a day or two once, I was struck by his high-toned principles. I remarked to one of the best of men, his law partner Judge Dillard, "Ruffin is a lawyer who can be relied on for utter fairness." Dillard smilingly said, "He is a rascal like the rest of us." He meant only that in the hot excitement of trials he might take positions which non-lawyers might think not strictly fair. But it should be remembered that lawyers giving their minds to the cases of their clients, studying mainly the arguments for their side, necessarily become biased. It is impossible for them to act as impartial judges. This is illustrated by what Judge James C. MacRae told me about a trial over which he presided. A certain lawyer made a speech advocating a construction of the law which did not meet the judge's approval and he said, "Surely you do not claim that to be law?" "Well, Judge, I can't say that I do, but I did not know how it would strike your Honor."

No lawyer ever had so sure control over the juries of his county as Thomas Ruffin, the younger. It was dangerous to try a case with him on the opposite side. His manner was so earnest and apparently sincere, his ability so real, and his personal traits so winning, that his neighbors trusted him as they would a judge.

George Edmund Badger was certainly one of the ablest men North Carolina has produced. In fact he was almost too clever. His mind was so strong, his powers of debate so superior, and his sense of humor so keen, that he would sometimes argue on the wrong side in order to tease his adversary. This was a real hindrance to his reputation and sometimes caused offense. When he was stirred to earnestness on a subject in which he was interested, he was well-nigh irresistible. In the early forties Rev. George W. Freeman, rector of Christ Church, Raleigh, of which Mr. Badger was a vestryman, denounced the wine and dancing parties then fashionable. Mr. Badger answered his scriptural arguments with such cogency of reasoning as to surprise the public and excel the preacher in his own field. Finding that his opponent had convinced his congregation, Mr. Freeman resigned his charge. Soon afterwards he was made Bishop of Arkansas.

Although Mr. Freeman failed in his attack on the convivial customs of his day, I think that those acquainted with the history of Raleigh will agree with me that the free use of alcoholic beverages has been a curse to its society. I recall a shocking number of men who failed to reach the eminence which their talents merited, men who were hurried to premature graves, men who failed in life because of sound judgment rendered unsound by the distorting if not poisonous influence of liquor.

After Mr. Badger's defeat for the senatorship in 1855 he was often in my law office and I heard that he spoke kindly of my wife and me. I recall some of his stories, mostly humorous. One was this. "When I went off to school my mother gave me twenty dollars.

Of course I must keep an account, so I gave ten cents for a notebook. I entered the twenty dollars as a receipt and the ten cents for a notebook under it. Then I bought a schoolbook and put that under it. A boy borrowed twenty-five cents from me and I put that in the same column. When the twenty-five cents was repaid, I put that under it. And so I went on buying, lending, and collecting, entering all the items in one column. Then I concluded to balance my account, and see where I stood financially. My books showed that I was worth $247 but my pocket-book showed that I did not have ten cents. And so, Mr. Battle, I concluded that the man who pronounced double-entry bookkeeping to be a device of the crafty Italians to enable employees to cheat employers was about right." I told my father this and he said, "Badger may not like figures but when he has a case requiring that he delve into complicated accounts, there is no man more clear-headed and patient than he."

As soon as he was admitted to the bar he won a reputation for intellect and persuasive oratory. He was honored with a seat in the House of Commons from the borough of New Bern when just twenty-one years of age, and had a large following for a judgeship at twenty-four and obtained one at twenty-five. Paul C. Cameron told me how he was at first defeated. Judge Duncan Cameron was a member of the General Assembly from Hillsborough and Willie P. Mangum from Orange. The judge had conceived a great liking for Mangum and appreciated his eminent ability. He wished him to be elected a Superior Court judge. So he called on John Stanly, who was speaker of the House and almost an autocrat, to ask his cooperation. Stanly rather curtly said, "No, I've made up my mind that Badger shall have the place. I know that he is fully qualified." Cameron, who had a will as strong as Stanly's, called to see his colleague, "Mr. Magnum, it has been in my power to my great satisfaction occasionally to aid you in your profession and now I have a favor to ask of you." "I know you have helped me," said Mangum, "and am deeply grateful. I will do what you wish, if in my power." "Well," said Cameron, "today is Friday. The election for judge will come off Monday. Stanly has picked out his kinsman Badger for the place. I want you to beat him and I think you can. I will help you." "Certainly. I can beat him, I feel sure." And he did beat him. A year afterwards Badger was elected to fill another vacancy.

Judge Badger told me that sometimes a law point was so exceedingly doubtful that he could not make up his mind which side was right. In such perplexity he would secretly take a quarter of a dollar and toss it up. "Heads for plaintiff, tails for defendant," and decide by the result. It hurt no one as the defeated party had the right of appeal to the Supreme Court.

His youthful zeal and abhorrence of lynch-law came near landing five or six of the leading men of Edgecombe in jail. A bad free negro was known to be corrupting the slaves on the river plantations by persuading them to steal from their owners and sell to him cheap. It was impossible to obtain legal evidence against him and five or six of those injured proceeded to give him a good whipping and made him leave the county. The County Attorney, Francis L. Dancy, pushed an indictment against the lynchers and aided the solicitor to convict them. Judge Badger talked of Magna Carta and the Bill of Rights and imposed a fine of $500 on each. He was with difficulty dissuaded from subjecting them to imprisonment in the county jail. Naturally the feelings of the victims were not kindly to the County Attorney by whose zeal they were prosecuted. Their sons and daughters, however, did not sympathize with the animosities of their fathers. It so happened that two of the sons and one of the daughters of Dancy married two of the daughters and one of the sons of one of the victims—a North Carolina Montague and Capulet feud.

Mr. Badger never complained of the loss of his seat in the Senate nor of the failure of the Senate to confirm President Fillmore's nomination of him to a Supreme Court judgeship. The cause in both cases was politics. Personally all the senators had a high regard for him and for his legal abilities. Webster especially admired his genius and learning, even though he once said to him, "Badger, you are the greatest trifler in the Senate."

He was a very kindhearted man. Once at the White Sulphur Springs in Virginia, when the ice-cream was brought to the table, a little girl was much distressed because her mother forbade her eating it. He called out, "Waiter, take these two saucers of cold stuff to the kitchen and warm them. The little girl and I want ours good and warm." And earnestly he praised the liquid dainty until he restored cheerfulness to his young friend.

Another example of his sense of humor. At Granville Court a man employed him in a simple four-dollar case which he gained. When payment was made, the client pulled out a buckskin purse and brought out one coin and then another until the amount of the fee lay on the table in shining silver, leaving the purse empty. With a theatrical air Mr. Badger thrust a dime back into the purse. "Take that back. It shall never be said of me that I took the last cent a man had."

Judge Romulus M. Saunders was one of the strongest men on the bench. He had decided talents and was a very forcible speaker but had little respect for dignity or grammar or the technicalities of law. He had been a general of militia and the title of general stuck to him. He had also been Minister Plenipotentiary to Spain. Judge Badger, a master of sarcasm, in a public speech in Raleigh said, "We all know the reasons for this appointment. It must be for his knowledge of the Spanish language. He knows nothing of Latin, or Greek, German, Russian, Italian, French, or Dutch and everyone recognizes his profound ignorance of English. All men must have some language and therefore the honorable gentleman must be versed in Spanish." Hon. D. M. Barringer, who was also Minister to Spain, told me that all the Spanish words he learned were "*Si, señor.*" The wags among the great lords around the throne made satirical hits at the *Americano*. In Spanish they would say, "You are very ugly this morning." "*Si, señor!*" "You must have been on a carouse last night." "*Si, señor!*" And so on.

He was never out of office except when he was in pursuit of one. This gave rise to many jibes at his expense, the most absurd being the grave publication that Hon. R. M. Saunders was a candidate for the bishopric in the Episcopal Church vacated by the deposition of Right Rev. L. S. Ives.

The satire of Mr. Badger that he was ignorant of the English language, of course not intended to be taken in earnest, was far from the truth. Probably he adopted the speech of the unlearned so as to be agreeable to unlearned voters. I heard him make a strong and valuable address at the dedication of the bronze statue of Washington in our Capitol Square. In his peroration he predicted, "The name and fame of Washington will survive when that there statute shall crumble into dust."

He carried his unconventional ways to the bench. A certain lawyer insisted on arguing a question of law. "I don't want to hear you," said the judge, "I've made up my mind." "But my client insists on my presenting the arguments." "Well, talk on, but I'm not going to listen." And he clapped his hands on his ears. It was likewise reported in Raleigh that in Burke County he threatened to jail a man who refused to take Confederate money for the amount of a judgment. Notwithstanding these peculiarities he was an able man and a good one.

His wife was very handsome and accomplished, a daughter of William Johnson, of Charleston, South Carolina, a judge of the Supreme Court of the United States. She survived her husband a few years. At the request of the family, including General Bradley T. Johnson of the Confederate army and a prominent lawyer of Richmond and Baltimore, I wound up the estate as administrator. I was amazed at the elegance and costliness of the furniture and paintings. I bought at the sale and have yet a set of steps which was used to mount the tall bedsteads of the old days.

Judge Saunders' indifference to settled legal notions not supported by his common sense led to a famous decision against former precedents. If A calls B a damned liar and B strikes him for the insult, the judge said that both are guilty of an affray. This was contrary to the ancient maxim, "Words do not justify a blow." He was sustained by the Supreme Court, however, as well as by public opinion.

I give another illustration of his rough manner. He was so rude at Franklin Court to Major Augustus M. Lewis as to provoke an angry retort. The judge did not reply to this, but on their way to dinner he clapped Lewis on the back, saying, "Gus, I didn't think you to be so stupid as to mind what I said. I meant no offence." Lewis was satisfied.

Judge Badger and he at breakfast one day had an argument on a point of law and Badger in the opinion of the company got the best of him. At dinner Saunders magnanimously said to him, "I have been thinking over our discussion at breakfast and honesty compels me to confess that I was wrong." "Well," replied Badger, "I've been thinking over it too and have come to the conclusion that *I* was wrong." So at it again they went and the hearers agreed that Saunders was again discomfited.

12. A Lawyer in Raleigh

BEING QUITE FAMILIAR WITH THE TEXTBOOKS prescribed by the Supreme Court I hoped to pass a perfect examination for admission to the bar. Chief Justice Pearson asked me one question not in the books and I answered it wrongly to my great disappointment. Getting my second or Superior Court license, I concluded to settle in Raleigh. I was warned against this on the ground that there were many lawyers there who had the people's confidence and I would be kept in the background many years. It turned out, however, that owing to deaths and retirements from practise, I was one of the older members of the bar in the short space of ten years.

With a heavy heart in June, 1854, I left my old beloved home and began what I thought was to be my life-work. My first act was indiscreet, if not foolish: I rented for law-office and dormitory a large room with windows facing west, under a flat roof covered with tin. Soon hot weather came and after twelve o'clock the summer sun blazing into the windows made the heat unbearable. Even after sunset the hot tin roof allowed little cooling and hindered or broke my sleep. Besides, I was too far from the courthouse.

Having never left the home of my parents for any length of time, I was naturally homesick. Learning that the candidates for the General Assembly were to speak at Wake Forest, I endeavored to change the color of my blues by being one of the people to listen to their wrangles. After an hour or so I could stand them no longer and joined a company who had left the scene of the speaking and were conversing on other than political matters. Feeling desperate, I relieved my despondency by telling old jokes suitable for such listeners. Their mirth satisfied me and I was especially flattered by a young man who amid boisterous laughter burst out, "I'll swear, Battle, I did not know you were such a good blackguard." I had never before heard this latter word used in a complimentary sense.

Right here let me give a short psychological lecture. The narration of piquant anecdotes is good medicine for depressed spirits. It diverts action from the nerve cells where melancholia is poisoning happiness to those which bring merriment. I have found by experience that the practise brings relief to the mind and health to the body. Let no one sneer at jocularity in its place. Inopportunely used it is a nuisance. Why was it given to us if we are to hide it in the recesses of the brain?

During my tutorship my parents gave me board so that I saved $1,600. I gave $500 of this to Quentin Busbee, who had been a partner of his deceased brother Perrin, for a partnership for one year and one-third of the proceeds. Busbee had been too fond of whiskey but had been an abstainer for some time. His ladylove, Miss Julia Taylor, had agreed to marry him and I felt sure that he would keep straight for a year.

On the whole I made an excellent trade. Our business brought in what the partnership had cost and a considerable amount more than what I would have gained if I had practised alone. But the gain in throwing me into full practise was incalculable. I did not have a pushing disposition by nature and my progress would have been slow if I had been alone.

I was soon cured of my nostalgia. In the first place the partnership with Busbee caused a change of residence to an apartment not lovely in appearance but pleasant in winter and summer, a room in the rear of our law office next to the Market House. Next it threw me into all the legal work I could do. At the August term of court, the first that I attended, Busbee took the laboring oar and I acted as his assistant in order that I might learn the details of trying cases. I sadly needed this noviciate because I knew absolutely nothing of actual practise. But at the November term, Busbee having accepted the position of Reading Clerk of the Senate, I had a criminal docket of over a hundred cases under my sole care.

My partnership with Busbee lasted only two years. At the end of the first year, as he had been straight all the year, I concluded to risk him a second. But, alas, at the end of about nine months he succumbed to his old enemy. Wild with spasmodic laughter and in almost perpetual motion, he walked rapidly from one barber-shop to another and called for a hair-cut until his scalp, of a yellowish hue with the blackest of bristles, had an unearthly aspect. A negro who had been long in his family was sent for him and succeeded in getting him home. It was several weeks before he was able to take up business. Of course I was uneasy for fear he would get me into trouble by misconduct or neglect of the affairs of the firm, but fortunately his temporary insanity made him despise business. Although I suffered some anxiety the firm lost not a dollar except to myself. It owed me some $300 but I bore that cheerfully in the joy of there being no loss to others. After this I practised alone for years.

It was pitiful that a man of such a generous heart, attractive manners, and bright intellect should have ruined his career. It was a grief to me but his infirmity actually brought me to the front. It happened this way. W. W. Holden, afterwards Governor, was in 1861 contemplating the formation of a party to be led by himself. Busbee was an adherent of his. I had been an active candidate for the General Assembly the previous year and many wished me to be a candidate for the proposed Convention of February, 1861. Holden engineered the nominations at a mass-meeting packed with voters from the districts where Busbee was born and raised. I declined to be a candidate and Busbee was nominated and elected. The people of the State, however, voted down the February Convention. When another Convention was called by the General Assembly for May, 1861, Busbee was incapacitated and I took his place on the ticket by general consent.

Busbee when sober was original and interesting, having a big brain and forcible oratory. I give some specimens of his humor. Once he lived in the same cottage with my Uncle Richard who was hopelessly in love with a lady named Delha and was despondent. Busbee, who was very athletic, solemnly lay on the floor and twisted his body successively into the shape of the letters of her name, D E L H A. It was so ludicrous that my uncle perforce lost his melancholy.

Sometimes I would catch Busbee in a mistake. He would gravely announce, "I will have you to understand that the Constitution of the United States guarantees to every man the privilege of being a damn fool."

Once Busbee was called by the plaintiff as an expert witness in a suit about the building of a brick house. The lawyer opposed to the claim questioned his being an expert. "Mr. Busbee, you are a lawyer. How is it that you claim to have peculiar knowledge on the subject matter of this action?" "Well, sir, when I was young I worked in a brickyard and helped make bricks. I have laid bricks in walls. I have superintended the building of my own brick house. I have paid workmen for their labor in laying bricks; and, sir, I have worn them in my hat." The judge allowed him to testify and the case was gained.

A country man came into his office one day and said, "Is Mr. Miller in here?" Busbee rose gravely from his seat, opened his many drawers and searched them, looked carefully under bureau and table, stepped into a chair and examined the tops of his bookcases and then confidently announced, "He is not here." The gradual dawning of the joke on the bewildered questioner was extremely amusing.

The elder brother and former partner of Quentin Busbee was Perrin H. Busbee, a man of more commanding influence and possibly of greater intellect. He had a high reputation as a lawyer. He had a strong sense of humor. The trick he played on General George Washington Haywood created much merriment. Once in trying a case in Nash court the general's speech was postponed until after dinner. Busbee and he were intimate friends. While he was at dinner Busbee slipped into his room and wrote on the general's brief, "This action will not lie but if necessary I will." The general was extremely near-sighted and was caught. He began, "Gentlemen of the jury, I contend in the first place that this action will not lie but if necessary I will." There was a universal laugh, and recalling what he read he turned to the trickster and said, gravely but not angrily, "Busbee, you done that."

Perrin Busbee was for a short while Reporter to the Supreme Court and if he had not died in middle age, he would have attained high office. His wife, daughter of Solicitor General James Fauntleroy Taylor, was noted for her beauty and intelligence.

General Wash Haywood was in some respects a remarkable man. Not a deeply read lawyer, not at all fond of books, he amassed a fortune at the bar, not by eloquent speaking or by learning but by his knowledge of the men of the county and his unerring commonsense. He seemed to know the views of every qualified juror and therefore in important cases the leading counsel hastened to engage him as an associate. When the war came on, he kept a discreet silence as to his opinions. He thought the movement unwise. The constant anxiety unsettled his mind and he became obsessed with the idea that detectives were watching for opportunity to deprive him of liberty and property. It was thought best to send him to his brother in Alabama. His escort was a notorious Raleigh man, James Fauntleroy Taylor II, son of the Solicitor General, and it was said that people on the road could not decide which was the crazy man and which the escort. The general died in Alabama, leaving most of his estate to his younger brother, E. Burke Haywood, M. D., the very able Surgeon-General of the State.

James Fauntleroy Taylor II was a very singular man. He was a promising boy until he lost the sight of one eye by the inexcusable carelessness of a fellow-student. Thereafter, though he had a sprightly mind and spurts of energy, he refused to employ his talents in useful occupations. He spent his time in riding first one hobby and then another, earnestly endeavoring to impress all acquaintances with the worth of his hobby for the time being. At one time he wrote short pieces of poetry, calling himself the Bard of Ram-cat, the southwest part of the county which he insisted should be spelt Rham-kart. At another he insisted on changes in current pronunciations, not hesitating to correct scholars and dignified officials. Once, when serving as a petty officer on the blockade steamer Advance, a position given him because his health did not permit him to be in the army, he actually interrupted a rebuke by the captain for some dereliction in order to correct the pronunciation of a word the captain had used. I remember a few of his corrected pronunciations: go-at for goat; to-ad for toad; ah-li-gah-tor for alligator. He would insist on his change as if it were a matter of life and death.

While the things which interested him were as a rule not interesting to his friends, often in the most serious manner he would make utterances very humorous. Soon after the war began I heard him explaining with the utmost gravity to some country people how they could in the fiercest battle avoid wounds and death. "A bullet, gentlemen, has a path called its line of trajectory. All you have to do to ensure safety is to stand to the right or the left of this line."

At a later date the news came that General Lee had opened out his army, the Federal troops had walked into the trap and had been almost annihilated, but the Southern army for strategic reasons had fallen back twenty miles. Such news was common. Taylor in most emphatic tones declared, "I am tired of whipping the Yankees and then falling back. I want to hear of our being defeated like hell and then advancing on them and cutting them to pieces."

Although opposed to any gainful work, he often volunteered to assist others by advice and temporary labor. For example, when Jonathan Worth (afterwards Governor) was in 1863 elected State Treasurer and removed to Raleigh, he inspected and improved the Treasurer's fish-pond, saying that no man with Quaker blood in his veins can make a sensible fish-pond. "See how instead of having it circular he has made it square. Without doubt the fish will dash their brains out against the corners."

13. Courtship and Marriage

IT HAD NOT BEEN LONG IN RALEIGH WHEN I FELL in love with a distant cousin Martha Ann Battle, of Edgecombe, universally called Patty. Her father James S. Battle and my grandfather Joel Battle were first cousins. I have already told of our hearing Jenny Lind at a concert in 1850 before we met and our meeting at West Point and Troy, New York, and Warrenton, North Carolina, the same year. I heard of her speaking kindly of me but we did not meet again for four years. In 1854 I was called to be the best man at the marriage of my first cousin Helen Battle to Dr. W. B. Ricks at the Falls of Tar River five miles from Cool Spring, Patty's father's plantation. I learned that her father, whom I called Cousin James, though not confined to his bed, was in bad health and that his youngest daughter, Patty, had stayed to take care of him while her two elder sisters had gone to some Springs. I called with my Uncle Dossey. We were asked to dinner. Cousin Patty's graceful manners and sensible conversation completely captivated me. Further acquaintance from time to time convinced me of the entire accord of our ideals.

It is impossible for me to describe the depth of my love and admiration of her. She was my ideal of what a woman ought to be. We were sweethearts fifty-eight years and I truly say that my love and my admiration of her never diminished. As a wife and mother she was perfect in my eyes. We had terrible trials in our married life—illness, loss of children, the anxieties of the war, loss of property. She bore all with serenity and fortitude. She was always ready to do anything, submit to any labor or inconvenience which I thought desirable in order to advance my aims in my profession or in politics or as President of the University or as Professor of History. It is a precious thought to me that not a cross word ever passed between us. I do not mean that we never differed in opinion. But when we disagreed, one or the other would yield without bad temper. She adopted my friends and my kin as her own and I am sure that she loved them as I did. In her religious views she was peculiarly reverential, loving such characters as George Herbert and Keble and their poetry. I was far behind her in such devotion but endeavored to sympathize with her. One thing makes me fear that I was not entirely successful. Before she became weakened by the stress of motherhood, she played beautifully on the piano, was noted for her exquisite touch. Her taste was for what might be called serious music, while mine was for the lively and gay. She discovered this and was reluctant to give me what she herself preferred. Just so, although she knew that our literary tastes differed somewhat, this did not prevent her being interested in the books most agreeable to me.

Before marriage her studies were beyond what the girls of that day achieved. She knew the Constitution of the United States by heart and the 119th Psalm with its 176 verses. She read the whole of Gibbon's *Decline and Fall of the Roman Empire*. But she was not a whit pedantic or fond of showing her learning. I discovered such feats of hers by accident.

She was always among the best at her schools. I have the record of her standing at one of the most eminent seminaries in the country, that of Miss English in Georgetown, D.C. Her marks were among the best in all her studies, and her deportment was perfect. While at Georgetown she and a teacher, Miss Rosa Nourse, and a schoolmate, Miss Fanny Reade, became such warm friends that we visited them after our marriage. Miss Fanny returned our visit in Raleigh. At a school in Warrenton, of which the principal was Mrs. Daniel Turner, wife of a former member of Congress, daughter of Francis Scott Key, she formed a close friendship with a teacher who was afterwards Mrs. Worcester of Rochester, New York. After many years we stopped a day in Rochester so that they might be together again. Mrs. Worcester was the mother of Rev. Dr. Elwood Worcester of Boston, the leader in the famous Emmanuel Movement which aims to effect cures of bodily and mental ailments by religious faith. Another of my wife's schoolgirl intimates was Miss Rebecca Spruill of Warrenton, a lady of high intelligence and lofty ideals.

My courtship and engagement lasted a year. My visits were by railroad, through Weldon and back to Raleigh by Goldsborough. My ladylove most of the time was at her brother William's at the Falls of Tar River, while I was made to feel at home with my cousin, Mrs. Helen Ricks, wife of Dr. W. B. Ricks. It is a grief to me that I felt compelled to break the friendship between the doctor and myself. Thinking him a man to be trusted I talked freely—too freely—about two relatives who were dear to me. For no good reason he reported what I said and wounded their feelings acutely. While I felt always grateful for his hospitality, I was too deeply hurt to show warmth of friendship afterwards. I mention this in order to recommend prudence about blaming people. My father was a model in this respect, while my own tongue has made enemies for me several times in my life.

I managed to win the hearts of the children of Patty's brother. One of them announced as a great discovery, "I declare I believe Uncle Kemp and Aunt Pat are favorites." Among other pleasant things that I carried them was a story in rhyme which had some amusing bits. For example:

> Daddy Longleggiano
> Had heard the soprano
> Of Miss Butterfly's
> Voice in a song.

The courtship was described and then the marriage ceremony came on.

> The priest, an old rook,
> Was there with his book.

The ceremony was interrupted:

> Down into the hollow,
> Pounced a fat swallow,
> And carried Daddy Longlegs away.
> The bride of course fainted,
> For she was acquainted
> With manners and knew what was right.
> They fanned her, then brought her
> Some brandy and water,
> And so they recovered her quite.
> "Is he gone," she did cry,
> "Without saying good-bye?
> I think it was very improper;
> So I'll cease all my sorrow,
> And early tomorrow,
> I'll marry old Gaffer Grasshopper."

Then the news came that a hawk had killed the swallow and that Old Daddy Longlegs with the loss of one of his strong pegs was in hot pursuit of Miss Butterfly and her new lover. Old Gaffer Grasshopper is frightened but declares:

> "The tale that they tell each
> Is gammon and spinach,
> My eye and Elizabeth Martin.
> Although I'm not frightened,
> I'll run a bit now."

I will not trust myself to write of our engagement except to express my gratification that the Rocky Mount Mills Company has laid out a park on the river bank where we used to stroll in the late afternoons. It will be very beautiful and interesting, embracing the woods on the north bank and an island of eight or ten acres. The flowing water dashing among the picturesque rocks gives a charming outlook.

Our marriage was intended to be on the 21st of November, 1855, but owing to some mistake in the arrangements it was postponed to the 28th of November. It was at Cool Spring, the original home of the Battle family in Edgecombe which had come to the brother of my bride, Turner Westray Battle. His wife, a woman of conspicuous charm of person, brain, and character, was daughter of Judge Joseph J. Daniel of our Supreme Court. There was a large company assembled and the festivities were on a grand scale. I must record a compliment to our family from Henry Mordecai, whose potations had carried him to the lively stage. My brother Richard was introduced to him and he burst out, "Dick Battle, son of Judge Battle, a good breed of dogs!"

There was no dancing. The day after the wedding there was a big dinner and that night another gathering of invited guests. It was all very grand but to me very tiresome.

I add part of a letter written by Cousin Livy, wife of Captain Turner Battle, to her sister, Mrs. Mary Long Gordon.

Cool Spring,
December 12th, 1855.

...We had forty guests who remained all night, and the following day and night, so you may know I was busy to make them all comfortable such cold weather. I had nineteen or twenty beds, and thus stored them away, two by two. The Misses Somerville, Miss Brownlow, Miss Sue Plummer, Miss Margaret Norfleet, Miss Bettie Parker, Mrs. Austin, Mollie Battle, Mittie and her little ones, were the lady part of the company who rested here all night, and such a nice clever set of gentlemen! I wish Brother George could have been here to have seen them. Pattie behaved in the most proper manner imaginable. She was a good deal frightened, but evinced her usual self-control. She looked more handsomely than I ever saw her, in a dress of white corded silk, worn under an embroidered lisse, with three skirts. Kemp, of course, was all smiles and happiness. Mr. Cheshire remarked that it made him very sad to perform a ceremony which separated from his flock one whom he so highly esteemed and warmly loved. Pat was a great favorite with him, as she is with all who know her. The girls accompanied

Courtship and Marriage

her to Chapel Hill on Friday, when there was to be a great feasting and merry-making....

The second day after the ceremony we took the railroad by way of Weldon to Raleigh, stopped at Guion's Hotel, and the next day journeyed by carriage to Chapel Hill. There we met with the warmest of welcomes from my parents, my Aunt Laura Phillips, and other relatives. My two sisters-in-law and William Jordan and Peter Hines accompanied us. A party was given us at my father's and there we settled down for a week or two.

From Chapel Hill we returned to Edgecombe and had a most affectionate reception from Patty's brother William and his good wife Elizabeth. Then we were warmly welcomed by Captain Turner Battle and his wife. Then we spent some days at Westrayville with my wife's uncle, the brother of her mother, Turner Page Westray, and his excellent wife. We spent several days also in Tarborough at the home of Rev. Dr. Joseph Blount Cheshire, whose wife's sister was Miss Arabella Parker, one of my wife's most intimate friends. It was here that I had the pleasure and honor of drawing on the front walk my only original picture—a huge cat, with little cats on back, tail, neck, and head; cats in front, underneath, and behind; cats in sundry other positions—for a future bishop, Dr. Cheshire's son Joseph Blount Cheshire, the younger, then a boy of five or six.

Afterwards, before settling down in our quarters, we accepted an invitation from a relative, Miss Susan Hines, to spend a few days with her and Cousin Rowena, an excellent pair of sisters. They lived in Raleigh with their brother, Dr. Peter E. Hines, and gave us an introduction to the city which my wife had seen only in her childhood.

14. My Wife's People

MY WIFE WAS NOT BORN AT COOL SPRING, her father's place on Tar River, but at Nashville, Nash County, where he had then a second home. It was found that the proximity of a millpond rendered the village malarious, and after a few years he sold the house. It is now used as a hotel, the marble mantel in the reception room still in good condition. On account of his wife's health her father resided for a time in Raleigh, then tried Jones's Springs and Shocco Springs in Warren County and finally the town of Warrenton. In 1840 he started with her to a Virginian health resort but her strength gave way and she was taken from the train to die at Hicksford, Virginia. Thus at seven years of age Patty lost the care of a mother, which to a child of a sensitive, retiring disposition was a peculiar calamity. Her lovable character, however, always attracted friends who discerned her worth and, as far as it was possible to do so, supplied the mother's place.

Patty and I were both descended from Elisha Battle and Elizabeth Sumner. My line was: 1st, William Battle; 2nd, Joel Battle; 3rd, William Horn Battle, my father. Hers was: 1st, Jacob Battle; 2nd, James Smith Battle, her father. My grandfather and her father thus were first cousins. The designations of kinship beyond first cousin are muddled. According to some genealogists my wife and I rate as second cousins, according to others as second cousins once removed, according to others as third cousins.

Patty's father, James Smith Battle, was an excellent neighbor, a wise farmer, exceedingly kind to his many slaves. He was of such a serious disposition when I knew him that I conjecture he was afflicted with the Bright's disease that carried him off at the age of sixty-seven. He had no liking for politics and office-holding. He was twice married, first to his cousin, a sister of Dr. Cullen Battle of Alabama. There was one child, Marmaduke, who died in Mississippi. His first wife died soon after marriage and after several years he married Sally Harriett Westray, the beautiful and attractive daughter of Samuel Westray and Sally Bradford Turner who was the widow of David Short. By her he had six children: 1st, William Smith; 2nd, Cornelia Viola, childless wife of John S. Dancy; 3rd, Turner Westray; 4th, Mary Eliza, wife successively of William F. Dancy and Dr. Newsom J. Pittman; 5th, Penelope Bradford, wife of General William R. Cox; 6th, Martha Ann, universally called Patty, my wife.

Of these I was most thrown with William Smith. For years he was an active and successful business man, but in later life he lost his fortune. Having unlimited confidence in him, I became surety on his paper for a large amount and his fall carried me down. After his death I wrote a notice of him which was circulated privately. I give the major portion of it slightly revised:

"The death of this splendid specimen of the fine old North Carolina gentleman removes an ancient landmark of Edgecombe and Nash. He was born October 4, 1823, eight years before passenger trains were run on the railroads of America. He died November 10, 1915, at the age of ninety-two, having lived to see distance conquered by man on land and sea and in the air.

"William was prepared for the University at the Louisburg Academy by one who had a high local reputation as a classical scholar, John B. Bobbitt. He graduated at the University of North Carolina with honor in 1844, in the class of James H. Horner, Judge Thomas Ruffin, Jr., Col. Walter L. Steele and other prominent men.

"His father had recently purchased the Rocky Mount waterpower and the cotton mill built by his cousin, Joel Battle, in 1818. Together with a large plantation and sufficient slaves, he conferred on William the sole management of the mill. In this William showed conspicuous energy and sound judgment and for years had the reputation of a highly successful business man.

"He soon happily married one of the most beautiful and attractive girls of his county, Elizabeth, daughter of the prominent lawyer, Francis L. Dancy. They were a loving couple for over half a century.

"Until the Civil War fortune smiled on him. His people chose him and Judge George Howard to be their delegates to the Secession Convention of 1861 and his legislative acts won their approval. He lived to be next to the last survivor. If he had died when the convention adjourned, his career would have been conspicuous for its happiness. But time had in store for him disastrous business losses and heart-rending family afflictions.

"In 1863 a squad of Federal cavalry rode rapidly from New Bern and applied the torch to his mills. After the war closed he rebuilt on a larger scale and with machinery of the latest model. Prices on all materials were greatly inflated. The work was finished at abnormal cost.

"Then the demon fire assailed him. On one plantation the gin-house with a large lot of seed cotton went up in flames. A month afterwards the gin-house at the Falls of Tar River and a grist and saw-mill not excelled in Eastern North Carolina shared the same fate. A fortnight later the cotton mill, which had absorbed so much of his capital, went in ashes. And then he fell into the grasp of the disastrous panic of 1873.

"If he had refrained from entering on the second rebuilding of his mills, he could have retired with a handsome competency, but his courageous spirit could not brook defeat. Besides, he felt that it was his duty as a citizen to provide work for those of his operatives who were unwilling to desert their old for a new home. With diminished resources, relying largely on money borrowed at a high rate of interest, he rashly entered on the work of reconstruction. The load became too heavy to bear.

"When the end of his struggles came he showed the greatness of his character. He met misfortune with serene courage. He gave to his creditors all his possessions and stepped down with dignified equanimity from a commanding financial position, without loss of self-respect or the respect of his neighbors....

"The loss of fortune was paralleled by the acutest family afflictions. To him and his precious wife were born nine sons and a daughter. All except two were cut down during his lifetime. Then his wife was taken. For a few years he lingered, bruised but not crushed, submitting to his afflictions without bitterness of spirit, with the serenity of a high and noble nature.

"I first met William Battle when I was nine years old. His kind manners won my heart. I have known him intimately ever since and without exaggeration I say that there never was in my acquaintance a more benevolent, just, and honorable man. There were few of a stronger natural intellect. To all thrown with him, relatives, friends, neighbors, employees, slaves, he was a comfort and a blessing."

One of his mistakes was the building of a large, handsome house at Tarborough. This removed him nearly twenty miles from his manufacturing and farming business. He entrusted the factory to his son James soon after he reached his majority. James married a beautiful woman, as lovely in character as in person, John Anna

My Wife's People

Somerville of Warren County, the two making the handsomest couple within my experience. Until the financial crash came to his father's fortunes, I was a frequent guest at his home. Of the seven children two, John and Marion, graduated at West Point and are colonels in the army; the eldest daughter, Mary, married Col. W. C. Rivers, U.S.A.; and William, the eldest son, Vice-president of the Norfolk and Western Railroad, is universally called Colonel because he was once a colonel on the staff of the Governor of Virginia.

My wife's brother Turner was a successful farmer as long as the price of cotton allowed anybody to be. He lived at Cool Spring all his life. He was a captain in the Confederate army. Late in life with his son-in-law Bennett Bunn he opened a commission house in Norfolk under the name of Battle, Bunn, and Company, but it was not a success. Of his large family two reached eminence: Jacob, who was a State Senator and a Superior Court judge, and George Gordon, who has made a remarkable success as a lawyer in New York City.

One of the family slaves at Cool Spring was Dick, the blacksmith. He gave me his history, a history that can hardly be paralleled. He was born the slave of Elisha Battle who died in the year of Washington's death, 1799. In the division of his master's slaves he fell to Jacob Battle, Elisha's youngest son. When Jacob died he became the property of Jacob's son, James S. Battle. On this master's death in 1854, Dick was allotted to Turner W. Battle, son of James S. He belonged to four generations but lived till after the war and died free.

Dick gave me some personal reminiscences. His first master, Elisha, lived on the part of the Cool Spring plantation on which were the cool spring and the dwelling; Jacob lived on the plantation eastward, later called Old Town because the slaves' cabins were grouped together like a town. Jacob's house later became the overseer's. Dick said, "Mars Elisha sent me wid a message to his son, Mars Jacob, about a mile off. On de way I seed some boys playin' marbles and I played wid 'em, and forgot the words Marster giv' me. Den I goes back to Marster and he say, 'Dick, did you tell Jacob what I told you?' I say, 'Yes, sir.' Den he say, 'What did you tell him?' en I couldn't say nothin'. Den he whoop me."

Dick seemed to love his Master James most of the four. He said, "Mars James lived in the gret house on the first floor arter his wife died. He never locked the outside door. He called me in to see him.

He say, 'Dick, I got some bad news to tell you.' 'What is it, Marster?' He say, 'Your wife's master is goin' to move to Mississippi. I went up into Nash to his house to try to buy her so you wouldn't be parted, but he said, "She is my wife's seamstress and I can't sell her." Then I asked him if he would buy you, and we agreed on the price, if you want to go with him. But, Dick, it depends on you. I am satisfied with you, I would rather keep you. But if you want to go with your wife, you can do so. I will not think hard of you.' I say, 'Marster, will you give me tonight to think it over?' He say, 'Yes, Dick. Come in the mornin' and let me know.' I study over it all night. I didn't sleep a wink. Next mornin' 'fore breakfas' I knock at his door. 'Come in,' he say. 'Well, Dick, have you made up your mind?' I say, 'Yes, sir.' 'Well, Dick, what do you say?' 'Well, Marster, I 'clude dat I'll never git as good a marster as you is, but I kin git as good a wife as I got now.'" So Dick stayed and true to his prediction he got really a better wife, known in all the neighborhood for her virtues.

Among slaves with whom I was thrown, marriages, although not legal, were about as happy as those of the whites in modern days and as enduring. Separations of families were not much, if any, more frequent than occur now. Whether this constancy was caused by fear of the owners I cannot say. Certainly there was not as much killing and brutal beating among the negroes as there is now, because the slaves were protected by the fact that they were worth money. Maltreatment met with punishment.

15. Our Home in Raleigh

FOR EIGHT OR NINE MONTHS AFTER OUR MARriage we had most agreeable lodgings with Mr. and Mrs. Rufus H. Page. We had two upstairs rooms and a hall between, facing east. Our hosts and their only child Erasmus (Ras) were all agreeable and friendly and we became much attached to them.

During the summer the brick residence of the late J. G. B. Roulhac was offered for sale under decree of court. It comprised two acres, an entire square, on lower Fayetteville Street near the Governor's Mansion at the other end of the street from the Capitol. As it was a judicial sale and an unreasonably low bid would not have been approved by the court, after careful inquiry among the older citizens of good judgment, I offered $8,000, and became the purchaser. My wife's health required that we should take possession as soon as the house was vacated, which was about the middle of December, 1856. The neighborhood was good. It was at a convenient distance from the courthouse, the stores, and the railroad station, and not too far from the Capitol and Christ Church. The front yard was shaded by seven large oaks and hence I named the place Seven Oaks. The house had been built of unseasoned timber and as the window sashes had been balanced before being thoroughly dried, the weights were too heavy and there was portentous rattling when the wind blew. This gave rise to belief among the servants that haunts infested the house. It seems that Col. Roulhac at the request of his wife, a daughter of Chief Justice Ruffin, had punished one of his girl slaves by fastening her to a table-leg in the basement. This was at dinner-time. He then went to his store, lit his pipe, and died suddenly in his chair. Hence the belief arose that his troubled spirit could be heard moaning in the room where his slave-girl was fastened. It required several hundred dollars to repair the house and hush the noises which were heard when the wind blew. It was thought by many that grass could not be made to grow under the great oaks, but by spading up and turning over the soil and scattering manure we succeeded in having a good sward. The soil of the garden was fertile. On the whole we were well satisfied with our purchase. We spent twenty years there in comfort, although we did not have the modern conveniences of piped water and electric lights. Nobody else did either.

There were born all our children except Herbert, who saw the light first at Chapel Hill. There we went through the terrible days of the war and Sherman's occupation of Raleigh. There we mourned the death of two little girls. There our daughter Nelly was married. It was with a heavy heart that we left the home of so many years in the fall of 1877 to go to Chapel Hill. Duty called and my dear wife made no complaint.

16. Plantations and Slaves in Edgecombe

UNDER THE LAW AS IT STOOD IN 1855 ON MY marriage I became the owner of a number of slaves and acquired a life interest in my wife's two plantations in Edgecombe. I offered to enter into a marriage contract settling my wife's property on her but her brother William on whom she relied advised against it and she declined. In fact I never heard her allude to her possession of property. It never seemed to cross her mind.

I can truthfully say that I treated our slaves as well as I thought possible. The law did not allow them to be taught reading and writing. One of my neighbors tried the employment of a chaplain for their spiritual growth but they found it irksome in comparison with frequenting the neighboring churches of their choice where they could meet their friends from other plantations. Little could be done for them except to feed and clothe them well and look after their health and provide overseers of high character and intelligence.

My wife's two plantations lay on Tar River five miles apart, the upper called Flagmarsh, the lower Walnut Creek. The upper was probably so called from a meadow where the sweet flag or calamus abundantly grew, the lower from a creek of that name bounding it on the west. The upper place had been the property once of my father's grandfather William Battle and his grave is on it. It then descended to my grandfather Joel Battle, who on his marriage to Mary Palmer Johnston exchanged it for hers called Shell Bank about five miles below on the other side of the river. His object was to have a country store on the main road half-way between Rocky Mount and Tarborough. Grandpa Joel is said to have kept a blacksnake in the store.

On the Flagmarsh place we had a white overseer, Jesse Norris. He served before and during the war and for several years afterwards. He was a bachelor until near the end of his time with us, when he married Miss Braswell. Her mother had known my father's mother's father, Amos Johnston. She gave me once a sarcastic rebuke which I claim was not deserved. I said, "I do not trouble myself about dying. It never occurs to me. I do not realize that I shall die." She replied solemnly, "Mr. Battle, I always thought that people who say they won't die haven't got good sense." I tried to explain my position but I doubt if her matter-of-fact mind understood me.

Mr. Norris had two pretty daughters and in the seventies moved to a plantation he bought in Wilson County.

During the war I kept Norris from conscription into the army by what was called the "Twenty Nigger" Law. This was the law of October 11, 1862, which granted a detail of one man liable to conscription to have charge of a farm of twenty negroes. After a while the law was repealed (May 1, 1863) and Mr. Norris notified me that I must employ a substitute in his place. I went to Edgecombe in a sad frame of mind because nearly all persons suitable for managing farms were in the army. One of my men met me at the station. After riding a mile or two I said, "Henry, has Mr. Norris gone to the army?" "No, sir, he is down at the plantation." "I thought the conscription had got him." "Well, sir, there was some talk of that. But he went down to Conetoe where he was born and raised and found two more years. They saved him." It seems that he had mistaken the date of his birth but after inquiry was able to prove satisfactorily to the proper office that he was forty instead of thirty-eight years of age. It was one of my good luck happenings of which I have had many during my life pilgrimage.

At one time in the course of this drive I crossed the Edgecombe and Nash line. For a mile I noticed that my colored driver gazed anxiously first on one side of the road and then on the other. So I closed my book to give him an opportunity to question me. He said, "Mars Kemp, I seed the curiousest thing back yonder I ever seed. There was a sign-board and no road for it to pint to." I replied, "Jim, that sign-board merely showed the dividing line between Edgecombe and Nash." With the most satisfied air Jim said, "I might have knowed we was in Nash ever since I seed a woman ploughing a steer." Jim's reason was not a good one because doubtless her husband was in the army. But at that time and for years before, Nash had a bad reputation. In public estimation its chief products were Nash brandy and drunkenness and fighting. It has in recent years greatly improved. My son Thomas a year or two ago took me in his auto to Nashville and through other parts of the county. I was amazed at the changes for the better, at the evidences of intelligent farming. Land had advanced in price from $8 and $10 per acre to $30 and $40 per acre.

On the Walnut Creek plantation I had Allen Battle, one of our slaves, in charge. He was a fine looking man, one-fourth white, as honest and honorable as ever lived and a very good farmer. His father was black, his mother a mulatto. They were slaves in a good

Virginia family in what is called the Northern Neck, that is, the peninsula between the Potomac and the Rappahannock. For some fault his mother was sold and bought by my grandfather Joel Battle. Her husband was infatuated with her and determined to follow her. He heard that her purchaser lived in the South and his county was Edgecombe. He turned his back to the North Star and walked through forests and crossed rivers until he found her. Grandpa sent to his owners and by purchase reunited the loving couple.

Allen when young was the playmate of the sons of his master. When he grew older, he was advanced to the dignity of foreman. While in this capacity he was the witness of the shooting of his fellow-slave Will with bird shot by the overseer, who was then slain by Will in a fight. This led to the celebrated case of *State vs. Will* in which the court decided that all killing of masters by slaves was not murder punishable with death and Will's conviction of manslaughter was upheld.

The estimation in which Allen was held by the neighborhood is shown by the fact that after my grandfather's death, when his slaves were sold at auction at a time of financial depression, Allen brought $500 while other negro men brought only $300. He served his new master, James S. Battle, with his usual faithfulness and intelligence. When James S. Battle's slaves were divided among his five children, Allen fell to my wife and was advanced to the dignity of overseer, about eighteen hands, as the workers were called, being placed under his charge.

Allen died worth about $2,000, leaving me executor of his will. His wife Suckey never had a child. He bequeathed to her all he had but requested me to keep the money in my hands and to pay over to her whatever she should ask for. "If she gets it all in hand," he said, "her kinfolks will eat her up." She tried the plan of living with one of them and they began at once to eat her up. They persuaded her to buy a $200 horse and other things too costly for her station. After two years she took alarm and came back to my care, rented a house at Flagmarsh, and lived economically. When she died, she had still about $800, which was distributed among her kin, so numerous that the share of one was only about $3.50. As a matter of law she could have called for all the fund but both she and her kin regarded the provision in the will as a legal check on extravagant expenditures. I was really vested with moral but not legal power.

In later years I was thrown rather intimately into business relations with another negro of similar virtues though not of equal brainpower. This was Henderson Oldham, who had no mixture of white blood. As executor of Miss Mary Ruffin Smith I sold Oldham his farm near Chapel Hill, a fine tract of about 350 acres. It is men like these that give us hope for the future of the negro race.

Although Allen lived from childhood a life of strictest probity, he never joined a church. He said to me, "If I get sick, I don't want a horse to be half-killed racing for a doctor. When the Lord sends for me, I must go." I think that he did not approve the ranting sermons usual in negro and other ignorant communities but he kept a discreet silence as to his views.

He died about 1876 and was buried in the graveyard on the Pork Island plantation, the residence of Gen. Cox. I caused a marble slab to be placed over the grave with an appropriate inscription.

Allen was the victim of bad treatment by a man who was unhappily a kinsman of mine in a trade of an old-fashioned buggy for one of modern make. He had requested an army officer to purchase the new vehicle and its style was not suitable to him and his plain old wife. It cost $200 and he swapped it for one not worth $50. He failed to show his usual good sense because he did not think it possible that the man with whom he traded would deceive him. He spoke of the deception with tears in his voice. "To think that I should have been treated so by a man who come from my old marster Joel Battle!" This thought hurt him more than the loss. He tried to have the exchange rectified. He said the man said something about "emptor" (*caveat emptor*) and laughed at him.

Allen was overseer for five years before the war, all during the war, and until his death. He met all new questions with his usual good sense. He was not educated in books. He would say, "Mars Kemp, I am glad to see you. I've been wanting to insult you about several matters." Some of his expressions were quaint but they had sense. My near neighbor, Gen. Cox, had an overseer named Hingson, who had been connected with the Northern army in some way. Being bothered by his debts he concluded to take French leave. Here is Allen's account of it. "About three o'clock in the morning my dogs barked. I got up, like I always do when they bark, and there was Mr. Hingson running away. I knowed he was running away because he was gwine to Battleborough to take the train, when Rocky Mount was his nighest station. He owed me fifteen dollars for the puppy of the fine dog you gave me named Uno. Mr. Hingson has sold that puppy and got the money for him and gone off without paying me a cent. And then my wife had lent his wife some cheers (chairs) for her visitors to set on and them cheers he had given to the darkies." Then Allen gave his opinion of Northerners in general. "Mars Kemp, North men have got more sense to be mean than South men."

When the election for state officers under the Congressional Reconstruction acts came on he said to me, "I want to vote your ticket (I was on it for the office of State Treasurer), but if I do, I cannot do anything with my hands on the farm. They think that everybody who votes the Democratic ticket is against them." Of course I told him to vote the Republican ticket. The Democrats had no chance of success anyway.

When it was evident in 1865 that Sherman would march on Goldsborough, I thought that he would lead his army northward from that town. It seemed best therefore to buy a farm in Wake so as to have something to fall back on if the Edgecombe places should be devastated. It was a mistake though not a costly one. Sherman came to Raleigh instead of marching north from Goldsborough but my place was eighteen miles from Raleigh and too much out of the way to be ravaged. My mules and corn and fodder were taken but there was no wanton destruction. After peace was declared, I told the negroes that they might cultivate the crops already planted and we would leave it to the agent in charge of the Freedmen's Bureau to divide the crops. I further agreed that I would at my own expense transport them and their household property back to Edgecombe. This satisfied them but when the Government officer (called by them the Bureau) made his award, he placed an undue estimate on the share to which the land was entitled. He gave me double what was usual and I at once reduced the allowance to one-third of the corn and one-fourth of the cotton.

I told my negroes early in the war that if the North succeeded, freedom would be brought to them. They would gain nothing by running off, on the contrary would incur danger and trouble. I doubt whether this was needed as other slaves than mine continued quietly at work. But it is a remarkable evidence of their docility and of their previous kind treatment that when the cotton factory at Rocky Mount was burned by Northern cavalry from New Bern, they loaded wagons with meat under supervision of my overseer, Mr. Norris, hauled the loads three or four miles into the piney woods, and remained quiet while the Federals passed by. Not one showed any disposition to join the soldiers. After the war at least half of my hands continued to work as freely hired or as tenants. Some thought that it looked more like freedom to leave "Old Marster" and work for somebody else but nearly all continued on the Tar River farms.

The railroad connections at Weldon were so bad, the trains being sometimes seven or eight hours late, that in attending to my business on the farms I often made the journey to Edgecombe by horse and buggy. A very convenient and most pleasant trip was to go by Westrayville, the home of my wife's uncle, Turner Page Westray, and spend the night there. Mr. Westray was a highly intelligent man, with such a well-balanced judgment that it was pleasant and profitable to listen to him. As I lived in the capital and often met leading actors in the strife going on, he gave me the impression that my visits were grateful to him. This and the winning welcome of his beautiful wife and only child, Samuel, made my evenings delightful. The roads were so good that the fifty miles to Raleigh were passed without injury to the horse, or horses, for sometimes I had two.

Mr. Westray was a man of pluck. Once a number of deserters from the army came armed at night to his dwelling and demanded a supply of bacon. He walked into his porch with his double-barrelled gun and with the fiercest vituperations drove them away. After the war he found it irksome to carry on his farm with hired negroes and accepted the invitation of his nephew and namesake Captain Turner W. Battle to live with him at Cool Spring. A short while afterwards he died of heart-disease while travelling on the railroad. He left his estate of about $250,000 to his son and after his son's death it was divided among his heirs-at-law. My son Thomas was his executor.

It is perhaps worth while to record a freak of the weather one day. I started from Westrayville in a cold, north-easterly drizzling rain. There was every indication that I would have a whole day of discomfort. But after going ten miles I reached a perfectly dry road and a pleasant sun. At another time, after going some distance, I struck a region where the young pines bowed their heads as if in mourning. There had been a heavy snow which had melted rapidly but the evergreens had not had time to right themselves.

The roughest household I encountered in my travels lived near the Nash line. I was desperately hungry and stopped to obtain dinner. The wife was pretty in face but unable to walk on account of some ailment. Her upper dress was loose and dowdy. While I was talking to her, she called to her daughter about twelve years old. "There's a fly down my back. Git him out." The daughter ran her hand down her mother's spine in search of the offender. The mother called out frantically, "Lower, lower!" Finally the young huntress captured the game. I asked the husband who was the father of his wife. "An old man who lived up in Wake. He had a good property too, but he never giv me nuthin. The naked woman is all he giv me." The dinner of bacon and greens and corn bread was not unpalatable, but the abundant dirt all around made me afraid much of it had got into the corn pone she had made with her hands.

17. Children

OUR FIRST CHILD WAS BORN ON THE 14TH OF January, 1857, the anniversary of the birth of my grandmother Mary Johnston. I rushed to the office in my yard that was the abode of my father when the Supreme Court was in session, with the joyful news that the child and mother were doing well. "Is it a boy or girl?" said Father. "I don't know, sir, but they are doing well." On this my good friend Aleck McPheeters, with whom I had shared desks at school, invented a story that I rushed frantically up Fayetteville Street, no hat on my head, shouting, "I've a baby! I've a baby!" and when people inquired as to the sex, I answered, "I don't know, but I've a baby!"

My wife expressed a preference for the name of her sister, beautiful and sweet-tempered Cornelia Viola, but knowing that I did not then like the name Cornelia, proposed that it should be shortened into Nelly, although that usually stands for Eleanor or Ellen. To this I gladly agreed.

Certainly no child ever gave more pleasure to all around her than our Nelly. She had a lovely face and a well proportioned figure. She had a strong mind, high principles, a religious temperament. She was faithful to every duty, fond of reading yet joining with delight in decorous sports: in fine, she was as perfect a creature as God allows to live on this earth. This is not alone the estimate of a prejudiced father but it met the concurrence of all who knew her.

She was always first in her studies and had a sweet voice in singing. When she began music, I insisted on her committing to memory the music and the songs that she learned. She did this so well that she played and sang accurately with or without notes. This accomplishment was a source of much pleasure in our social circle as well as in amateur concerts. Her simple, unaffected manner was admirable.

She married a man in every way worthy of her, Richard Henry Lewis, a physician who became a specialist in diseases of the eye, ear, nose, and throat and gained a high reputation. Our daughter seemed perfectly healthy but on October 13, 1886, was taken from us.

Our next child was a boy born March 9, 1859. His name, Kemp Plummer Battle, like mine commemorates three of the families whose blood is in our veins, the Battles, the Kemps, and the Plummers. He was of healthy frame and stood high in his classes. He was of thoughtful temperament but skilful in athletic exercises. Always having control of his temper and of his tongue, he was influential among his fellows. I inherited the liking which my grandfather Kemp Plummer had for giving nicknames to his children. I called the boy Plum Blue-eyes, shortened into Plum Blue.

He early showed fortitude. Falling on a piece of iron he cut open one side of his nose. It was necessary to sew it up. He submitted to the operation with the nerve of a seasoned soldier. In all his boyish difficulties and excitements at school and at the University he was never known to lose his self-possession.

Graduating at the University in 1879, he studied medicine a year at Chapel Hill, then after a year's work took the degree of M.D. at the University of Virginia, then a second M.D. at Bellevue Medical College, New York City, in 1882. For two years he was an interne first in the Charity Hospital, Blackwell's Island, New York, and then in Blackwell's Island Insane Asylum. He then secured by competitive examination a position as Assistant Surgeon in the U.S. Marine Hospital Service. This work he gave up in 1885 and took a special course in London in the branch of medical science devoted to ailments of the eye, ear, nose, and throat. He then settled in Raleigh as a partner of Dr. Richard H. Lewis, his brother-in-law. He was Professor of Physiology in the Leonard Medical School at Raleigh 1885-1913 and Professor of Diseases of the Eye, Ear, Nose, and Throat in the Raleigh branch of the Medical Department of the University from 1903 until the discontinuance of the Raleigh branch in 1910.

His baptism was accompanied by a most thrilling event. It was at Morning Prayer on Sunday. I was unpleasantly impressed with the 2nd Lesson, which was a part of the Burial Service. While I was kneeling afterwards, the sexton summoned me to the door. There I was informed that the horses had run away with my carriage in which were the nurse and child. Hatless I started down the street but was stopped and told to get my wife and hat and jump into her sister's carriage. We soon found that our driver had been thrown from his seat, the carriage had collided with some stone steps, and the horses had broken away. The collision tore off one side of the carriage. The faithful nurse held the child so tight in her plump arms that he was not in the slightest degree injured. He was in the parlor of our physician, his house being nearest to the scene of the disaster, placidly sleeping on the lap of an excellent neighbor of ours, Mrs. Alfred Williams. She said his crying from fright lasted only a few minutes. Ordinarily horses that run away are afterwards unsafe. In this case they were not really frightened but galloped off because of a defect in the harness and were soon stopped. They never repeated the trick. A horse really frightened is a maniac and is liable to lose his mind again.

My second son, Thomas Hall, I nicknamed Tommy Two Crowns, or Tommy Two, because like his father he had two centers in the hair at the back of his head, commonly known as crowns. In my case my mother declared this showed that I would live in two countries, as a Minister Plenipotentiary perhaps, but her prediction failed. In character and talent Thomas was equal to his brother but lacked his calmness and deliberation. He was more aggressive, mixed more with others. After graduation at the University he taught for a year and then studied law. He settled for a while in Tarborough as a lawyer, was elected County Solicitor soon after he reached the town. It was not long, however, before he removed to Rocky Mount, served as mayor for years, and is credited with turning a town noted for drunkenness and rowdyism into one distinguished for good conduct and progressive spirit. For some years he has been President of the Bank of Rocky Mount and Treasurer and General Manager of the Rocky Mount Mills.

He was born early on the morning of election day August 2, 1860, when I was a candidate for the General Assembly, and mother and son were so well that I was able the same day to go eighteen miles to a precinct and attend to the electioneering.

The next child was also a son, born May 29, 1862, the only one of all the family with a fancy name. As my wife was a devotee of George Herbert, the saintly poet of Bemerton parish in England, we concluded to honor him. Very seldom will be seen in our family connection a name not found among our ancestors.

When the time approached for the coming of our third boy, there was a possibility of a cavalry raid on Raleigh by Federal troops from New Bern. Entrenchments had been thrown up around the capital but they were of little strength. It was therefore deemed best for my wife to undergo her confinement in my father's home in Chapel Hill. The two-roomed cottage that is now my working office was assigned to her. Herbert was born in the front room. Like the other children he was a healthy, vigorous, good tempered little fellow. He had little hair and I dubbed him Herby Wedgehead. As he grew up, he showed a decided liking for scientific studies, and his standing was especially high in chemistry. He was awarded the degree of Bachelor of Science at the University in 1881, then became assistant chemist in the Agricultural Experiment Station. In 1887 he received the degree of Doctor of Philosophy, and was elected Director of the Agricultural Experiment Station and State Chemist. He performed the important duties of this office to the public satisfaction for ten years. Then the executive department of the State passed into the hands of the Republican party, Hon. Daniel L. Russell being Governor. For party considerations Governor Russell devised the plan of turning over the duties of State Chemist to the Agricultural and Mechanical College, thus displacing my son and obtaining a short-lived reputation for economy. After Russell's term was over this policy was reversed but in the meantime Herbert had organized the Southern Chemical Company at Winston-Salem, with himself as president and manager. The manufacture of fertilizers was conducted with success for several years, but the chief stockholders became interested in other enterprises requiring much capital and sold their stock in Herbert's company to the Virginia-Carolina Chemical Company, which then purchased the residue of the Southern Chemical Company stock at a figure that saved the stockholders from loss. Herbert afterwards organized the Battle Laboratory at Montgomery, Alabama, and built up a valuable business.

The next child was a girl born February 2, 1864. We named her Susan Martin, the name Susan honoring my sister and earliest friend next to my mother, the second name recognizing my grandmother Susannah Martin Plummer. Our little girl was a bright, pretty, affectionate child. She had a religious temperament, repeated the hymn "Nearer, My God, to Thee" with an appropriateness of utterance that was charming. I recall an amusing incident connected with her. Once, when her mother's sickness made it convenient for her to spend the day at my brother Richard's, I took her there through Capitol Square. We passed near a flock of goslings, to my eye unsightly fowls. She was entranced, "O Father, they are so beautiful! Are they partridges?"

Her lovely life was cut short by a most tragic accident. While I was attending a Diocesan Convention in Edenton in 1870, her mother took her on a visit to her cousin Sally Watson in Petersburg, Virginia. There Susie and some other children were playing in the yard and one of them found a pistol which had been lost by a soldier of one of the armies. In the course of play the pistol was discharged and the ball went through the body of our little girl. She died the next night, May 7, 1870, mercifully with little pain. The telegram conveying the tragic news hastened me home of course but the journey was so slow that the burial was over before my train reached Raleigh. I found that my wife was bearing the trial like a Christian, like a saint. But it was a terrible blow.

Our next child was a girl, born August 27, 1866. We named her Penelope Bradford after her mother's sister, Mrs. Cox, and called her Neppie. Neppie was very pretty and sweet-tempered, uncommonly graceful and winning in her ways. Our Maker loaned her to us for a short while only. All her digestive functions gave way at once. Neither food nor medicines had the normal efficacy. Her mother had sick-headache and I watched and waited on the child continuously. A day or two previously I had read a strong medical article in a great London review in which the author detailed the symptoms of starvation. These symptoms were exactly those of our daughter. In the afternoon of the night when she became sick I was in the front porch with my uncle Alfred Plummer, watching her in the absence of my wife confined to her bed. She found in the grass a small Siberian crab-apple. She brought it to me, saying "Peel it." I stole it from her and hid it in my pocket. After her death I found it and still have it on my bureau, preserved in alcohol.

After the death of Neppie my wife's health became seriously impaired. It was deemed advisable to consult Dr. Austin Flint, the elder, in New York. He found that she had no specific disease, and prescribed rest as far as possible and freedom from household labors and cares. We succeeded in procuring a competent housekeeper and my wife in large measure recovered her strength.

Our last child was born November 30, 1870, and was named in honor of his two grandfathers, William James.

Those who believe in the transmission of qualities by heredity can pick out traits of the following families in our stock: Battle (English), Sumner (English), Horn (English), Johnston (Scotch), Williams (Welsh), Hayes (English), Plummer (English), Kemp (English), Smith (English), Westray (English), not taking into consideration the numberless unknown families prior to the John Battle who came to America in 1654. Notwithstanding the impossibility of identifying the characteristics of so many families, all observers must admit that descendants do show traits similar to their ancestors. I am persuaded from inquiry into the character of Elisha Battle, whom we humorously call Elisha the Great, that as a general rule his sincerity, his liking for public position, his reliability, his temperance, his freedom from ostentation, his desire to do well whatever he agreed to do may be found in most of his descendants. The failure to possess these qualities can easily be traced to our other strains. My father, for example, closely resembled Elisha Battle while several of my uncles resembled their Williams kin, some of whom were wild.

William James, our seventh child, was a remarkable boy. He was larger than other boys of our acquaintance and had an unusually thoughtful look for one of his age. My usual baby talk to him was, "What are you thinking about?" because from his earliest days he had a look of thoughtfulness. He seemed to be trying to understand the occurrences in this new world into which he had recently entered. Owing to the four years' gap between Neppie's birth and his and to the death of Neppie and Susie, William was almost in the position of an only child. He thus had more attention given to him than is usual in larger families. There were eight years between him and Herbert, the nearest living child.

It is an interesting fact that on the day of the birth of our youngest son, I joined with four other men, Dr. W. J. Hawkins, Colonel A. B. Andrews, Col. William E. Anderson, and Philip A. Wiley, in the founding of the Citizens National Bank of Raleigh. Romeo, our faithful and beloved Newfoundland dog, saw the light the same day. This good animal lived to be eighteen years old and one morning was found on the lawn at Senlac with his head resting on his paws, fast asleep forever. He had been always watchful to do whatever we wished him to do. In fact he was a high-toned gentleman.

An amusing incident will illustrate my manner towards my children. Our youngest, when about three years old, behaved obstreperously one day as we sat down to dinner which in our Raleigh home was in the basement. When he disobeyed my order to behave properly, I seized him and started upstairs. He saw I was in earnest and shouted, "I give up, *I give up*, I GIVE UP!!" Of course I took him back to the table. After dinner was over, I took him lovingly in my arms and carried him around the sitting room and pointed out the figures in the pictures and told stories about them. I said, "You are sorry you behaved so downstairs, aren't you?" He said, "Yes, *sir*, and you whipped me, didn't you?" I replied, "No, I didn't whip you!" "Well, you went for me, anyhow."

Another time, after our removal to Chapel Hill, I said, "William, there is a hollow tree in the woods, in which I once found an owl and afterwards a Molly Hare. Don't you want to go and see it?" "Yes, sir!" "Come on then." The bushes in the way were very thick and a switch struck him, with smarting violence. He indignantly said, "If you hadn't brought me over here, I wouldn't have been hurt." Notwithstanding these anecdotes, he was a good, pleasant boy, with an inquiring mind.

After obtaining the degree of A.B. in 1888, and A.M. in the following year at Chapel Hill, he entered Harvard University and was made Ph.D. in 1893. He was the same year at the age of twenty-two elected Associate Professor of Greek in charge of the department in the University of Texas. In 1898 he became full professor. He has since studied a year abroad, mostly in Athens. For some years he was Dean of the University and on the resignation of President Mezes was appointed Acting President. My son declined, however, to allow his name to go before the Regents of the University for the permanent Presidency because he and Governor Ferguson differed as to the construction of the act of the legislature appropriating money for the support of the University and he thought that this difference might be of injury to the institution. He therefore resumed his old place as Professor of Greek and Dean of the University.

Our children looked on their parents as their friends as well as their father and mother. We spent much time with them, showing interest in their games and reading. I have known excellent people who gave most of their spare time to charitable and church objects. We took care to avoid this and have been rewarded. One mistake especially we took care to avoid. Whatever censure was needed was administered with no one else to witness it. A normal child loses much benefit from correction if resentment is engendered by the thought that others are triumphing over his humiliation. I was often struck with admiration at the gradual fading of angry temper, a frown replaced by a smile, as my wife whispered soothing words. Her influence over children and grandchildren alike was extraordinary and it never ceased. It continued undiminished until she left us and the memory of her guides them now. She was never severe in punishing them but she had a firm, determined manner which awed and conquered. As for myself, if the children showed an ugly defiance of authority, I convinced them by rough but not painful handling that I was the stronger and was determined to be obeyed. I never did this more than once to any child and no parent ever had more respectful or more obedient children.

We took care to follow any expression of displeasure by adopting means for their happiness. We did not wait for them to beg us for a desired pleasure. We often surprised them by proposing schemes of enjoyment which they had not thought of, not only circuses and the like but excursions to mountains or ocean. This was practicable because we had in A. P. Bryan, the Raleigh agent of the Southern Express Company, an excellent man and warm friend who was very fond of boys and took pleasure in accompanying them to the seaside or to his mother's summer hotel on Long Island Sound. Of course they often went with their mother and me on our journeys of business or pleasure. I made it a habit to walk with them on Sunday afternoons and to encourage them on other days to fish and hunt and engage in sports with other children. Occasionally we gave them a social dance in our parlor. One of the most beautiful scenes I ever witnessed was when Nelly was a little girl. We gave her a Christmas Tree party. I sent a wagon ten miles in the country and procured a holly tree as high as the ceiling, full of berries. I wrote to New York for the gifts. They were fastened to the tree by colored glass chains and interspersed were tiny colored wax candles all lighted. The base was fastened in a box full of earth. On the box was colored paper and on that were shell and other bright objects. About sixty girls and boys, rosy and well dressed, danced and frolicked in a radiant circle. It was all charming.

18. The Courts in Wake County

THE SUPERIOR COURT WAS HELD ONLY TWO weeks in the year. Capital cases had precedence and in consequence civil cases were continued from term to term for years. There was little work for young lawyers. My practise was therefore at first confined chiefly to the County Court. The statutory name for this was Court of Pleas and Quarter Sessions, i.e., a court for the trial of pleas (an old name for law-suits) and the quarterly meetings of the justices of the peace for the transaction of county business.

The Quarter Sessions were held on Monday and a busy day it was. A majority of the justices was necessary for a quorum. Business of a general nature was transacted. Sometimes there were exciting disputes; for example, as to the propriety of laying out new roads or the change of old roads. Large numbers of people took advantage of the day to come to town, and it was a favorable opportunity for public sales, speeches of politicians, popular meetings, and private business. Some counties preferred Tuesdays for this miscellaneous business.

For the trial of criminal and civil cases the justices of Wake elected five of their number to be a special court, one of them being chosen chairman. They had jurisdiction when the punishment did not extend to loss of life, limb, or member. The court could order whipping on the bare back for stealing, but could not have ears cut off for perjury.

After the criminal cases were disposed of, generally in two days, the civil docket came on. Usually the civil cases were of minor importance, as great suits were brought in the Superior Court, but occasionally the litigation aroused much feeling and led to protracted trials. The chief work of the County Court, however, was in criminal cases, which in the large county of Wake were numerous. Indictments were often vigorously fought and hot temper engendered among the lawyers.

The presiding justices, five in number, elected by the whole body of justices of the county, were as a rule not lawyers. Occasionally a retired lawyer who had the confidence of the people was induced to accept the office and made the tribunal of as great dignity as the Superior Court. In Wake for several years we had one of the ablest lawyers in this or any other State, George E. Badger. Of course the other members of the court deferred always to his ruling although he courteously asked their opinions. Judge O'Brien of the District Court of South Carolina was once forced to spend some hours in Raleigh by a delayed train. County Court was in session. He asked the hotel proprietor what was the occasion of the assembling of so many people. The reply was, "It is court week." "What sort of a court?" "County Court." "Who presides?" "The justices of the county elect five of their number, any three of whom can hold the court." "I will go over and see how they manage." After a while he returned and inquired, "Who did you say presides in that court?" "Five justices of the county." "Well," said the judge in wondering tones, "I don't understand it. There is an old bald-headed man in the middle who is no fool, I tell you!" He was informed that it was ex-Senator Badger, who had been publicly praised by Thomas Hart Benton as not excelled in his knowledge of the common law by any man in the Union.

When we did not have Badger as our chief, the presiding justices were unlearned in law. The chairman was long a retired Baptist preacher, Rev. Thomas G. Whitaker. For a time after the retirement of Mr. Badger he endeavored to imitate him but with little success.

As a rule the lawyers had their way unchecked and many and fierce were the wrangles and sometimes fights. Once a man rushed at another and the other drew a pistol and pulled the trigger with the muzzle pointed right at the breast of his assailant. Fortunately the pistol did not go off. Once in Nash County two men named Miller and Lewis clinched. When pulled apart Miller held Lewis' coat-tail in his grasp and shouted, "I have made Lewis what people call him, a bob-tailed lawyer!" After the conflicts were over, the court would fine the fighters. Presently they would make friends and beg the pardon of the court and the fines would be remitted. Duels had gone out of fashion before my day.

I think that the County Courts were very useful. They brought the people of the county together four times a year and as appeals could be taken to the Superior Court at will without giving reason, no harm was done by reason of having unlearned judges. Numerous disputes of small moment were finally settled in them. They were excellent practise grounds for young lawyers.

The Superior Courts were well conducted, some judges being more strict than others. Judge M. E. Manly was the most exacting. I heard him once fiercely stop the wrangling of two of the leaders of the bar, Moore and Miller. "I do not sit here to hear this wrangling of counsel back and forth. You must stop it." And they were as meek as lambs. No fun was ever attempted when he was presiding.

19. Practice in Wake County

ALACK, AND ALAS, I LOST THE FIRST CASE I tackled. Hinton Franklin struck a newly imported Irishman, name unknown to the witnesses. There were two counts in the bill of indictment, one giving the name of the man struck, the other for striking a man unknown. There were six witnesses endorsed on the bill. I called five, who said they saw the blow but didn't know the name of the man struck. I did not call the sixth. The lawyer for Franklin was one of the ablest men at the bar, Henry W. Miller. He sent for Archbold on Evidence and showed that the jury could not say the man's name was unknown because the sixth witness might have known it. I had not the right of reply and the jury said, "Not guilty." To increase my mortification the foreman of the jury said when I met him afterwards, "The jury blamed the State in this case." I was never caught in such a slip afterwards. I ought to have asked the court to call in the last witness, but I had announced that my case was closed and the justices would have refused. If Mr. Badger had then been chairman he would himself have called in the sixth witness.

Judge J. H. Dillard, one of the ablest judges of our Supreme Court, told me that he too lost his first case. He declared on a note as due at its date, whereas it was payable three months after date. He said, "I took a non-suit and paid the costs out of my own pocket. It was the best money I ever spent."

When I began appearing before juries I was exceedingly nervous before rising. I was agreeably surprised to find that, after a few sentences, I lost all trepidation, my ideas became more clear, my recollection of the testimony more distinct. It was then the oratorical fashion to shout into the ears of the jury, with frantic gesticulations. The conversational plan of calm reasoning now used seems more sensible but I have often wondered whether vigorous action of the body did not help the flow of ideas. There were not wanting lawyers at that period who used the modern style, George E. Badger and William A. Graham, for example. But as a rule the jury ten feet away were subjected to shouts which could be heard far beyond the courtroom.

I recall a case of an affray between two young men of the extensive Olive family. My client admitted his own guilt, but was eager to have his antagonist convicted in order to share the costs and the odium of fighting. He was so excited that he imparted to me a portion of his spirit and I did my best and gained my case. A juror named Morris came up to compliment me. "Battle, you made a fine effort today. The jury praised your speech mightily. And if ever I have a plain, easy, four-dollar case, I will give it to you."

The best speech I ever had in my mind was not delivered. My client was, while in his little shop, visited by a man stronger than he was who had repeatedly threatened bodily violence. My client was afraid of him and when he advanced in a threatening attitude struck him with a hoe which he had in his shop for sale and knocked him senseless. If he had done no more, we might have secured his acquittal on the plea of self-defence. But in the extremity of his terror he continued his defence with further blows. His adversary died after an hour or two and unfortunately for my client gave a false story of the encounter. Our danger was that death-bed declarations are generally believed to be true because the dying man is about to face his God. I fully believed that my client told the truth and my anxiety to save him gave me such nerve-tension that I felt as if I would make the speech of my life.

We finished the evidence by dinner time. During the dinner-hour the judge sent for the attorneys of the prisoner and offered that if we would submit to a verdict of manslaughter, he would not fine or brand our client but give him only a short imprisonment. We consulted our client and his mother and they accepted the judge's offer rather than run the risk of a verdict of murder. Our client told us afterward that he had four friends on the jury who would have voted for acquittal. On the other hand they might only have caused a disagreement of the jury and a new trial.

One of the few times in my life when I appreciated the expression "beside myself" was when the county solicitor, J. Kemp Marriott, asked me to try a case for him so that he might get his dinner. As there were five justices, of whom three could transact business, they refused to take a recess and slipped out one by one and satisfied their hunger. I consented to act as prosecutor *pro tempore*. The indictment was against a man named Griffin for retailing whiskey without a license. The witnesses were two young men who had been living as workmen with the defendant's father-in-law Brown. In order to break down their testimony Brown charged them with stealing. On going into the case I became satisfied that the charge was false. It became necessary to break down Brown's character. The atrocity of trying to ruin the characters of two innocent youths excited me greatly. I actually was transformed into another man. I became "beside myself." Fortunately for me there were neighbors of Brown accessible who could prove his bad character, and the jury rewarded my passionate denunciation and convicted Griffin.

A lawyer sometimes must acquiesce in propositions which may injure his case. I was once employed by Hockaday, the owner of a mill. He raised his dam a foot and thereby flooded some of Squire Law's low grounds. The law required the question of damages to be tried *in pais*, i.e., in the locality of the dam, the sheriff presiding, and the jury must inspect the land alleged to be flooded. The day of the trial proved to be cold and rainy. The jury accompanied by the parties, their counsels, and the sheriff, trudged through the cold mud up the creek bank for half a mile or so and then returned to the mill for the trial.

The discomfort and even danger to health of sitting in wet clothes for hours without a fire were apparent. The plaintiff had a country store a mile off, with a large back room well warmed. He proposed that by general consent adjournment should be had to this place. My client and I were bound to acquiesce. On arrival at the snug quarters the plaintiff asked us if we had any objection to his treating the company to a drink of peach brandy. If we had refused these hospitable offers, there was the probability of incurring the ill will of the jurors. We were forced to try our case in the plaintiff's warm room, with a balmy glass of his beverage inside the jurors. Notwithstanding these allurements to partiality the verdict was reasonable, $150 a year for five years, at the end of which period the question would be again open for suit or compromise. Probably the owner of the mill bought the plaintiff's land. At least he died soon afterwards and the suit was never renewed.

My habit of keeping in touch with the decisions of our Supreme Court enabled me to gain in Mr. Badger's court a triumph of which I was proud. My client was on trial for selling whiskey to a slave without the written permit from his master prescribed by the statute. The state's attorney proved the sale and rested the case. I asked the court for a verdict of not guilty. "On what grounds, Mr. Battle?" "Because the State has not proved that there was no written permit from the master." "Mr. Battle," said the judge, "surely you do not mean that the State must prove a negative! Let your client prove that there was such writing." "I know, sir, that such was for years the opinion of the bench and bar. But the Supreme Court has decided that if the State alleges the absence of the permit, it must prove it." "Can you produce that decision?" "Certainly, sir." The judge read the case carefully and said, "Gentlemen of the jury, we are bound to acquit this man, and I am sorry for it." As the slave in this case was allowed to drive a hack for hire acting as a freeman, the defendant did not think that he was breaking the law.

As hard work as I ever did in my life was in behalf of a degraded free negress who was charged with aiding the killing of one paramour in order to secure another. I was assigned by the court with two others, Cantwell and Marriott, for her defence. In order to get her version of the facts I went into her dungeon. I remember it well. It was about six feet wide, the floor and walls of heavy stone blocks, the window about a foot wide with a heavy iron bar in the middle. After the homicide, blood was found on the woman's dress. Fortunately we had a witness who swore that she had killed a chicken and carried it to the kitchen with head down and we contended that the blood on her dress was not the blood of the deceased. There was evidence against her of a circumstantial nature but we saved her. We worked as hard and as earnestly for this degraded creature for charity's sake as we would have worked if we had been heavily feed.

I have seen nothing more pitiable than the sickly, sallow complexions of those confined for months in the dungeons of that day. It is gratifying that others more comfortable and healthy have been substituted.

Once I assisted in the defence of a slave who had killed another slave belonging to his master. Notwithstanding the loss, Robinson the master paid my associate and me a good fee for defending the slayer. We succeeded in reducing the homicide to manslaughter, the punishment for which was branding, or fine, or imprisonment, or any combination of these at the discretion of the court. The judge sentenced our client to be branded only and as counsel I was compelled to witness the punishment. The hand of the prisoner was strapped to the railing of the bar and the sheriff pressed on the brawn of the thumb a red hot wire bent to the shape of the letter M until one of the counsel repeated three times the words, "God save the State." The process was very disgusting. The negro was an elderly man, his hands hardened by the work of a lifetime. A white smoke shot up to the ceiling and the odor was offensive. But he uttered no cry and on account of the thickness of the skin, I doubt if the pain was very severe.

I always shunned the sight of corporal punishments whenever possible. This branding was my solitary experience but I once met a man coming out of the courthouse who had just had the letter B (for Bigamy) burnt on his cheek. I am glad such punishments have been abolished.

20. Old-Time Treatment of Criminals

HANGINGS IN THE EARLY DAYS WERE NOT AS uncommon as they are now. Sentimental objections to taking life have had effect both on juries, inducing them to acquit, and on governors, inducing them to pardon. The day of execution was a general holiday and the town was full of ardent sight-seers. As the grog shops were all open and drinking spirituous liquors was common, there was disgraceful drunkenness. Women were present in numbers. Indeed in Granville County a newly married couple once made their bridal tour to the scene of execution. Boys were carried by parents in the belief that it would aid their moral training: it showed the youthful mind the punishment of crime. It is an indication of public sentiment on the subject that some well raised, refined school girls at Louisburg started to join the concourse, but when they saw afar off the convict brought out of the jail, clad in a long white shroud, they became panic-stricken and fled to their homes. Not only was the condemned man clad in the dress which was the clothing of the dead, but he was driven in a one-horse cart, sitting on his coffin. He was allowed to make an address to the crowd and men of nerve often spoke impressively. Once when a great crowd came into town to witness the much-desired spectacle, the Governor reprieved the prisoner. To complete the crowd's disappointment a dismal rain set in. We then lived three miles from town. Some of the woefully wet women stopped at our house on the way home to get warm. They were voluble in denouncing the Governor for depriving them of their rights. One old hag heaped abuse on the poor prisoner. She vowed that she "never would come to see him hung if he never was hung." Her language seemed to imply that she was conferring an honor on him.

I never witnessed a hanging but was told that there was much exhibition of brutal rowdyism and the old argument for their publicity that they discouraged lawlessness was proved by experience to be unsound. They did harm.

The machinery for carrying out the sentence of the law was rude but effective. The rope was fastened to a limb of a tree, the lower end in a slipknot placed around the neck of the prisoner seated in the cart on his coffin. The horse fastened to the cart was made to move on and the unhappy man was left hanging to the tree. An eye-witness told me that he could see the feet holding to the cart

Above, Campus of the University: Cameron Avenue, looking west. South Building, Gerrard Hall (the Chapel), and Memorial Hall (later taken down). Photograph taken about 1888.
Below, Cameron Avenue, looking east. Memorial Hall is in the foreground; Gerrard Hall next; and South Building beyond.

DIALECTIC SOCIETY HALL AT THE UNIVERSITY
This room was later dismantled. From a photograph taken about 1885.

to the last moment of time. A handkerchief hid the facial distortions from the eyes of the crowd. A clergyman accompanied the prisoner as at present. The prisoner was always exhorted to confess his crime as a prerequisite to salvation. Some refused to do so, hoping for a pardon or reprieve at the last moment.

The foregoing primitive arrangement was superseded by the erection of a gallows. This consisted of two upright beams, with a crosspiece on top. At a convenient distance from the ground was another crosspiece to which was fastened a platform, connected with the cross-beam by hinges. This platform was kept in a horizontal position by a rope carried over a pulley fastened to the top cross-beam. The criminal stood on the platform until the sheriff cut the rope and the platform dropped, the prisoner falling with it. Occasionally the rope would break and the poor victim painfully half-strangled would be hauled up again. Sometimes there was a trap door in the middle of the platform and the prisoner fell through it. If the neck was broken by the fall of about four feet, death was sudden; if the bone was not broken, the strangulation lasted several minutes. It was to secure instant death that execution by electric discharge was adopted. The sheriff selected the place of execution. At Raleigh in early days a pine-covered hill which had been devised to the city by John Rex was selected. Then the extensive hole called the Rock Quarry, whence came the stone for building the Capitol, was used. The spectators looked down from the rim.

I remember attending the trial of a young negress for killing her mistress. She was defended by a lawyer of some brilliancy, Hugh McQueen, once Attorney General. No one saw the killing but there was no one who could have done it except the accused. I was about ten years of age and had never witnessed a trial before. I was amazed to hear the lawyer quote case after case of men hung on circumstantial testimony and afterwards proved to be innocent. McQueen showed how easy it would have been for someone intent on robbing to enter the woman's house and murder her. He so solemnly warned the jury not to have innocent blood on their consciences that I was glad that I was not a juryman. But his eloquence did not save her.

Public sentiment was in favor of capital punishment. In the case of murderers the argument was from the Bible, "Whoso sheddeth man's blood, by man shall his blood be shed." In the case of other offences, burglary, arson, slave stealing, rape, highway robbery, it was urged that dwellings are poorly defended, especially at night, all the more defenceless when the State was sparsely settled; that offenders are so wicked that they cannot be reformed; that in the interests of society they should not be allowed to propagate their kind; that there are no prisons strong enough to hold them; that if they should not escape from prison, soft-hearted governors would pardon; that in executing offenders society was acting in self-defence.

While I was at the school of J. M. Lovejoy, a crime was committed which caused great excitement and introduced the boys to the mysteries of grand jury investigation. The school-yard adjoined the garden of a bad-tempered neighbor who was offended because the pupils occasionally entered his premises through a hole left in the fence by a broken plank. Once a gun was fired at a boy but either it was not well aimed or was shot only to frighten. If the latter, it was a dangerous experiment as the shot did not miss the lad more than a foot. The grand jury made a thorough inquiry into the facts but could not find the perpetrator, though the owner of the garden was suspected.

Some people are worried at the idea of the possibility of the execution of an innocent person. I give my testimony that in all my practise I never knew of a person not guilty being convicted. But I saw undoubtedly guilty persons acquitted. Moreover, I am sure that the juries before which I practised were entirely just to colored people, slave or free. I appeared once for some free persons of color seized by a trader who claimed that they had not been lawfully emancipated. We had no difficulty in defeating him. A few years after Nat Turner's bloody insurrection in Southampton County, Virginia, in 1831, there were excited stories of similar insurrections in our State, in Northampton, Bertie, Duplin, and other counties. There probably were hasty punishments but I know nothing about them. An elderly resident of Raleigh told me that there was a panic in Raleigh in fear of a rising of negroes. A silly rumor spread that an armed band of them from the Roanoke valley was marching on the capital. Horsemen were sent as scouts to bring advance tidings of the invasion. There was only one bell in town, that in the steeple of the Presbyterian Church. It was agreed that on the approach of danger this bell should be rung and women and children should take refuge in the church. It so happened that a blacksmith shop caught fire about midnight and the bell was rung to summon the fire-fighters. There was a wild rush of the women to the church, frantic for fear of murder or rape. My informant, James D. Royster, who was one of the city guards, had after forty years a vivid remembrance of the scene, many in their extreme terror not having changed their night clothes. We are apt to be surprised at such conduct of the people of old times. But we should remember that many slaves were recent importations and not nearly as civilized as they later became, that Nat Turner and his gang had lately slain some of the farmers before being dispersed, and that undoubtedly hostile conspiracies really were planned in certain localities but were discovered in time to prevent outbreaks. The fact that the negroes lived among the whites, in a few feet of their dwellings, enhanced the feeling of insecurity. People felt as if rattlesnakes were under their beds and hidden in their shrubbery. Moreover the country was thinly settled, the roads bad, and intercommunication difficult.

But many false suspicions were engendered, increased sometimes by jovial wags who found delight in terrifying others. There was a flare-up at Chapel Hill about 1846, when it was alleged that an abandoned cottage had been found containing a number of scythe-blades and other like weapons. There was a temporary scare but it was allayed when two or three resolute men visited the supposed arsenal and found it a myth. The remark of Sam Green, an old darkey who led an idle life by pretending to his master, Professor Green, that a sore hand prevented his working, made the whole story a joke. "When I rises, I rise to do my master's work."

It is certainly unjust to blame our ancestors for habitual cruelty in punishment. They made their laws to suit the circumstances of their day. For example, when the country was thinly settled and roads almost impassable, highway robberies were often accompanied by murders and robbers were not easily caught. Hence the offence was punished with death. It was found necessary in some of our territories to organize Vigilance Committees, who inflicted swift punishment for horse-stealing. I remember that years ago before the advent of railroads and telegraphs one John A. Muir organized slave and horse stealing so well that his crimes went undetected for a long time. He had associates stationed between his home in Guilford County and the lands bordering on the Mississippi River. His booty was rapidly transferred from one set of his accomplices to another. He was not run down until one of his followers was induced to betray him.

Our ancestors thought that instead of putting a bigamist in prison it was better to brand the letter B on his cheek so that other women could see it and beware of his guile. A similar reason existed for branding the letter M for manslaughter in the hand that had killed an adversary in a fight.

21. Practice Outside Wake County

AS MY FATHER WAS UNCOMMONLY POPULAR in Franklin County, it appeared reasonable to me that some favor of litigation would incline my way. Although a long-headed friend warned me of probable disappointment, I concluded to try the experiment. Accordingly I attended the Franklin courts for two years. Although old friends of my father took my hand cordially, and some told me I was bound to do well on his account, I met no practical encouragement. There were four or five good local lawyers, among them Joseph J. Davis, afterwards a judge of the Supreme Court. Evidently they would get the preference and in great cases clients would employ men of established State reputation to act with the local lawyers. On the other hand Wake was the most populous county in the State. It had its own six courts. It was the seat of the State Supreme Court. In it were held the United States courts. I concluded therefore to confine myself to this single county, the first lawyer who pursued this policy.

The old custom of lawyers to follow the judge from court to court had serious evils. Many were inevitably not engaged. "Satan finds some mischief still for idle hands to do." Naturally there was much gaming and many convivial potations. Very many men, bright, well-gifted in manners and capacity for usefulness, fell victims to these temptations. Another disadvantage of circuit riding was the possible loss of employment at home. And time which might have been utilized in study was consumed in the long buggy rides and loitering about the hotels. On the other hand it must be said that many counties were too small to afford a living from their own law business alone.

At the request of my partner I attended one term of the County Court in Johnston County with instructions to continue his cases to the next term. I succeeded with all but one. One client named Earp (pronounced Harp) insisted on a trial and I felt bound to comply. The plaintiff sued Earp for a wagon. There was only one witness and he swore pointedly in Earp's favor. I asked the plaintiff's attorney, Rogers, to give up the case. He said, "I prefer to go to the jury." After our speeches the jury brought in a verdict for the plaintiff, without a particle of evidence! Before the jury was impanelled, I asked Earp if he was satisfied with the jury. He said they were all right. Greatly wondering that my client should lose, I sought the private reasons for it. I learned that there were four jurors who knew that Earp's character was bad and that he paid the witness to allow him to keep his wife as a paramour. These four jurors told the rest that it was the neighborhood belief that the witness was bought by Earp. The verdict was against law. The four jurors ought to have declined to serve and been examined as witnesses but the verdict was probably right. Earp was regarded as a bad man. It was said that he kept his insane wife in a pen like a pig.

On the way from Louisburg to Raleigh once I had an adventure which resulted in a woe and a blessing. It was necessary to stay in Franklinton all night and take a very early train to Raleigh. After supper I took my candle and went to my room to write my first letter to my ladylove. I was deeply interested of course. The candlestick was a cheap tin flat-bottomed affair, with a half-burnt candle. When I finished my letter, I noticed that the room was full of smoke of a burnt-hair odor. Investigation discovered that I had written without removing my high silk hat, formerly called a beaver, recently purchased at a cost of four dollars and a half. There was a charred hole in it, utterly beyond repair, burnt as I leaned over the table. On the cars next morning I sat hatless and in Raleigh I walked a back street to my lodging, with the burnt spot behind. But the answer to my letter was a healing balm to my sad mishap. The hole in my hat did not cause a hole in my heart.

I had a subsequent experience with a high-crowned hat, indicating that such ambitious style does not accord with my temperament. When in 1865 I spent three months in New York City endeavoring to secure immigration to North Carolina, I bought a hat in the prevailing city style, with the shape of a truncated cone. The style was so common there that I did not realize how odd it would appear, with none like it in Raleigh. When I got home, I was laughed at. One day I saw coming towards me the sheriff of Johnston County on whom I had conferred a favor by some legal advice. As he approached I noticed successive changes of his countenance from mere curiosity to wonderment, ending in pity and disgust. When he reached me he said plaintively, "Mr. Battle, that hat does not suit you!" I utterly failed as an introducer of fashions.

I appeared in some cases in Franklin at the request of Mr. Fourney Green, who was a candidate for the House of Commons and was afraid he would make enemies of those whom he would be compelled to denounce if he should try the cases. One was about an account against the husband of a country school teacher for a debt contracted by her before marriage. I was praised for my successful ridicule of the defendant. I took up the account item by item and conjectured that the lady incurred the debt in order to make herself agreeable to her favored suitor. The jury laughed especially at my denunciation of him for refusing to pay for the sugar item which I said sweetened the toddy prepared for him by her fair hands. I gained the case.

I lost another case, however—the defence of one Acril Pearce for striking the prosecutor with a cane. I proved that another man had struck Pearce on the head and argued that the blow so dazed him that he was unconscious of his acts. The lawyer for the prosecution, Col. Leonidas C. Edwards, was uncommonly skilled in pointed, sarcastic oratory. He treated my position as a plea of insanity and so ridiculed the idea of Acril Pearce, who was a noted hard-headed fighting man, being insane that he carried the jury with him. The courtroom was filled with merriment in which I shared.

Col. Edwards afterwards had the table turned on him. He was in Reconstruction days canvassing for the State House of Representatives, his competitor being a negro named Cuffee Mayo. He assailed vigorously the General Assembly of 1868-1869 of which Cuffee was a member, then seeking re-election. In particular he was eloquent in denouncing the extravagance of the General Assembly. He gave as an item, "$1,500 of the people's money to cleanse the privy of the people's representatives." Cuffee looked up at him and inquired, "Mars Ed, would *you* do it for that?" The colonel lost his balance. "Not to save your life, you durned scoundrel!" The laugh was against the colonel.

In the days when I attended court in Franklin County I made the acquaintance of that excellent gentleman and lawyer, afterwards a judge, Robert Ballard Gilliam, one of the most genial and kindly of men. He was full of anecdotes gathered in a long practise at the bar in the old days when it was the custom to accompany the judge from county to county. One of his stories was about a neighbor of his in Oxford, Marcus Lanier, a very learned man of great simplicity of character. Once when arguing a case before the Supreme Court, Lanier earnestly set out some very elementary principles of law, known to the veriest tyro. Chief Justice Pearson interrupted him, "Mr. Lanier, the court is presumed to know *some* law." Mr. Lanier answered gravely. "Well, sir, I thought so myself until last week when the court decided against me in a perfectly plain case." The simplicity of his manner showed that he did not intend to be sarcastic.

When Gilliam was a member of the General Assembly and a candidate for a judgeship of the Superior Court, he asked my influence on the ground of old intimacy with my father. I did what I could but he did not need my aid. He was a favorite among the members. Afterwards, near the close of the war, he called at my house and breakfasted with me. The day being cold, I gave him a toddy out of a bottle of corn whiskey, which I had just bought for medicinal purposes. I paid $100 in Confederate money for it, although I suspected that it had been grievously watered. After testing it, with a look of sadness he said, "You are right. It was watered." Then he showed me that no bubbles arose when the whiskey was shaken. He was a fine specimen of the old-time lawyer, not averse to taking a drink, nor to a brotherly game of cards to relieve the tedium of waiting until his case was called. He was a master of pathos. I recall a case of his in which he defended a client who had acted brutally in a fight. His intense earnestness and tender, sympathetic voice brought the judge to a mild sentence. He made the impression that a heavy fine would break his heart. He was not dissembling—*altogether*.

On the whole, while I made little money in the Franklin courts, I had a pleasant time and never regretted my attendance on them.

22. Extra-Legal Activities in the Fifties

ONE OF THE KINDEST MEN TO ME WHEN I came to Raleigh was John H. Bryan, Jr., and it was a real grief to me that, after I had been elected a director in the Bank of North Carolina, I felt bound to vote against him for teller of the bank. The president, George W. Mordecai, and the cashier, Charles Dewey, both strongly advised against him because of the enemies he had made by ungracious manners, at the same time bearing testimony to his integrity. As a matter of course I was governed by the opinion of the officers whom we had placed in charge of the institution. Happily, our friendly relations were not disturbed.

When Bryan was at the University, graduating in 1844, he was enthusiastic over the poetry of Keats and the nickname, Keats, was affixed to him by the students. When his younger brother William S. entered the University he was known as Young Keats. About the same time Peter Brown Ruffin was a student. He told a thrilling story of an adventure, his hero or heroine having the disaster of being overturned in a stage coach. The narrator in consequence acquired the name of Stage Ruffin. When his brother Thomas became a student the college wit called him Hack Ruffin, a hack being smaller than a stage. His old acquaintances often accosted him as Hack Ruffin even after he became a judge of the Supreme Court.

A year or so before the war I had a gratifying triumph. The Bank of North Carolina succeeded the Bank of the State of North Carolina with a larger capital. I was the first young man ever elected a director of the leading bank, those who held the office theretofore having been men of considerable age and widely known in the financial world. I had shown my confidence in the bank by subscribing for a good block of stock, $14,000. But it was mainly my avoidance of evil habits and strict attention to business that procured the favor of the veteran financiers. Probably President Mordecai controlled the choice. It was a pleasing thought to me that at the school of his father, Moses Mordecai, in Warrenton he was a teacher of my mother.

Mr. Mordecai was an excellent bank-president—clear-headed, firm yet pleasant-mannered, accurate, with good knowledge of the law, of perfect integrity, and thoroughly reliable. Born a Jew, he had years before joined the Episcopal Church. He lived a bachelor until past middle age, when he married the wealthy daughter of Judge Duncan Cameron. Dying before her, he bequeathed to her nearly all his property, including all that came to him in consequence of the marriage. Though he had been a member of the Constitutional Union party, when the war began he sided with the extreme war party to an extent that surprised his friends.

Charles Dewey had been connected with banks in New Bern and Raleigh for years. "C. Dewey, Cashier," was, or had been, on a boundless number of bank notes. He was trusted by everybody and was well versed in the routine of his profession but was not learned beyond it. I was amazed at his limited knowledge of the laws relating to financial business.

I was honored also by being chosen a director of a Mutual Fire Insurance Company. The premiums were paid partly in cash but chiefly in notes. There were losses which exceeded the cash on hand. An assessment was necessary which was collected with difficulty and caused dissatisfaction. President Solby had been a merchant but had no special knowledge of insurance. The secretary, Hampden Smith, had talent but was content with performing his clerical duties. I took the trouble to go over the past history of the company, ascertained what cash payments ought to have been required to avoid assessments, and made certain recommendations to prevent trouble in the future. My recommendations were adopted and the changes met with success, but the war wounded the company so that it went out of business.

A compliment was paid to me in 1857 by the General Assembly in electing me a director of the State Insane Asylum. The annual meetings were agreeable as we had confidence in our superintendent, Dr. E. C. Fisher. Among our actions should be recorded our diversion of part of the waters of Rocky Branch for the use of the asylum. It was good for the asylum but it caused complaint from the owner of a mill, Sylvester Smith by name, who alleged that our taking the water from the branch had injured his mill. We referred the question to Paul C. Cameron and Dr. Thomas D. Hogg as arbitrators. They awarded him $300 in damages. I was surprised to hear that Chief Justice Ruffin said that the asylum was not bound to pay anything. The large amount of water taken from Rocky Branch above the mill which had been in use for many years was not returned to the branch, but what was not diverted to irrigation of the asylum garden flowed into Walnut Creek. It was certainly equitable that some compensation should be paid for the obstruction of the motive power of the humble corn grinder. Perhaps the judge was not cognizant of the facts or was misunderstood.

Then the asylum was sued by William Grimes for emptying on his land the sewage not used in the asylum garden. He declared this made his land offensive and unhealthy. He offered, however, to stop the suit if we would allow all the sewage to pass out of the asylum land. This was accepted but subsequently we bought the Grimes land and added it to the asylum holding.

The tin on the asylum roof became loosened by a storm and it was necessary to fasten it down. In order to protect the spikes from corroding, they were driven through old-time big copper cents of which the bank had a keg full and a heavy coat of solder was melted over the coins. This is perhaps the only building in the land whose covering is secured with coined money.

Before long I was placed on the Asylum Executive Committee whose duty was to inspect all the wards once a month and generally to note anything wrong in the management. We always found things in good order. One day, in a room occupied as a parlor by the well-behaved lady patients, I found a group engaged in sewing. The superintendent introduced me to them. All shook hands very naturally except one. She was handsome and ladylike. When I stretched forth my hand, she declined to take it saying pleasantly, "Mr. Battle, I hope you will excuse me. I mean no offence but I can't help it. I fear that there is grease on your clothes." That was her mania. Her husband had built for her a new house, with every precaution against the introduction of grease, but it did not cure her.

23. Running for the General Assembly

THE WHIG PARTY MADE A MISERABLE BLUNder in allying itself with the American or Know Nothing party. I was so disgusted with this that without losing my dislike of the Democrats I gave my first presidential vote for Buchanan. An old Democrat, Samuel Whitaker, often State Senator, disgusted me by praising my good sense in siding with the party which was especially strong in Wake. He was mistaken. Instead of turning Democrat I became an ardent partisan of the Constitutional Union party and was appointed a member of the executive committee, Sion H. Rogers being chairman.

When the election of 1860 came on, I entered with enthusiasm into the state-wide canvass. I made several speeches in Wake, abstracts of which were printed and circulated. I showed by extracts from the speeches of William L. Yancey of Alabama and others that they were carrying the South straight to disunion and war.

The executive committee concluded to have a grand rally at Salisbury to catch the western vote. It was very successful. The crowd was large, the speaking was by eminent orators such as ex-Senator Badger, W. N. H. Smith, a member of the national House of Representatives, afterwards Chief Justice, Nathaniel Boyden, afterwards a judge of the Supreme Court, and above all, one who had gained and deserved an exalted position as a stump speaker, Congressman Zebulon B. Vance.

These were the appointed speakers in the morning. Then came a copious dinner and a grand torchlight procession followed by more orating at night, free and easy short talks, full of animation, jocularities, and denunciations. I was called on vociferously but I did not feel in the humor and silently dodged. *Non sum inventus*. I concluded afterwards that I was wrong in this. Having embarked my little boat on the sea of politics, I ought to have taken advantage of every breeze.

We had a special train back to Raleigh and with Dr. Thomas D. Hogg, Dr. Dick Haywood, and a few others like me tired by the strenuous day's exertions, I went to the train in advance of the time of starting. A tall countryman named Gaston Utley from what was wrongly called the "Dark Corner of Wake" was along. Following him was a young man of a good appearance, but given to intemperance. He had a flask in his hand and was hospitably inclined.

Running for the General Assembly

He said, "Mr. Battle, won't you have a drink of peach brandy?" "No, I thank you." "Dr. Haywood, have some peach brandy?" "No, I thank you." "Dr. Hogg, let me give you a drink of peach brandy." Dr. Hogg also declined. The young man turned off with a much disappointed air. Then I heard a deep voice from the corner where my Dark Corner friend was seated. "If you will extend that invitation over this way, you will shorely be accommodated!" And they made for the water bucket, a joyous pair. Poor young man! An only son, handsome, able; in a few months he was in a drunkard's grave.

Wake County had always been considered one of the deep-dyed Democratic counties of the State. It did not share the general enthusiasm for "Tippecanoe and Tyler Too," and the defeat of the opposing party had always been sure. The old leaders of the opposition were thoroughly disheartened and discouraged a canvass for the General Assembly as certain to end in defeat. Some of us younger men thought there was a chance to break the serried ranks. Sion H. Rogers, a good jury lawyer who had won a term in Congress because two Democratic candidates, Venable and Lewis, divided the votes of their party, was one. He was a son of a farmer, of popular manners, who had gained honors at the University but was not much of a student afterwards. He was fond of mixing with the people, was acquainted with almost every man in the county, and was a shrewd electioneer. Another was J. P. H. Russ, a jovial farmer, and a teller of amusing jokes, some of them too broad for good society. I was asked to be the third because of my hard work as executive committeeman. Really I did not desire to be a member of the General Assembly. I thought that the time spent in acquiring the office and attention to legislative duties would impede success at the bar. I was not fond of mixing with the people. On the other hand the delivery of speeches in every part of the county and becoming acquainted with the "sovereigns" would increase my practise and give me confidence in speaking. I had no experience in haranguing miscellaneous crowds and it was irksome to me, but I soon rather enjoyed it although at times I longed for quiet and my books and business.

Besides the charge that the leaders of the Democracy were Secessionists, carrying the country straight into disunion, war, and ruin, we had a lovely state issue, one in advocating which we could at the same time be demagogical and conscientiously right.

When the Constitution was amended in 1835, there was a strong demand for building railroads, plank-roads, and turnpikes, digging canals, and making rivers navigable, largely at the expense of the State. The slave-owners living in eastern counties were satisfied with the water transportation of their products, and were fearful of heavy taxation on slaves. So they forced the provision into the Constitution that all slaves between the ages of twelve and fifty and free males between the ages of twenty-one and forty-five should pay the same capitation tax and no other person should be subject to such tax. Thus a large amount of property, namely slaves under the age of twelve years and over the age of fifty years, were exempt from contributing to the support of the State. Inasmuch as slave-owners were much less numerous than non-slave owners, manifestly such inequality could not stand permanently.

Being a member of the executive committee of the Union party, I threw myself into the contest with the utmost vigor. I prepared a document showing the inequalities of the old taxation, and the reasonableness of all property paying for the support of the government according to value, exempting a small amount to each person on the same principle as the exemptions to insolvent debtors. My document, under the name of *Ad Valorem Taxation Explained by Questions and Answers*, was published by the hundred thousand, and Hon. Richard S. Donnell republished fifty thousand copies especially for his congressional district.

The Democrats made little effort to show the justice of the constitutional provision but contended with earnestness and ability that it was a compromise after excited controversy between eastern and western counties and that it was unfair if not dishonest to repeal it. They moreover declared that as long as the slave question was prominent in national politics it was playing into the hands of Free-Soilers and Abolitionists to stir up feelings of hostility to slavery in our State. They insisted that the consideration of the question should be postponed. Although we lost the governorship, the correctness of our position was proved by the fact that all parties in the Convention of 1861 united to make the changes we advocated.

My only hope was to make a conspicuously good run. I was sure that we could elect Rogers but no one else. One thing was in our favor. The last Democratic state senator, Moses A. Bledsoe, a strong debater, had made a speech in favor of *ad valorem* taxation, which caused his party to drop him and nominate George W. Thompson. We induced Bledsoe to run against Thompson, promising that no Whig should be a senatorial candidate. The sheriff and county court clerk, William H. High and Thomas J. Utley, who had the control of many votes, we persuaded to take no active part by the simple argument that their candidacy was two years off and if they should interfere, we would certainly bring out opposition. As they were uncertain as to the strength of our movement, they did not work actively for our opponents.

One thing puzzled my conscience. The custom of treating to whiskey was fixed in the county. A temperance man, Everard Hall, had been a candidate two years before and aroused a bitter prejudice against prohibition, getting very few votes. I was not a drinking man but I did not then feel so strongly against the practice as I do now. I consented therefore not to take a stand publicly on the subject and to pay my share of electoral expenses, including such treating to whiskey, lemonade, and cakes, as Rogers should deem necessary. I now regret that I did this much, but then I thought I should injure the other candidates as well as myself by refusing. Further, I was so much troubled for fear the Secession party would get control that I thought desperate efforts ought to be made to secure the prestige of a victory in the county of the capital. At that time opposition to treating would have been fatal.

There were other expenses which were necessary, such as having men at every precinct to provide a sufficiency of tickets, to prevent intimidation of our voters, to convey invalids to the polls, and such like. I paid my share.

Our opponents for the House of Commons were Ed. Graham Haywood, William R. Cox, and Henry Mordecai. Haywood was considered to be the finest orator in the Democratic party. He was liable to get on sprees but kept himself straight when he had work to do. In such case he would labor without stint. Once at Smithfield he was asked to meet a Whig antagonist next day. He rode to Raleigh in a buggy twenty-eight miles, studied all night and was back in Smithfield fully prepared by 12 o'clock. He had already spoken in this campaign and each time consumed two hours. To embarrass him we insisted that each day two candidates should have one hour each, the candidates for the senate one hour each, the remaining four only seventeen minutes each. Haywood went home, cut off one-half of his two-hour speech and was ready for us next day.

William R. Cox, afterwards a brigadier general in the Confederate army, was a young lawyer recently entering the State from Tennessee. As Mordecai gave up his right to the one-hour speech, Cox and Haywood each had that hour on alternate days. Cox, although he had not the reputation of his colleague, was a good speaker, but being a newcomer was not well acquainted with the people. After the war he became a solicitor, a judge, member of Congress, and secretary of the U.S. Senate. The third Democrat, Henry Mordecai, was a man of strong natural ability and kindly heart but too fond of the pleasures of life. He refused to make set speeches but his generosity in lending money and dispensing liquor made him formidable. He was accused of getting the crowd so hilarious before the speaking began that they lacked the disposition and the wits to profit by the sensible arguments of the speakers. On the night before the election he gave a big frolic in his gin-house to a large number of men always in search of free drinks and next morning sent them to the polls, shouting, "Hurrah for Mordecai!" Similarly, Squire Drake, who had a grog-shop on Hillsborough Street, "liquored up" one hundred twenty-five Mordecai men and forwarded them down the street in goodly array armed with Mordecai tickets.

By a rather odd combination there were two pairs of brothers-in-law in the campaign: Haywood against Rogers, and Cox against me. Cox and I were always friendly but on one occasion Rogers, owing to a misunderstanding, struck at Haywood but missed him and friends made peace between them. The sheriff had appointed eighteen places for the listing of taxables and the collecting of taxes and the candidates followed him around with their speaking and electioneering. It was trying work in the hot days of July, eighteen consecutive days, omitting Sundays. Seven liquor booths followed us around and there was much intoxication with occasional fights but none fatal. I came out about as fresh as when I started, having really enjoyed the novel experience. I attribute this to several causes. In the first place what flesh I had was all muscle. I had not an ounce of fat. Then I had learned from a book called Warren on Health that it is healthy for young people to stand when studying and I had been adopting that attitude for ten years. The exigencies of speaking and circulating among the "sovereigns" the best part of the day did not greatly tire me. And I contend that the joviality I employed in my conversation and speeches was distinctly salutary. But above all I was not an intimate friend of John Barleycorn. There were thirteen candidates in all and I was the only man who did not miss a day or two from indisposition. I do not

FACULTY GROUP IN THE EARLY SPRING OF 1888

Standing, left to right, F. P. Venable, Chemistry; George F. Atkinson, Natural History; James Lee Love, Mathematics; Walter D. Toy, Modern Languages; Joseph A. Holmes, Geology and Natural History; J. W. Gore, Natural Philosophy and Engineering. *Sitting, left to right*, R. H. Graves, Mathematics; N. B. Henry, Science and Art of Teaching; A. W. Mangum, Mental and Moral Science; President Battle; John Manning, Law; Thomas Hume, English. From a photograph taken on the Campus.

KEMP PLUMMER BATTLE
From a photograph taken about 1900.

MRS. KEMP PLUMMER BATTLE
From a photograph taken about 1900.

mean that their resting came in all cases from over indulgence. By no means. Some were temperate, but some had real carousals occasionally.

I had an amusing and unusual experience at Seth Jones's Cross Roads. Haywood had been on a frolic the night before—I have a right to speak of his habits as he did it himself with perfect frankness. It was his turn to speak eighteen minutes. He said to me, "Battle, what am I to do? I am drunk, as you see, and my time has come." I said, "Haywood, I have heard your speech so often that I know it by heart. I will sit near you and if you get out I will prompt you!" He tried and to my surprise while his eyes had a vacant look, as if he did not understand what he said, he did not miss a word.

An incident something like the above occurred the same morning. It was the turn of Col. Russ to occupy the hour on our side. He preferred not to attempt a logical discourse but to amuse the crowd with anecdotes, some of them too coarse for the ears of ladies. Just before he started, four or five of the best ladies in that end of the county came out with chairs and took seats in front of the speakers' stand. Russ turned pale. He said to me, "Battle, I'm in a fix. You know some of my jokes won't do for ladies to hear and I've not time to sort them." I said, "Colonel, I've heard all your jokes. Give me the list and I'll put a cross mark to those you can tell." He brought out his list. I cross-marked the decorous anecdotes and he got off with flying colors. He could have marked them himself but was too much flustered.

I must chronicle the thoughtful act of an excellent lady, Mrs. Montague, a daughter of Seth Jones, a farmer of high standing. She and her husband invited us to spend the night with them and when we reached the house, we were shown our room upstairs, cool and pleasant. And there were two tubs half-full of fresh water from the well with soap and towels attendant—a grateful luxury for men tired and heated.

The day after this the boys got the laugh on me. The meeting was at Rosenburg, near where four counties cornered, Wake, Nash, Johnston, and Franklin, on Moccasin Creek, there so small as to be called a branch. There were few trees, no breeze, and the sun was as hot as in the Sahara. Looking around to find something wherewith to make myself agreeable, I espied an old woman with a large basket of ginger cakes, called "gungers." I bought them all and invited the bystanders to help themselves. They did so expeditiously. One young man, whose yellowish complexion and protuberant abdomen indicated that he was an eater of dirt, was quite frantic in his efforts. He secured three or four cakes and, wrapping them in an imitation bandanna handkerchief, turned to me in a sheepish way and said, "Mr. Ba-atle, I'm much obleeged to you for the cakes but I'm sorry I kaint vote for you. I lives tother side of the bra-anch." He had the instincts of a gentleman.

It is a commentary on the intelligence of a portion of the sovereign people about political questions that one day, as I rode to the home of my host for the night, I passed a man on a wagon shouting, "Hurrah for old Valorem! He is the best man in the gang. I'll vote for him *every* time!"

Another time when I bought cakes, I was amused at the sight of a man being teased by some jocular fellows. He vigorously scrambled for the cakes and obtained several. A rough man ran against him and scattered his prizes on the ground. He was thrown into an ecstasy of rage. With a scream of anger and violent gesticulations he shouted, "What is the use of being a coward all the time?"

We never lacked for invitations to spend the night. Indeed it was said that families felt honored in having the candidates with them. We met with warm receptions and excellent entertainment. We always carefully considered whose invitation it was most politic for us to accept. If an invitation came from a dyed-in-the-wool Democrat or Whig, nothing would be gained by accepting it. But if it came from a man whose position was doubtful, an evening's conversation and the honor of a visit might gain him permanently. In such matters Rogers was my guide. He knew everybody and was as shrewd as a red fox. But sometimes he slipped up. One day he advised me to accept the request of a man above the ordinary in manners and appearance. When we reached his home, I was kindly received by his handsome wife and among others a beautiful daughter of fifteen. After a savory supper there was a grave assembly of all the family, and then appeared the reason for the honor which had been done me. There was an acrid church quarrel going on. My beautiful maiden had been tried and convicted before a church court of falsehood, of slandering an associate. My advice as a lawyer was sought for. Of course I tried to be noncommittal though sympathetic. The next day a bitter looking man said to me, "I know what that fellow wanted you to go to his house for. It was about the trial of his lying daughter." It is likely that I was quoted as being on her side, for I fell four votes behind my ticket in that precinct.

When the votes were counted, it was found that we had gained a surprising victory. All our men were elected except me and I had beaten Haywood and Cox. Mordecai was ahead of Russ and me because of his control of the liquor-loving part of the population. However, I gained what I worked for, some reputation as a canvasser (Haywood said I was the best on our side) and still more as a worker. It cost me some hundreds of dollars because it so happened that I had to pay nearly all the bills but this was a good investment. We bribed no one. It was said to be the best race ever had in the county. The Democratic majority in the preceding election was over 700 and was usually not less than 500. Rogers carried the county by about 200, and Pool, the candidate for governor, nearly the same. I never asked a vote for myself but worked for the ticket. A constable who often came to my office for the free advice usually given to constables said to me, "Why didn't you tell me you wished to be elected? I would have voted for you and carried forty other votes."

The vote of one precinct was unaccountably delayed in reaching Raleigh. Russ and I were tied. If the tie should continue, the sheriff would be called on to give the casting vote. I asked him to give it to Russ as the country people ought to have a representative. When this became known, the country people were much pleased and one of them mounted the courthouse steps and nominated me for the General Assembly two years afterwards. The missing return however came in and I was two or three votes behind Russ. My pretty girl's church quarrel lost me the election.

24. My Part in Secession

UNTIL LINCOLN'S CALL FOR TROOPS TO PREvent the seceding states from leaving the Union I had been a violent Union man. I had worked hard for the Constitutional Union party. Although I believed that the Republicans did the slaveholding states great injustice in excluding their slave property from the territory which belonged to all the states, although their refusal to return fugitive slaves was a flat violation of the Constitution, although I was sure that the tariff laws built up the North at the expense of the South, I believed that by party management, by argument, by appeals to fairness, we could always maintain our essential rights. I felt sure that secession would lead to war and that war would certainly bring on us all the evils of which we complained. Although the triumph of Lincoln was a notable evil in theory, another election would come in four years and again in another four years, and so on, and in the mutation of politics the bidding for Southern votes would probably result in just legislation. There was no pressing necessity for an immediate solution of the question. Senator Hammond of South Carolina in a speech in the Senate stated that counting the vacant lands of Texas and other slave states there was land enough for the slaves and their increase for four hundred years.

Notwithstanding their opposition to secession and prediction of probable dangers, the Union men of the State thought that the party in power should have shown a more conciliatory spirit and not have declared war against the seceding states, which the call for 75,000 troops amounted to. President Jackson declined to order troops to enforce the mandate of the Supreme Court in the disputes about the Cherokee Indians and his wisdom in delaying was shown by subsequent legislation which forced the removal of the Indians. The Unionists hoped for similar wise action. When the call for troops inaugurated war, they decided to cast their lot with their own section. As I told an inquirer as to my position, "It is better to go out together, even if we are whipped back together. If we do not go with the South we shall certainly have civil war at home. That will be much worse than fighting the North."

The people by a small majority had voted down the State Convention proposed for February, 1861. The excitement was so great after Lincoln's call for troops that the Governor convened the

General Assembly, and both Houses by a unanimous vote called for the election by the people of delegates to an unrestricted convention to meet May 20, 1861. Mr. Badger's service as chairman of the County Court caused him to be a favorite of the people and when the Union men held a mass meeting to nominate candidates to represent Wake in the Convention conditionally called for February, he, with W. W. Holden and Quentin Busbee, was chosen, and the three were elected by about 1,800 majority. Mr. Badger was much pleased at this evidence of his popularity, especially because in his earlier days he was thought to be of aristocratic tendencies.

After the firing on Fort Sumter, even the anti-secessionists determined to resist the attempt of the general government to crush secession by force of arms. I had been chosen chairman of the Wake County Union Club. We had regular and most enthusiastic meetings during the winter and early spring of 1861. Popular speakers aired their oratory before large assemblies in the courthouse, a choir of six members of the General Assembly sang for us. But in the midst of our labors came the news of the attack on Sumter and Lincoln's call. Like most men of my party, I concluded that coercion should be resisted. Zeb Vance rode a day's journey from Asheville to make a Union speech. Before speaking time next day came a swift messenger with the news of Sumter and the call for troops. Vance began his speech. "Fellow citizens, I died last night a Union man. I am resurrected today a Secession man."

This was the general attitude of the Constitutional Union or Bell and Everett party which gathered in the fragments of the old Whig party. As the war went on, they increased in numbers and were called Conservatives.

Naturally Badger and Holden, who received so large a majority as candidates for the abortive Convention of February, were considered the logical aspirants for seats in the Convention of May. Busbee would have been with them but was incapacitated by sickness. Rogers was a colonel in the army, and Russ was Secretary of State. Having been an active canvasser the year before I was called on to take Busbee's place on the new ticket.

But the Secessionists, although discredited in the preceding election when they were defeated by a vote of almost two to one, made a strong effort to gain control of the county. They called a meeting of the people on short notice and this rump convention nominated three strong and popular men against Badger, Holden, and Battle, under the name of compromise candidates. They were ex-Governor Charles Manly and President of the Bank of North Carolina George W. Mordecai, both Old Line Whigs, and ex-Governor Thomas Bragg, a Democrat but not a violent Secessionist. These were men of the highest character, and the movement was a formidable danger to the other ticket.

Seeing this danger, I took horse and buggy and visited as many of our known friends as possible, explained to them that our opponents were named by the original Secessionists desirous of regaining their influence in the county so signally lost in the preceding February. It was admitted by all that my exertions saved our ticket. We prevailed by only a small margin, Mr. Badger and myself having a majority of about sixty, while Holden's majority was only five.

The old Unionists had a majority in the Convention but in the early days there were a number who voted with the original Secessionists because they thought that a firm front might dispose the national administration to avoid a bloody war. By their aid Weldon N. Edwards, a kinsman of Nat Macon, one of the old leaders of the States Rights party, was elected President of the Convention over ex-Governor Graham, the leader of the ex-Unionists. A like division was in favor of the ordinance claiming secession as a right introduced by Burton Craige, as against the ordinance of revolution proposed by Mr. Badger. And the same line was drawn on the question of adopting the Provisional Constitution of the Confederate States, the ex-Unionists insisting on a formal guaranty of equal rights in the instrument of adoption, while the majority thought it best to trust to the fairness of our sister states.

The formation of a distinct party by the ex-Unionists was caused by what they considered unfair treatment by the executives of the State and Confederacy. The General Assembly had authorized the raising of ten regiments of state troops, the appointment of all field and company officers being vested in the Governor. Governor Ellis, an ardent Secessionist, as a rule selected those of his own way of thinking and it was thought that President Davis concurred in this policy. It really seemed as if those who were not early in favor of secession were considered so lukewarm that they could not be trusted with leadership. Certainly President Edwards by no means ignored party but in his appointment of committees gave a marked preference to men of his own way of thinking.

This feeling grew so strong that the ex-Unionists determined to call a caucus for the nomination of delegates to the Provisional Congress. The old maxim that politics make strange bedfellows was verified. The strange spectacle was seen of a meeting in the parlor of W. W. Holden presided over by ex-Governor Graham so often severely criticized in the columns of the *Standard* newspaper of which Holden was the editor. I attended and made a talk showing the partisan appointments of Governor Ellis. Some of the nominees of the ex-Unionist caucus were elected showing a breaking up of the Secession party. This continued until, before adjournment, the ex-Unionists had a decided majority.

Most of the delegates to the Convention were leaders in their counties and some had state-wide experience. Many of them seemed to think that they were expected to give their views on every question that came up. Being a young man, comparatively speaking, and in my first legislative body, I did not speak often. My most elaborate oration was made at the suggestion of ex-Governor Graham, who said that the young men were not standing up to their party. It was in advocacy of requiring proper guarantees of equality to be inserted in the Confederate Constitution. It was printed in the *Standard*. I made another studied speech showing the importance of State aid to reach by railway from Raleigh the coal and iron of Deep River. In addition to these set speeches I made some short talks so that I was at least not among the dumb members.

When the question of final adjournment came up, I voted for holding a special session to consider constitutional changes. Able committees had been appointed and had made their reports. But many members thought that notwithstanding the high standing of the delegates individually the people expected the General Assembly to pass needed laws, and that the Convention was a useless expense. And I think that the Secession party desired adjournment because they had lost control of the body. The last session was held May 13, 1862.

I have in two publications (Sprunt Monograph No. 1 and the North Carolina Booklet of April 1915) given other recollections of the Convention of 1861. There is no need to repeat them here.

25. President of the Chatham Railroad Company

ALTHOUGH AS ATTORNEY OF THE CITY OF Raleigh I was exempt from war service by the act of Congress which excepted from conscription state and municipal officers, I determined to enter the army as soon as I was released from convention duties. I had two offers of a lieutenancy. The first was from John Devereux who was then raising a company. We had a meeting in the mayor's office. There was some discussion of the matter. Nothing was said against our plan but it came to nothing. I suppose that other aspirants for military honors offered superior inducements. Mr. Devereux had never mixed with the people and had few acquaintances in the county. He was afterwards employed in the Quartermaster's Department.

I then had an offer from Willie D. Jones, one of my political friends who reached the dignity of state senator. He came to me and promised me that if I would learn military tactics so that I could drill the company he was forming at Avent's Mill, he would certainly have me elected first lieutenant. I agreed to this, came to Chapel Hill and took lessons under Col. W. J. Martin who was about to enter the army. The only blood I shed for the South was from a wound then received. I was going through the manual of arms with a heavy musket of the old pattern on the hard ground in front of the South Building. When the order to ground arms was given the butt of the weapon came down on my toes like a maul of iron. Several weeks elapsed before I left the ranks of limpers.

I stayed with the boys at Avent's Mill some days, though a kindly neighbor would not allow me to sleep on the mill floor but took me to his hospitable home. The voting day came. The neighbors assembled in picnic style to hear speeches by Daniel G. Fowle and me urging young men to volunteer for the army. A friend of mine, John W. Smith, took me aside and kindly said, "I am for you. But Fab Perry has joined us and persuaded the boys that it would be a disgrace to prefer a town man to a country man. It is my duty to tell you that he will be elected." I thanked him and told him that I came on the assurance of their captain that I was wanted, that I never had any idea of entering into a scramble for the place, and requested him to withdraw my name, if any one should nominate me. So I was not voted for. It was a lucky miss. The company made no reputation, was soon captured at Roanoke Island, and was never heard of afterwards. My chief regret was that I made a poor speech. Fowle had an earnest, tearful kind of eloquence, and portrayed the dangers of invasion and the necessity of meeting it so vividly as to thrill the people. I was so chagrined at the defeat of my lieutenant plan that I am sure my speech was a failure. A week or two afterwards, when my plans were settled satisfactorily, I was invited to the same neighborhood for another speaking and by sawing the air and vehemently denouncing the Yankees I regained the little reputation I had as a stumper. A country man told me before I began, "Mr. Battle, you must do better than you did at Avent's Mill. You didn't do yourself justice there." I knew it as well as he.

It soon became evident in the progress of the war that receipts of coal and iron from the Virginia mines would be very precarious. It therefore became important that other sources of supply should be sought. Among these was the Deep River region in Chatham and Moore Counties. I made a speech in the Convention of 1861 advocating substantial state support for the Chatham Railroad Company to build a railroad from Raleigh to Deep River. I also published an article advocating that the city of Raleigh should subscribe fifty thousand dollars to the stock of the company and pay for the same with bonds of the State procured by exchange for Raleigh bonds. The plan met with favor, and on account of my labors for the road I was elected president. The place suited me well. It gave me honorable occupation in behalf of the Confederacy.

I had little trouble in providing for my household during the war as I easily had corn and meat hauled by my own wagons from the plantations in Edgecombe. I had a tract of woodland which supplied me with wood and I hauled by wagon Deep River coal from Lockville in Chatham County. At Lockville was a dam that made the river navigable to Egypt, where the mine was. This coal made a quick fire which melted the coal on the surface. By breaking up the crust a very satisfactory combustion was obtained.

I went down this mine once. It was 480 feet deep. Ventilation was secured by fires, one of the shafts being the chimney. I heard the dangerous gas (carbureted-hydrogen) sizzling from the coal. The seam of the good coal was four feet thick. Above that was a foot-wide layer of earth and above that another seam of coal. But the coal was not as good as English coal. It is said that as long as the blockade runner "Advance" was able to procure English coal it could outsail the blockaders but on its last trip it had Deep River coal which caked so that rapid heat could not be created.

In his famous controversy with State Geologist Emmons, Dr. Elisha Mitchell contended that there are no evidences of a coalbed at Egypt but only of a seam, sloping about 18° with the horizon. Certainly the angle continued unchanged at a depth of 480 feet and I believe that Dr. Mitchell was right. I was confirmed in this opinion when I learned afterwards that Dr. Emmons had bought Deep River land but had sold it. I noticed that it was situated where coal would have been if the deposit was a bed instead of a seam.

This reminds me that when State Geologist W. C. Kerr and I visited Williams College, Massachusetts, in 1876, the Professor of Geology (Tenny) showed us the collection of specimens of North Carolina minerals made by Dr. Emmons while he was in the service of the State and bought from his son for $4,000. In the collection was the renowned jawbone of the *Dromatherium sylvestre* Emmons, an insectivorous marsupial, one of the only two examples, says Dana, of mammalian remains of the Atlantic border. It was found in the Triassic stratum in which the Deep River coal lies. When Professor Tenny examined the Emmons Collection, this relic was absent and he retained $500 until it was produced. The evolutionists say that all the mammals come from that animal by the operation of the law of the survival of the fittest.

This Triassic formation is said to be the bed of an ancient arm of the ocean, extending with varying widths from Staten Island to Georgia. The Piney Prospect elevation at Chapel Hill overlooks it. About sixteen miles wide there, it lies about 250 feet lower than the high land on which stands Chapel Hill. I cannot understand why this collection, made while Dr. Emmons was working for North Carolina, was not the property of the State. Perhaps if alive he could explain it.

Dr. Emmons left in the Capitol at Raleigh a mass of specimens of the rocks and minerals of the State. When war was being waged, the military authorities needed the room where they were stored and they were donated to the University. They were transferred to Chapel Hill under the supervision of Col. W. J. Martin, Professor of Geology, who in addition to directing the transfer worked arduously with his own hands.

Dr. Mitchell was never afraid of controversy. Besides his bout with Bishop Ravenscroft on a theological question, he and General Clingman had a battle royal as to the first discovery of the highest mountain east of the Rockies. There was some probability that Clingman would gain the victory because of his influence at Washington, he being a senator, but the tragic death of Dr. Mitchell on the mountain was potent in inducing the senator to withdraw his claim.

When I was in the University Dr. Mitchell told our class that the land in the old Triassic formation was generally unfertile because the potash had been washed out of the disintegrated sandstone. Moreover, because of the porous nature of the soil, fertilizer placed upon it was carried by rain too deep for plants to benefit by it properly. The exceptions to this rule were the farms adjacent to the hills. He mentioned the plantations of Paul C. Cameron on Flat River, of Mr. Hargrave (now R. L. Strowd's) on Bowlin's Creek, and of Mr. Solomon Morgan on Morgan Creek. It so happens that by the will of Mrs. Mary Elizabeth Mason, a daughter of Solomon Morgan, one-half his lands, amounting to eight hundred acres, is now the property of the University.

The first step in building the Chatham Railroad was to let out the grading by contract. The contractors were A. Frank Page and D. E. Murchison. Page was a successful business man who, after the war, accumulated a fortune and raised a remarkable family, one son being Ambassador to England, another a member of Congress. Murchison stood high in Harnett County. None of us had had experience of the effects of war on prices. It was soon found that the rapid advance of prices, the difficulty of procuring labor and other causes rendered it impossible to carry out the original contract. The directors of the company granted the contractors a release and determined to carry on the work by their own agents. Captain D. E. Allen, an excellent business man acquainted with railroad construction, was engaged as superintendent.

The chief engineer was Colonel Elwood Morris of New Jersey, a man of very unusual ability. For many months he did good service, giving an excellent location from Cary to Lockville. In order to have coal delivered eight miles nearer their shops at a town now called Burlington, then known as Company Shops, the directors of the North Carolina Railroad Company gave my company the privilege of widening their cuts and embankments from Cary to Raleigh. This was of great advantage. After the war and after the Chatham Railroad was absorbed by the Raleigh, Columbia, and

Augusta Airline the North Carolina Railroad Company endeavored in vain to get rid of this contract.

Col. Morris proceeded rapidly with the location of the road to the crossing of Haw River. It was amusing to hear the comments of the country people on his work and his quick retorts. "Mr. Morris, that is not the best way. This is the levellest." "Sir," was the reply, "the directors of the Chatham Railroad Company employed me to locate a line from the village of Cary by the nearest and best route to Lockville in the County of Chatham. They did not order me to run it over every level piece of ground in the county. Good day, sir!" The country man reported, "That man Morris is very curus." Col. Morris told me that he had directed the building of forts at Hatteras and other places on the coast because he was in the service of the State and the work was done for the State. But after they were transferred to the Confederate government, he resigned his position.

There was a railroad being pushed from Cheraw, in South Carolina, northward. It was to our interest to connect it with the Chatham Railroad in the Deep River valley. It was hotly urged by certain members of the General Assembly that there were formidable difficulties in the way. To examine into this I judged it best for Col. Morris and myself to take a horseback ride to Cheraw by one route and return by another through Montgomery County. The southward journey led through Moore and Richmond Counties. The first night we had to listen to music played on a piano so much out of tune that even the beauty and charm of the performer could not keep it from being painful. Next morning we had to ride up a stream five miles in order to cross its swollen waters. The next night we were warmly welcomed because during the previous night some deserters had plundered the storehouse of a country merchant and we were regarded in the light of reinforcements. The road through Moore and Richmond was peculiarly dreary. Years afterwards in a speech I made at the Commencement of the South Carolina Medical School in Charleston I described it as so like a desert that we travelled sixteen miles of sand hills, wiregrass, and dwarf pines without a sign of animal life, not even a horsefly. At the end we came to an abandoned mill, with a solitary grasshopper sitting on a burnt lightwood-knot, the tears rolling down his cheek. This was true with the exception of the gushing tears; yet in recent years by proper treatment the soil has been made productive.

President of the Chatham Railroad 177

When we arrived within ten miles of Cheraw, we found that the only inhabitants of houses near the roadside were free negroes. We were so tired that the colonel proposed that we should seek a night's lodging with one of them, but I had too much Southern prejudice in me and so we pressed on to the town, a bright moonlight ride, arriving there at nine o'clock.

Next morning we found that the president of the new railroad was in Charleston. So we went there and discussed with him his plans for the Cheraw Railroad. He seemed disposed to come to our view but the exigencies of the war prevented practical results.

In Charleston I had an experience which touched me deeply. I went to St. Michael's Church at the hour of service and was shown by the sexton the strangers' seat near the entrance. An elderly lady dressed in black, probably on account of a relative lost in battle, came from a cushioned pew not far from the chancel and invited me to sit with her. It was the cup of cold water to the thirsty traveller.

I found some new books brought in by a blockade-runner from England, among them Dickens' *Great Expectations*. As the book was small enough to fit in my saddle bags, I bought it and on the way back when we walked our horses I read it aloud to the colonel. I finished it as we rode into Haywood, then his temporary home. I doubt if any other novel was ever read in North Carolina on horseback.

Our route back was through Anson County and then by Carthage to Haywood. The colonel was of opinion that there was no difficulty in building a railroad by either of the routes from Cheraw to the coal fields.

While at Charleston we were introduced to many of the leading business men and were struck by their cordial manners, their freedom from self-importance and frigid dignity. We visited the historic Fort Sumter and were not surprised that Col. Anderson did not attempt a prolonged defence against the greatly superior force assailing him.

In carrying on the work of the Chatham Railroad we were surprised and disappointed that labor was scarce. The general opinion had been that slaves brought from threatened points into the interior would be a drug on the labor market. Not so. The scarcity of hands was a serious drawback. In 1864, however, Edmund and John Wilkes, having finished their contract on the Piedmont Railroad, were induced to enter on the grading of the Chatham Railroad.

Not only did the government aid us by exchanging supplies bought near the railroads for supplies stored under the tithing law, but power was given to impress trees for crossties. And iron was obtained from tearing up an unused side-line in Virginia.

I am proud to record that the directors of my railroad and the public generally gave me credit for doing all that could be done under the adverse circumstances of the stormy times. The road would have soon been finished to Lockville whither coal could be transported by water, the dam on Deep River being in good order at that point. But the advent of Sherman's army destroyed all my prospects. All the mules and other property of the company were appropriated by the Northern army. I applied to General Schofield for restitution but he peremptorily refused, doubtless on the ground that they were to have been used in carrying on the war. I also asked him to order citizens who had seized our mules to restore them. He refused this also. When I became State Treasurer I resigned the presidency of the railroad and was succeeded by Gen. W. R. Cox. The stockholders then by authority of an amendment to the charter changed its destination so as to make it a through line under the title of the Raleigh, Columbia, and Augusta Airline Railroad Company. It is now a part of the Seaboard Airline Railroad Company. The change was very proper as it was found that the coal and iron of Deep River could not compete with the larger deposits of Virginia and elsewhere.

26. War Pictures

EARLY AFTER THE WAR BEGAN I VISITED MY brother Junius in camp on the outskirts of Norfolk. I slept in his tent with about nine soldiers. As a favor they let me lie on the outside. I tried to make myself agreeable by telling jokes but the stern voice of a sentinel outside ordered silence. All the soldiers seemed happy. Next day a party was formed to visit Gloucester Point about four miles from Old Point and the Rip Raps, a little rocky island about a mile off in the bay. There was no firing then but I saw fragments of shells and large shells not exploded which had been fired a few days before. One of these had been picked up and carried into one of our tents. A young fellow, a Granville boy named Taylor, recklessly struck it with a hammer and was killed. He was son of one of the best citizens of Granville County, C. H. K. Taylor.

A wrestling match was got up between a large strong man in a Catawba company and one of smaller stature. To the surprise of all bystanders the strong man was thrown so suddenly that it was impossible to see how it was done.

From Norfolk I visited our troops at Yorktown. Gen. D. H. Hill was in command. Here too the soldiers seemed contented. To give an idea of the character of the early volunteers, I chronicle that I was invited to a tent of privates. One of them raised a trapdoor and treated me to a glass of good wine. I added up in my mind the fortunes of the occupants of the tent. They were worth at least a quarter of a million.

I then took a steamboat on James River for Richmond and spent a night at an old hotel called the Atlantic. I had been misinformed. It had lost its ancient prestige and was now only second-class. I was shown to a room and given a cot to myself. There were seven other cots, all occupied. It was too late at night to seek better quarters at the Exchange or Spotswood. I met one of our University graduates named Christmas. He was partly intoxicated. After getting onto my cot I heard a cry of "Murder, Murder!" One of my neighbors ran to see what was the matter. It was the cry of the hotel clerk being beaten by Christmas. As Christmas was a general, the clerk was afraid of him. This was the only disturbance which came under my observation during repeated visits to Richmond. After some months the sale of spirituous liquors was prohibited as a war measure. The decree did not stop the sale but it made men more prudent. Once at the Exchange Hotel a friend came into my room smiling triumphantly. "I have found out how to get a drink. You knock at No. 12 on this floor. A servant opens the door. You ask, 'Does Mr. Livingston room here?' Then you are admitted and you can get what you ask for."

It was remarkable that men who were abstainers in peace times should change their habits under the excitements of war. It was seldom that a soldier would refuse a drink. The hotel at Goldsborough was so crowded that the bar was in the waiting-room. Once a young soldier came in, ordered whiskey. He drank it without water and, with a benignant smile, in a loving tone ejaculated, "Old Corn!"

Goldsborough was seldom without soldiers. I stopped there once on a visit to my brother Lewis, a lieutenant in an Anson company. I was carrying him a ham of a plump porker. I left it in the porch while I stepped into the hotel to register. When I came out my much-prized intended gift was gone. Soldiering is a monstrous enemy to good morals. I have heard men of good character at home boasting of their skill in eluding their colonel's notice while they were on the hunt for green corn, melons, chickens, and other eatables.

I visited the battlefield of Malvern Hill. On the way I passed several miles through lands, cleared and uncleared, where the enemy's foot had never trod. All looked barren and desolate. The battlefield was a frightful sight. There were mounds over dead soldiers, divers swollen bodies of defunct horses lay on their sides with the upper legs high in the air. The charge of our men up the long, open, sloping field towards the height where stood the farm-houses, in the face of cannon and muskets pouring out their ammunition, was plainly a desperate venture. The long slope of Gettysburg gives the same impression of fearful odds against the assailants.

We could not always be critical in war times. Once I dined on a single sweet potato, and that not thoroughly cooked. On a journey to Weldon from Petersburg, I ran for breakfast into a baker's shop and bought a pone of light-bread. It contained such a large proportion of alum mixed in to economize flour that it kept my jaws wagging all the way to Weldon so as to be able to swallow it at all.

A man in the course of his life finds all his natural gifts useful. On one occasion starting from Petersburg the coaches were loaded with wounded soldiers just from a battle north of Richmond. Entering a car I found the air charged with the smell of half-putrid blood so offensive that I could not bear it. The platforms were also filled with soldiers but I noticed room for one on a step. So I asked the nearest soldier if it would incommode him for me to stand by him on the step. There was room for one foot only but it was important for me to get to Weldon. He readily acquiesced and off we started. Then I called on my memory for some of my raciest anecdotes. We had not proceeded over two miles before my laughing listeners made way for both of my feet on the step. I continued to bombard them with side-splitters and it was not long before I was invited to take a seat. As the weather was fine, I had a really pleasant time. It was a fair exchange. I gave them fun in return for a comfortable seat. In addition I had a modicum of pleasure in telling the jokes. It certainly whiled away the time of the journey both for myself and the soldiers.

Many of the companies had a member who was the champion witty man. I was fortunate in witnessing an encounter between two of these, one from Virginia and the other from North Carolina, near the train in which I was sitting. A number of soldiers formed a ring around the combatants. Their cuts at one another were very amusing and were vociferously applauded. As the large majority of the bystanders were Tar Heels, the Virginian did not have a fair showing. Much of the applause of his wit was of the mock variety in the nature of jeers and he retired defeated.

Another time I was present at a contest of wit in the waiting-room of the station at Rocky Mount between a Martin County soldier going home on furlough with his pal with instructions to obtain recruits for his regiment, and a local civilian named Weston, who was taciturn when no liquor was in him but talkative otherwise. The Martin man was an expert wit-slinger and soon had the laugh on Weston. He then announced, "Gentle*men*, gentle*men*, I am authorized by Colonel Hoke to get recruits for his regiment. He is the best officer in the army, takes good care of his men. He will pay $15 bounty for every recruit." Now the Convention had just raised the amount to $50 and anyone who could persuade a certain number to join him would obtain a company office, the rank to be according to the number. A man named Collins here interrupted, "Gentlemen, I am authorized to offer $50 bounty." The Martin man shouted, "It isn't true! Col. Hoke said it was $15 and he never told a lie in his life." Collins replied, "The Adjutant General gave me the paper just this morning." The Adjutant General, not wishing to throw away the old blanks, had erased with a pen the $15 and had interlined $50. The Martin man said grimly, "Show me that paper." Glancing at it, he sneered, "I thought so. Don't you see, gentlemen, that this is a forgery?" Collins then appealed to me, "Mr. Battle, you are a member of the Convention. You know that $50 was voted." "Yes," said I, "as the Convention was about to adjourn a motion was made and carried to increase the allowance to $50. I voted for the ordinance. The soldier from Martin County is authorized to offer a bounty of $50." The Martin man saw that everybody believed me and was silent. Just then the whistle announced that the Tarborough train was ready and we all got aboard. I had two seats to myself; the Martin man and his pal had one next to mine. It was a mixed train, taking two or three hours to go the eighteen miles to Tarborough. I put my hat over my eyes and "courted the balmy," as Dick Swiveller said. I overheard the Martin man talking in a low tone to his pal. "This is the derndest, lyingest country ever I was in. Col. Hoke, who never told a lie in his life, authorized me to offer $15. A liar named Collins brings out a forged paper offering $50. Then he calls on a man named Battle. Battle is a dernder liar than Collins. And he says Collins is right. I believe in Col. Hoke every time." I was so amused that I lost my nap. The remark was confidentially made to his pal and it would have been folly to take offence. Doubtless the Martin man became convinced of the truth when he reached Williamston.

When the soldiers were off duty, they frequently had a jolly time. I will give several of the jokes which were regarded as peculiarly piquant. Jake Harshaw was a good soldier when he was kept away from spirituous liquors. He invariably became intoxicated when he could get enough. After one of our victories he walked over the battlefield to see what he could find. To his joy he discovered a flask of whiskey in the haversack of a dead Yankee. He rapidly transferred the contents into his stomach and was soon in a drunken sleep, face towards the sky. A turkey buzzard came soaring along looking for a dinner. Seeing Jake in the semblance of death, he lit on his knees and prepared for a meal. Just then Jake opened his eyes and with horror said, "You are too derned smart." The disappointed bird believed him, flew off to find a real corpse.

After a rainy spell a regiment of Tar Heels was trudging through a narrow lane knee-deep in mud. They met a negro boy as ragged as a boy of that color can be in the summer time, one gallus fastened by a thorn and legs naked up to his knees. He was riding bareback on an aged mule whose hide showed years of ill-fitting harness and cruel treatment. The soldiers hailed the boy with all kinds of jocularity. "What are you going to do with that bag of bones?" "How far is it to the bone yard?" "What do you ask for them bones by the pound?" "How many chaws of tobacco did you give for your mule?" And other like witticisms. The boy kept stolid silence until he had passed the last of the regiment. Then he turned half around, showed his white teeth, and exultantly shouted, "But I'm a-ridin den!" The boys who had aired their wit at the little African's expense were unmercifully jeered by the others.

A sarcasm at the expense of an aged Baptist clergyman was much enjoyed. The scene was in Georgia. As no immediate fight was expected, the regiments were camped out in an extensive forest. The clergyman went to visit his son. He passed through several regiments before reaching the one he sought. His dress was peculiarly old-fashioned—a high-crowned hat, a long coat-tail. The boys were bound to have their fun and he was good-natured in submitting to it. One called out, "What is the price of butter, old man? I see you've got your churn on your head." "Your fire's gone out. I see no smoke coming out of your stovepipe." "Come out of that hat. I know you are in thar, I see your legs hanging down!" "Did you get that coat-tail from General Washington or your great-grand-daddy?" And such like. As he passed by the tent of the colonel of the regiment next to that of his son, a dapper young orderly stepped out and with mock politeness touched his cap and said, "Parson, I perceive by your dress that you are a servant of God. I hope you will excuse our boys for their rudeness. They have been so long from home and free from civilizing influences, that the colonel and I can't keep them from hollering at every dern fool they see!"

The explanation usually given of the term Tar Heel, generally applied to North Carolina boys, and the reason why far from being offended at it they considered it complimentary, was as follows. A number of negroes in Mississippi were playing at a game said to be peculiar to them. A coin, generally an old-fashioned copper cent, was placed in the centre of a ring and one after another of the contestants, dancing to a lively tune on the banjo, with bare feet endeavored by a single flirt to kick the coin out of the ring. If he succeeded, the coin belonged to him. He had the right either to flirt it out by a single motion of his foot, or to seize it with his toes and so transport it out of the ring. One day the game had gone on for some time. A young fellow succeeded so often that a suspicion of fraud arose and watchful eyes tried to detect it. Suddenly the cry was heard. "Dat nigger got tar on his heels!" He was searched and convicted of the cheat, then banished ignominiously. As the old geographies stated that North Carolina was famous for the production of tar, pitch, and turpentine, a Virginia company wit charged that the North Carolinians had tar on their heels. This was after a battle in which a Virginia regiment ran away. "Oh yes," retorted the North Carolina wit, "that is the reason we North Carolinians always stick in a fight and don't run away as you Virginians do." The story ran like wild fire throughout the army and survived the war. The student paper at the University is called *The Tar Heel.*

After the Conscription Law was passed, one of my clients, a simple-hearted fellow, came to me for advice, "Mr. Battle, I wish you would tell me whether I am obleeged to go to the war. If I am obleeged to go, I'd rather volunteer." This sounds absurd but really it is not. Volunteers were allowed to choose their company and my client desired to be among his county men. Conscripts were assigned at the will of officers and he dreaded to be among strangers.

It was in one sense amusing, in another disgusting, to witness the conduct of some blatant secessionists when they were called on to make sacrifices. An order came to seize good horses for the artillery at government prices, about $500 in Confederate money, equal to about $25 in gold. One of the very fieriest sort sent his matched horses out of the county away from the eyes of the government officer. Another, a physician who had been using a single nag and a buggy in his practise, suddenly found that his wife's carriage horses were necessary for his work in treating his patients. Another, who had denounced me before hostilities began as a "hatchet-faced lawyer speaking for the Union," now saved his horses by a palpable fraud. I showed my horses without a murmur but only one was accepted.

I recall a pathetic incident connected with the seizure of my horse. Before I became his owner, he was seen in a wagon team going to Fayetteville. My driver, Jim Trisback, liked him, inquired about him, and reported to me that he thought he was fit to take the place of one that had recently died. Jim had belonged to a Goldsborough man who sold him to a preacher in Raleigh to place him in the same town with his wife. For some cause not affecting his character the preacher became angry with him and sold him to a trader. I was satisfied that he was a good man, and being in need of a driver, bought him and came to have implicit confidence in his equine judgment. So I sent him to Fayetteville with instructions to buy the horse he had seen if on further investigation he should conclude that he would suit us. He returned with the animal and I found that I had made no mistake. It was a fortunate purchase. Of course Jim was very proud of this animal. The Confederate official also approved his judgment and the conscripted animal was turned with numerous others into the Baptist Grove (officially Moore Square) which had been fenced in temporarily. Next day Jim told me with tears in his eyes that he called by the Grove and stopped at the fence; that the horse recognized him, came to the fence, and as good as talked to him.

This story illustrates the relation in an immense majority of cases between master and slave. I was born and raised among slaves and after I was grown was a slave owner. I not only never whipped a negro, say over twelve years of age, but my father never whipped one. And if a boy or girl received punishment, it was for a fault for which a white boy or girl would have been similarly punished. I am confident that such was the usual treatment in North Carolina. Indeed Raleigh, a fair sample of our towns, had the reputation of spoiling negroes. I knew families where it might have been truthfully said that the black folks owned the white folks.

27. Trips to Richmond in War Time

IN THE COURSE OF THE WAR MY DUTIES REquired occasional trips to Richmond. One of these was to obtain the exchange of forage delivered by us in eastern North Carolina at points accessible to the Confederate army for the tithe forage, i.e., that paid the government under the ten per cent tax deposited on the line of the Chatham Railroad. Men familiar with governmental red tape predicted that I would be hanging around the offices a fortnight but I determined to test the effect of a little wide-awake energy. So I prepared my application and at nine o'clock was at the office of F. W. Sims, Lieutenant Colonel and Quartermaster. Getting his approval, I hastened to the office of A. L. Rives, Lieutenant Colonel and Chief of Transportation, then to Lt. Col. St. John of the Nitre and Mining Bureau, then to Col. J. G. Gorgas, Chief of Ordnance, and obtained their approvals. Accompanied by Col. R. R. Bridgers, who was exceedingly kind in forwarding my scheme, I called on Secretary Mallory. He did not answer decidedly but wished to consult a subordinate officer. I then hastened to Secretary of War Seddon. In about an hour the score or more of those ahead of me were dismissed and I was introduced. The Secretary seemed to be suffering from tuberculosis, stooping and coughing. He said, "It would be odd if I could not do something for you with all these endorsements." He read my paper carefully and approved it, referring me for details to Quartermaster General Lawton. I hurried to this officer but he was out of town and I could not secure the necessary orders until next day. They were then given although it was Sunday. If the general had been in town, I should have secured the approval of five officers and of the Secretary of War in four hours. My success enabled us to feed our laborers and mules in part without long hauling.

To get meat for our laborers I was forced to send an agent, W. J. Hollaman, to southern Georgia. He succeeded in purchasing the meat but a military officer objected to its being transported out of his territory and I had some trouble in applying to Richmond to have him overruled. When my agent, a worthy man, brought in his accounts, he said, "You must not be surprised at finding an occasional bottle of whiskey charged. There is such congestion on the railroads that I had to treat officers sometimes to induce them to give our car the preference."

I had the honor of being sent to Richmond with Thomas Bragg, ex-Governor of North Carolina and ex-Attorney General of the Confederate States, by Governor Vance on a special mission to President Davis. It seems that the conscription officers in North Carolina threatened to disregard the decisions of Chief Justice Pearson and other judges in releasing under *habeas corpus* cases soldiers held in the army under the conscription laws. Governor Vance was desirous of sustaining the Confederate authorities to the full extent of his powers but was determined that the maxim *Inter arma silent leges* should not apply to North Carolina, and Governor Bragg and I were instructed to urge upon the President the revocation of the order detaining conscripts in defiance of the decision of the courts.

I had a night ride by way of Danville but did not regret it, because one of the travellers was that excellent gentleman, lawyer, and humorist, William A. Wright of Wilmington. His anecdotes of public men and his reading of extracts from *Father Tom and the Pope* made the night memorable. I had not before heard how the Pope asked Father Tom if he would take his whiskey-punch hot or cold; how in his dream he chose hot; how, while the Pope was in the kitchen heating the water, Father Tom awoke from his dream and missed his punch; and how grieved he was that he did not choose cold.

As President Davis did not come to his office until eleven o'clock, we called on some members of the cabinet at their posts, Secretaries Mallory and Benjamin, and Attorney General George Davis. All were cordial and did not show gloom in their faces and manners at the magnitude of their tasks. I noticed on Benjamin's mantelpiece an ordinary flour biscuit, and wondered if the grease it was made with was lard or the fat of a goose. I have read since then that he gave up the Jewish faith. I was struck with his kindly manners.

President Davis came promptly at eleven o'clock, walking alone through Capitol Square. He was courteous but kept a business-like gravity. After Governor Bragg stated our case, the President sent for General Preston, the head of the Conscription Department, a tall, handsome old man with an abundance of gray hair. General Preston thought there had been a misapprehension of orders, and with the President's approval promised to give instructions in accordance with our request. The President then arose to show that the audience was ended. Despite this, as requested by Governor Vance, I brought to his attention a misunderstanding between the

Confederate naval officers at Wilmington and those of the blockade-running vessels. He emphatically declined to discuss this question, referring me to the Secretary of the Navy. We called on this gentleman at once and found him well disposed to effect harmonious action.

I give a list of eatables at the Spotswood Hotel which took rank with the Exchange as the best in Richmond. The date is August 12, 1864. Mutton-broth soup; Fish—none in market; Boiled—Bacon and Cabbage, Leg of Mutton with Egg-sauce; Cold Dishes—Ham, Roast Sirloin of Beef, Loin of Veal; Hot—Stuffed Shoulder of Bacon, Roast of Mutton Braised with Vegetables, Porter House Steak with Onions, Veal Cutlets Breaded; Vegetables—Beets, Stewed Tomatoes, New Irish Potatoes, White Beans, Green Corn, Simblins (so spelled), Lima Beans, Cabbage, Peas. The relishes were Assorted Pickles, Pickled Beets, English Mustard. The dessert was Green Apple Pies, Apples, Water-melons. Breakfast was 6 to 10; dinner at 2:30; tea at 6:30. It must be admitted that this bill-of-fare does not look like starvation.

In the fall of 1864 after one of my Richmond visits I called on my brother William, who was a brigade surgeon in Lee's army, stationed on the edge of Petersburg. He borrowed the horse of a quartermaster for me for a trip to the breastworks opposite a part of Grant's army. I had never before ridden a perfectly trained army horse. Mine this time noticed nothing on the right or left, cantered so smoothly that I could have comfortably written a letter while in motion. Passing near Gen. Lee's tent, we turned to see his cock and hen which he kept for fresh eggs at breakfast. The General was writing just inside the door of the tent. We did not speak to him but there was no soldier near to prevent it. Near the tent was a large oak tree and two fine mules were fastened to the branches. As we returned from the breastworks, a thunder storm drove us into a deserted blacksmith shop. When we passed again by the General's tent, the mules were lying dead from a stroke of lightning.

I was struck by the perfect quiet of both the Federal and Confederate lines. Not a sound was heard to indicate that two great armies were watching one another with loaded rifles and cannon. Deserted Petersburg was a sad sight but only occasionally could be seen shattered walls. The meagreness of the rations may be estimated from the remark of my brother, a most hospitable man, to Captain Dancy who had called on him, "Captain, I won't offer you a share of my small bits of bread and meat and onions. You are a quartermaster and can do better."

But although the soldiers seemed satisfied, there was no enthusiasm and desertions were not infrequent. One who went home and voluntarily returned exhibited a letter from his wife beseeching him to come back as their children were starving. Furloughs were granted only to allow men to be married. One soldier filed a letter from his sweetheart saying, "Dear Jim, Ask General Lee to let you come home to get married. I am ready, willin, and waitin." Col. R. T. Bennett is said to have endorsed an application for the purpose of marriage in the following words. "The application of A. B., private, for a twenty days furlough is approved. The Colonel Commanding is of opinion from personal experience that the time asked for, twenty days, is not more than sufficient to consummate the nuptials and recover from their effects."

Col. Bennett was noted for strength of character. He was fond of lofty and original language. Writing the history of his regiment he closed thus. "These bloody accompaniments but adminiculate the aphorism of Burke that the seed of liberty is the blood of the brave." Someone said, "Colonel, where did you get that word *adminiculate?*" "Out of the dictionary, sir!"

During one of my visits to Richmond I attended a reception given by President Davis. The honor of passing with a stream of visitors and shaking his hand was dearly bought by one who was not one of his warm admirers. There was no time for conversation and even the half-sentence sometimes vouchsafed had a dreary sound as if it did not come from the heart. The reception line extended through three rooms. Such formal handshakings are tiresome to me and I retired as soon as decency permitted.

At another visit I fell in with Mr. Atkinson, a brother of our beloved bishop. As the agent of citizens of Lynchburg (or Danville), he was commissioned to present to Gen. John H. Morgan, then in Richmond, a silver cup as a memorial of his gallant expedition with his cavalry troop through southern Ohio. The presentation took place in the parlor of the hotel with a goodly number of civil and military witnesses. It was in good taste, without undue boasting. Gen. Morgan was a handsome man whose words and manner showed the self-possessed gentleman.

I shared a room with a Confederate congressman from Kentucky, that state being allowed to send representatives, elected generally by soldiers, who had fled from the state and embraced the Southern cause. He was of good appearance and intelligence but his education had been curtailed. He was writing a speech or communication of some sort and asked me about the spelling of some words not at all difficult. I have forgotten the words but the following story told about two lawyers of the day shows the character of his mistakes. A: "How do you spell *equinomical* (economical)?" B: "I'll look in the dictionary and tell you." B. runs his finger down the column looking for *equinomical* and failing to find it says, "I cannot find it. If I had known that old Daniel Webster omitted so common a word as *equinomical*, I would not have bought his dictionary."

My last visit to Richmond on the business of my railroad was in January, 1865. Times were gloomy. I stopped at the Spotswood Hotel and to my surprise the meat on the tables was roast turkey. Apprehension of the approach of the invading army induced owners of flocks of that savory bird to drive them to be exchanged for Confederate bills. There was general gloom among the members of Congress. I was told confidentially by a number of them that our cause was regarded by intelligent men as hopeless; that as soon as the roads should harden, Grant's attack could not be resisted; that many were in favor of treating for terms of peace, but President Davis obstinately refused to move, saying that Lincoln demanded the restoration of the Union and he could not annihilate the Confederate government, that he could not commit political suicide. After this Governor Graham corroborated what had been told me. He stated that many members of Congress desired that steps should be taken looking to peace but they were so bound by pledges at home that they could not act. He urged that the General Assembly should be called together to consider the situation. Governor Vance did not see the possibility of legislative action remedying the troubles: any separate action by North Carolina would not only be fruitless but would bring on her the odium of causing our defeat. So, although we were already beaten, by the chivalrous obstinacy of Jefferson Davis many lives were uselessly sacrificed, much property destroyed, and we were driven to surrender at the discretion of the conqueror. It was chivalry but not statesmanship.

I have in my library an interesting record of a court-martial reviewed by General Hill. A captain and a lieutenant were charged with being intoxicated in the presence of the enemy. They were acquitted but General Hill in review says, "The finding of the court-martial is technically approved, but the General Commanding is of opinion that the captain was drunk on liquor and opium and while being so got his lieutenant drunk on liquor alone."

28. Last Days of the War in Raleigh

I COME NOW TO THE CLOSING SCENES OF THE Civil War, so far as came under my observation, *quorum pars fui*, though not *magna pars*.

When Johnston's army was passing through Raleigh and over the roads near it, a cavalry soldier called at my house with a story that General Wheeler had heard that I was a liberal man and had sent him to obtain one of my horses. Having heard much of the misconduct of Wheeler's men, I declined and he went off threatening to get authority of seizure from General Hardee, then in command of Raleigh. He said he was a courier with an important dispatch and that his horse had been taken sick. Thinking it possible that he might impose on General Hardee, I obtained a letter from Governor Vance to the general in my favor on the ground that the horse was needed for my duties as president of the Chatham Railroad Company. Subsequently, when the Federal army approached Raleigh, I offered my pair of horses and double buggy to Thomas C. Powell, afterwards a physician, a nephew of General Cox, to take them by way of Warrenton to Edgecombe out of reach of the approaching army. He accepted the offer with alacrity as he was much averse to being made prisoner. In Granville the buggy broke down and Powell rode off on horseback, leaving the other horse with a farmer. One of Wheeler's men, it was reported to me, carried off this horse—probably not the Raleigh deceiver.

The only time I ever carried a weapon with expectation of possibly being called on to use it was to defend my horses against robbery by one of our own soldiers. General Wheeler may have been maligned but the lawless conduct of some of his soldiers was generally credited.

When we heard that Sherman's army was marching towards Raleigh and saw Johnston's slender force retreating through it, I concluded to inquire for something more valuable than the Confederate currency which I had on hand. I recall that I paid $200 for the poorest cotton umbrella I ever saw. In a bookstore with a meagre collection of books which I did not want I found a number of bound pamphlets, principally proceedings of stockholders' meetings of railroads and other corporations left for sale by my former law partner. Partly to help him and partly because they might possibly be useful to me in the study of North Carolina corporations, I bought them for $500. After my term as State Treasurer was over, I was employed as attorney for several railroad companies and my purchase became very useful.

Ex-Governors Graham and Swain were sent by Governor Vance to meet the Northern general and obtain protection for Raleigh and the University and especially for state property. It was suspected by some hot-heads that they were treating for the surrender of the State and it was commonly believed that General Robert F. Hoke was instructed by President Davis to arrest all three if the attempt was made. Governor Vance left the city, stopped a while in Hillsborough, and thence proceeded to Greensborough to confer with President Davis at his request.

A party was requested by Mayor Harrison of Raleigh to ride into the country and meet General Kilpatrick and formally surrender the city. I was one of those invited but I had taken cold and was so hoarse that I could with difficulty talk so as to be understood. So I declined to accompany the party, which was sufficiently large without me, anyway.

The mayor and his party met General Kilpatrick and his troops. Hon. Kenneth Rayner made a speech to which Kilpatrick made a short reply. Protection was guaranteed, a guard promised to each dwelling, and the conquering army marched into the city, uniforms all new and bright, and bayonets sparkling in the morning sun, the horses rejoicing in their spirited beauty. All of my family were in our front porch admiring however regretfully the splendor of the pageant. When the head of the column came opposite my house, an officer pointed towards it and a trooper rode into the yard. He dismounted and started to hitch his horse to a young tree that was a favorite with my wife. I requested him to change to a larger tree which he did. He was my guard until relieved by a foot-soldier.

Just then I saw a part of the cavalry dash forward at full speed. I learned the cause afterwards from ex-Governor Swain who was at the Capitol to surrender it to the troops.

A Texan lieutenant named Walsh, a straggler from Wheeler's cavalry, was with several others seeking in a jewelry store what might have been left behind by the owner. As the cavalcade approached, all rode rapidly towards the west except the Texan. From the middle of the street he fired five or six shots in the direction of the Federal troops and dashed off at full speed. Pursuit was immediate. He rode across Morgan Street and then turned so as to reach Hillsborough Street, the only road to the west. The sharp turn at break-neck speed caused the horse to fall and the rider was captured and carried to Kilpatrick, then in the Capitol Square. Walsh had forfeited his life by the laws of war. His desperate act, if his aim had been accurate, might have roused the invading soldiers to madness. There was no element of heroism in his conduct, only reckless courage. And yet a young lady for many days kept fresh flowers on his grave in an obscure part of the city.

As soon as I found that my place was well guarded, I walked rapidly towards the home of my wife's sister Neppie, the wife of General William R. Cox, who lived near the North Carolina Railroad about two miles from my house. Passing by the railroad station, which had been burnt by our troops as they retreated westward, I met General Cox's faithful colored driver, John O'Kelly, now free but still faithful to his owners. Rev. Bennett Smedes had agreed to protect Mrs. Cox and I felt secure as to that part of my charge. But John excitedly informed me that the bummers were stealing what they could lay hands on and paying no attention to the expostulations of Mr. Smedes and Mrs. Cox. He stated that General Sherman with other officers was at the Capitol and in order to secure protection I must apply for a guard. I hurried to the Capitol, introduced myself to General Sherman, stated that the wife of a general who had surrendered under General Lee and was on his way home was being plundered and asked for a guard. He said, "Certainly. Go to General Mower yonder." I hurried to Mower and met with a prompt refusal. Ascertaining the locality he said, "I cannot do it. I can't trust Wheeler's men. They will steal up at night and shoot the guard." I reported this to General Sherman but he made no reply. He was asking, "Where is Governor Vance? What did he go away for?" Evidently he was giving no further heed to my request and was unwilling to overrule Mower, who was thinking of Walsh's misconduct. Much troubled, I walked to the south door of the building to think the matter over. Thence I saw an elderly officer, Captain Burns, assigning guards to applicants. I requested one and he graciously granted my request. I hurried to the Cox home as fast as I could induce the soldier to walk. I met a friend who said, "Hello, Battle, have they got you?" "No," said I, "I've captured one." When I reached my destination, I saw one soldier emerging from the house with a jar of preserves and another with a bag of flour. I said to my soldier, "Make the men put down those things." He replied coolly, "I wasn't sent to make anybody put down what they have got but to keep them from getting things after I have arrived." They used no insulting words to my sister-in-law but one was so urgent for a ring that Mr. Smedes satisfied him with one from his own finger, though he valued it highly on account of its having been the property of an ancestor.

My troubles were not over. A brigadier general asked Mrs. Cox's permission to pitch his tent in her front yard. She agreed as her guard belonged to his command. The next day he marched away and without explanation carried off the guard. As soon as he was out of sight, the robberies were resumed. O'Kelly was sent to me in hot haste. I hurried to the Capitol, procured another guard, and put a stop to the marauding. This time the chief offenders were ransacking the houses of the servants and many thanks were showered on me for my timely arrival. One miscreant, an Irishman, was ripping planks from the stable for his campfire. He grumbled at my stopping him, claiming that the loyal soldiers were entitled to gain comfort from rebel property. General Cox arrived home on this day and I had no further trouble. General Henderson of Kentucky pitched his tent on the edge of the grove of St. Mary's School near by and guards became unnecessary.

Prior to the surrender of General Joseph E. Johnston there was much marauding by the Federal troops. I took a ride into the county and heard many stories of the depredations. I was told with accents of horror how the soldiers stripped the house of old widow Lee. It was mentioned with especial indignation how one impious rascal took a pair of her drawers from her trunk, and tying the ends of the legs securely, filled them with flour and straddled his neck with the booty. Evidently no effort was made to put an end to such conduct until after the terms of surrender of Johnston to Sherman were settled. Indeed Sherman, in a letter to President Swain concerning the seizure of the property of Rev. George W. Purefoy, seems to admit this. The letter is given in Mrs. Spencer's *Last Ninety Days of the War*. It was reported that Hon. Curtis H. Brogden, State Auditor, and Esquire William R. Pool, one of the justices of the County Court, were treated with great indignity in the endeavor to extort money. Doubtless there were numerous other cases.

One day a Federal captain, Keeler by name, from New York State, on the staff of General Terry, applied to me for a room in my house. I was glad to have him as a tenant for greater protection. Lincoln's assassination was greatly resented by the soldiers en-

Last Days of the War in Raleigh 195

camped on the edge of the city. Sheriff High reported that he had heard among them threats of sacking the city in revenge. I asked my guard if the guards would not protect us. He answered, "The guards are as angry as the rest of the troops." Captain Keeler called on me and said, "There is danger of an outbreak tonight. The soldiers are greatly aroused. You must have every vessel on the lot filled with water. You and your wife must not take off your clothes. General Sherman has promised to protect you if possible and General Terry will aid of course. We will do our best." Of course I was uneasy but I was comforted by the knowledge that Sherman had strong control of his troops. There was no disturbance at all. Six thousand picked men guarded every approach to Raleigh and at intervals all night I heard the tramp of cavalry patrolling the streets. We were saved.

A week or two later we had another cause of anxiety. A few men belonging to the Holden party took it into their heads to get up a torchlight procession in honor of the capture of Raleigh by Union men. Threats were thrown out that the houses of all who did not illuminate their windows would be stoned. The movement was largely intended to humiliate the followers of Governor Vance. I called on my new friend Captain Keeler who had changed his quarters to a house on Hillsborough Street occupied by his chief, General Terry, and earnestly urged on him to induce the general to forbid the procession. I stated that I was acquainted with the authors and was persuaded that they acted from vindictive motives, to triumph over the leading citizens, and not from joy over the restoration of the Union. Of course there would be a possibility of collisions as there might be men whose combative tempers would rouse them to fight back, if stones should crash through their windows. Captain Keeler kindly presented my arguments to General Terry and orders were given to forbid the celebration.

I give another instance showing the sensitiveness prevailing between citizens of the North and South. After Captain Keeler left my house Colonel Hayes, an Ohio man in the Quartermaster's Department who occupied my law office in a corner of my yard, requested me to give him a room in my dwelling for himself and his wife. I very willingly did so. The staircase was opposite the front door. My wife's bedroom was on the left of the front door and the colonel and his wife were obliged to pass by the door of the bedroom. Once, while my wife was in her room, the colonel came in. For some good reason she did not wish a stranger to see what was going on, so she closed the door. I learned soon that he thought her action was prompted by hostility to him as a Northern man. My informant said that he went so far as to say that if we continued to insult Federal officers, he would have us banished to our plantation in Wake. I explained matters to him and soothed his wounded feelings. He was kindly and courteous to us and to show appreciation of our willingness to board him and his wife for a fortnight, he allowed us to buy some provisions from the commissary department. His wife was a very agreeable and handsome woman and we became good friends.

The officers of the government became much excited about the treatment of Federal prisoners in the South as was shown in the trial and execution of Wirtz on charges of inhuman conduct to those at Andersonville, Georgia. An effort was made to prove that Governor Vance was responsible for the suffering of the prisoners at Salisbury. Pending the investigation he was arrested at Statesville where he and his wife were sojourning and brought to Raleigh on his way to the Capitol prison at Washington. He and the officer who escorted him tarried in the office of Colonel Hayes. I called at once and invited Vance to breakfast. At his suggestion I included his attending officer in the invitation, but he declined laughingly, holding me responsible for the production of the prisoner. Very soon we walked to the train, Col. W. H. H. Tucker on one side of Vance and I on the other. The Governor kept up his usual spirits. Soon after his arrival at Washington Senator Tom Corwin called to see him. "Vance, what are you doing in prison?" "Well," said Vance, "Holden pledged the last man and last dollar for the Confederacy. I stood his security and am imprisoned for the pledge." He alluded to an article in Holden's paper containing that notable boast, although afterwards Holden posed as a steadfast Union man. Investigation showed that the Governor had actively urged humane treatment of the prisoners and he was honorably released.

The air was full of stories of the finding of hidden treasures. My observation was that such finds were made because the hiding was not intelligently done. The soldiers, when they saw a clump of bushes, or a thick bunch of weeds or other dark spot, naturally reasoned that an owner of valuables might have selected it for concealment. Where a hole in the ground was dug, the loose dirt was like a signboard pointing to the subterranean contents. And sometimes, though not often, the colored assistant proved to be

Last Days of the War in Raleigh 197

treacherous. The servants were generally faithful, eminently so. When a squad of cavalry neared Wadesborough, the cashier of the bank thought it best for him to leave the town. He left $20,000 with his old colored cook, with instructions to throw the package into the well if the soldiers entered the town. The soldiers did enter. Into the well went the package. The money was saved. I had two jugs of brandy, a gallon or so. Not knowing that I would have a guard, I ordered my driver to pour it out for fear that the soldiers would be more brutal if they should find the liquor. After things became quiet, my man brought me one jug. "I just couldn't waste all that brandy, so I poured out what was in one jug and here is the other. I hid it where nobody could find it. Here it is. It hain't been touched." Needless to say I forgave him, presented him the major part of the salvage, and had the pleasure of giving a good drink to my guard. Whether this last was against military law I did not inquire. It surprised me that my guards always consumed all the food sent to them at mealtimes but refused to accept any more.

A goodly quantity of silver and jewelry had been entrusted to me for safe-keeping by our relatives in Edgecombe when it was thought that Sherman would march through that county. We also wished to save some of our own. I had also a large quantity of securities belonging to clients and some of my own. My brother Richard was similarly situated. So with horse and buggy we rode into the country looking for a safe place. But we met a great many people and I became afraid they would suspect we were on a hiding expedition. So I said, "Let us return and after supper go to the head of Pigeon House Branch and cover up all our articles in a mudhole." He agreed and we easily found one that suited our purpose. I had enclosed the securities in ale bottles, driven in the corks, and poured melted wax upon them.

The soldiers came and encamped on the hills and slopes about our hiding place. After waiting several weeks and seeing no signs of their departure, I lost patience and asked General Cox to go with me to call on General Henderson. I took with us a servant with a meal-bag. I asked General Henderson for a guard and got it. In the presence of many soldiers we drew the treasures from their watery bed all uninjured. The bottles I broke and placed the contents in my pocket.

Then occurred the most remarkable case of lost and found I have known. My wife had three coupons paid her for rent of our office worth then $45. She asked me to take care of them. They were in the fragment of a yellow envelope. Three months after Sherman entered Raleigh she asked me for them. I thought that I had placed them in my iron safe. I made a careful search in vain. Sunday morning I took our daughter for a walk. We went to the hospitable mudhole and there in the grass with the print of a footstep in half a foot of it, within a few steps of the tents on the hillside, was the torn yellow envelope and its coupons uninjured. The fragmentary appearance of the envelope saved its contents.

Many people think that lawyers are too severe in their cross-examinations of witnesses—that an honest witness should not be closely questioned as though he might be lying. My father's experience in hiding money shows that the lawyer's right to question is essential to justice, that even witnesses of integrity and of the highest reputation for veracity may tell what is untrue, in other words may be mistaken.

My brother William, while retreating with Johnston's army, was able to spend a night at the home of our parents. My father asked him to accompany him into the forest adjoining our home and hide five packages of bank-bills and jewelry. A month afterwards I came up from Raleigh and Father took me to the place of concealment in order to bring the packages home. We readily found four. Father said, "I hid the fifth under this beech." I replied, "It is strange that there are no signs of the earth having been disturbed." He was positive that he buried it there with his own hands. I had a grubbing hoe, dug until I was exhausted, then procured a faithful servant to uncover all the ground under the tree. Father concluded that a rogue had stolen the package.

A month after that Brother William came home again. On Father's telling him of the loss of $500 in bank-bills he said, "Father, I am not satisfied about that. Let us go into the woods and see about it." Father took him to the beech tree saying, "I remember distinctly burying the package under this beech." William replied, "You are certainly mistaken. I saw you put it under that old log yonder." And there it was safe and sound. Now Father was at the time a justice of the Supreme Court, only sixty-three years old, and perfectly temperate. Scores of witnesses would have sworn that his character for truth was unimpeachable and always had been, and yet he would have testified in court what was not true. The explanation is that he had resolved to bury the package under the beech but changed for the log. Then, his mind being in a state of excitement from the unusual nocturnal work amid the strange surroundings, he forgot the change and remembered only the first intention. A skilled lawyer would have surmised the possibility of such bewilderment.

Months before this, when no one believed that the enemy would reach Chapel Hill, my wife and I sent to Father and Mother a silver coffee-pot and other silver articles for safekeeping. But a cavalry brigade under General Atkins did reach Chapel Hill and encamped in the woods adjoining our home. Mother became uneasy and let the silver down our well tied up in a bag. The troops used the well two or three weeks but did not find the bag. After they went away, the bag was hauled up and the silver found intact though black and battered. We later took it to the makers in New York and it was made as good as new.

I am rather proud of my success in hiding valuables. When I got back from the expedition to the aforesaid mudhole with my brother Richard, I found that I had overlooked one bottle of jewelry. My first thought was to bury it in our wood-room which had a dirt floor. Then, turning it over in my mind, I concluded that it would certainly be detected by the broken earth. So I exhumed it and hid it in the middle of a bed of running-box. Then it occurred to me that my steps in the shrubbery would be discerned by a sharp eye. So I carried it into the middle of a bed in the garden recently spaded over. I went to my room satisfied. There half-undressed I thought, "You fool! The soldiers will certainly see your tracks in the soft ground; go and do better! The fourth effort was successful. I walked along the beaten path, scratched a hole in the soft earth next to the walk and sprinkled some dry dirt over it. The Yankees never found it.

Col. H. A. Dowd, whose wife occupied a house not far from mine, handed me a $20 gold piece and asked me to give it to his wife after things settled down. I hid the coin under a strawberry plant, noting carefully its position. It was never discovered. The adjoining bed had holes filled with fertilizer for planting cantaloupes. Two of the holes were left unfilled. Fresh earth being thus exposed, some simple soldiers stabbed the bed all over with ramrods seeking for treasures which were not there.

I heard of a bank cashier hiding $20,000 in one of the stone walls at Chapel Hill, and of another at Company Shops so adroitly concealing the funds entrusted to him that a tent of the enemy was pitched right over the spot without discovery.

It must be remembered that the incidents under my observation happened after the Federal officers were satisfied that peace was near. Doubtless in Georgia, South Carolina, and parts of North Carolina robbery was winked at by the officers in order to terrorize the inhabitants and diabolical threats were made in order to force surrender of valuables. I think that rape and arson were as a rule forbidden but there were isolated instances of both.

The most valuable public records were sent to various points on the North Carolina Railroad, the custodians accompanying them. My brother Richard, who was State Auditor, went with his books and papers. As his dwelling was outside the corporate limits, his family abode with me during his absence. So did Mrs. Lydia Wiley and her children until her husband, Philip A. Wiley, who was Chief Clerk in the Treasury Department, returned from a like mission.

I heard of one case of the truthfulness of a dream. A Granville farmer hid a much valued watch under an oak tree. He forgot the location but three months afterwards remembered it in a dream.

29. Battle, Heck, and Company

ANDREW JOHNSON, WHO LEFT RALEIGH IN HIS youth to avoid prosecution for stoning the house of an old woman, was now President of the United States. One of his early acts as President was to issue an amnesty for men who had held office in the South during the war. There were certain excepted classes and I was in one of them, viz., those worth $20,000.

Col. Jonathan M. Heck, originally a land trader in West Virginia, later employed in the Quartermaster's Department of the Confederacy, was the first man in Raleigh to endeavor to break up the business lethargy prevailing after the surrender. His plan was to make known in all feasible ways the lands in North Carolina for sale and to induce Northern people to buy and settle among us. There had been expressed by soldiers who had traversed the State much admiration of our climate and other advantages so that it seemed reasonable that an immigration of land buyers could be secured for cultivation of the soil, converting forests into lumber, mining, fisheries, and the like.

Colonel Heck secured as partners Dr. William J. Hawkins, President of the Raleigh and Gaston Railroad Company, and Captain Bailey P. Williamson, both having a great reputation as business men and both possessed of good fortunes, and then applied to me to join them. Having faith in the intelligence and standing of the other three I agreed to become a member of the firm, which was called Battle, Heck, and Company, the order of names being adopted solely for alphabetical reasons and because two of the firm preferred to be the "Company."

The first step was to obtain our pardons for participation in the "Rebellion." President Johnson claimed the right to bring back the seceding states into the Union by virtue of being Commander-in-Chief of the army. He had appointed W. W. Holden Provisional Governor of North Carolina. Naturally he was willing to pardon whomsoever his appointee would recommend. We therefore explained our scheme to Governor Holden. It met with his warm approval and the pardons were promptly issued.

Colonel Heck was a very able man and of much experience in attracting the notice of the public. We opened an office in Raleigh and advertised extensively. We even published a weekly newspaper, circulated without charge, devoted to making the resources of the State known and exploiting the excellences of the lands placed in our hands for sale. It was called the *North Carolina Advertiser* and contained many valuable articles throwing light on every phase of our industry. The enormous area of 146,700 acres of land was placed in our hands for sale, besides seven manufacturing establishments, eight residences, and 138 building lots, fifteen of which were in thriving towns. Much of the land was mountainous or swampy and not immediately productive, but there were about ninety properties ready for cultivation.

After a time we left the office work at Raleigh in the hands of my brother Richard, assisted in the editorial work by Major Seaton Gales and in the investigation of titles by Alexander W. Lawrence, and Colonel Heck and I went to New York City and opened an office at 62 Broadway. On our arrival we called on the financier Jay Cooke, who warmly recommended our scheme. Of course we had favorable notices from some of the great newspapers, equally of course paid for. We magnified the importance of our enterprise by taking rooms at the St. Nicholas Hotel, then first-class, frequented principally by southerners. Seldom did an enterprise have greater prospects of success, seldom did an enterprise so suddenly and completely collapse. Was the failure from the stupidity of the projectors? I think not. If they were stupid, the same must be said of many of the wisest and most prudent men, north and south, who applauded our exertions as well planned and certain to aid in restoring the prosperity of our State and the dissipation of feelings of hostility between the sections. Hundreds of would-be purchasers visited our office in New York inquiring for lands. Still greater numbers of letters were on file for the same purpose. We were negotiating with railroad companies for special terms for our customers. The cause of our defeat was the rupture between the Republican majority in Congress and the President, ending in 1868 in upsetting the State Governments inaugurated by him. The rupture was accompanied by threats of confiscation of vast areas of land and this caused general distrust of Southern titles. Colfax's speech announcing the hostility of the Republican leaders to the President and their determination to have a Republican reconstruction of the Secession states, still more the confiscation bill of Thad Stevens, necessitated the dissolution of Battle, Heck, and Company. On taking account of profit and loss I found that individually I had lost about $1500 but as an offset to this I had for months had active, interesting work in exchange for gloom and despondency and I made connections which led to fees and commissions that more than offset the loss.

One episode I ought to chronicle. It became necessary for me to return home and be absent from New York for a few days. Travelling day and night and change of dietary habits—eating lunch in the middle of the day followed by a luxurious dinner and late tea at night gave me jaundice. My food felt like lead in my stomach. A Nash County physician calling on me prescribed a whiskey toddy. It was the worst medicine possible; it gave me extreme discomfort. A German physician, lately surgeon of a Confederate regiment, whom we had given a desk for a week or two in our office, explained the cause of the trouble. The ducts between the liver and stomach had become clogged. He was opposed to mercury in the shape of blue mass or otherwise because mercury is so heavy that it stays in the system and is poisonous. Instead, he prescribed the following:

$$\left.\begin{array}{r}\text{Ext. Taraxici}\\ \text{Colocynth.}\end{array}\right\} aa\overline{3}i$$
$$\text{F't Pil. xxiv. 3t. daily}$$

and a diet requiring little call on the digestive organs. I recall dried figs, soda crackers, lemonade in place of water. Following his advice, I ate without discomfort and was soon well. Our Raleigh physician told me afterwards that the remedy was recognized by the medical profession.

30. My Term as State Treasurer

RETURNING TO RALEIGH, I RESUMED THE practise of the law with my brother Richard as partner, courts being now open. Governor Jonathan Worth had been elected over the military Governor, Holden. I had not got warm in my practise, when in December, 1865, I received a message from Governor Worth, stating that he was dissatisfied with the public treasurer appointed by the President and requesting me to run for the office, then filled by the General Assembly. Under the law at that time the State Treasurer was the authoritative expounder of the tax laws, subject of course to appeals to the courts. These laws were in a state of confusion and there were grave difficulties in regard to the public debt. The office of Treasurer was therefore of much importance. The position would throw me among the leaders of the State and would be more agreeable than the practise of the law. Moreover, the extensive acquaintance the Treasurer forms would probably be of permanent value when the term of office should end. I make this explanation because my wife did not approve my course. I do not recall any other difference between us and in this matter she merely expressed a preference which had no other reason than the loss of income, the salary of $2,000 being certainly less than my law practise would yield.

I agreed to be a candidate and with Governor Worth's aid and some prejudice against my opponent I was elected by a considerable majority. I never regretted my course. In fact, I am inclined to regard the two and one-half years I spent in the Treasurer's office as the most improving and pleasant of my life.

My official bond was $250,000, the law providing for individual sureties not then required to make oath as to the amount of their property. My sureties were my brothers-in-law, William S. and Turner W. Battle, and my father and brother Richard. My colleagues in the State Government were all good and pleasant men. Governor Jonathan Worth, of Quaker descent though he did not affiliate with the Quakers, was a model of the true, sensible, and steadfast gentleman of the old school. His only oath was "ding." His principles were like the eternal rock. I was fond of and admired him greatly. He treated me always in the most friendly way. He had generally a most equable temper but sometimes boiled with rage at the interference of the military with the courts or other func-

My Term as State Treasurer

tions of the State. I give an example although it involves a compliment to me. The northern General Avery had lost a leg in battle and was said to feel vindictive towards our citizens in consequence. He had prohibited the hanging of a negro in Granville County who was convicted of raping a white woman, wife of a soldier in our army. The Governor was very angry at the interference and wrote Avery a denunciation. It was like the request of old Peggy Harward to Sion Rogers directing him to write a letter to an enemy who had offended her. "Call him a derned liar and scoundrel to begin with and then get hotter and hotter to the end of the fourth page." The Governor brought into my office a long letter and said, "Kemp, you are the most prudent man, I will not say of your age but of any age. Sometimes I consult you when I do not intend to take your advice unless it suits me. But I want your advice about this letter and I promise to take it whether it suits me or not. It is to that dinged scoundrel about keeping that raping negro from being hung." Then he read me his letter. It was terribly vitriolic. I regret that I did not ask for a copy. It would have rivalled Cicero *vs.* Catiline. I felt bound to say, "I think it will do more harm than good," and he suppressed it. He said afterwards that he agreed with me.

Mr. Burgin, the State Auditor, who had lost a leg in battle, was a most charming young man. He and I became quite intimate. We once overruled the Governor. Kendall Waitt, an old acquaintance, once the University carpenter, an honest man but a poor calculator, had contracted to build a small house for the State at a certain price. He found that even with proper care he had lost money and petitioned the Governor for reimbursement. The Governor's straightforward habits made him say that "a bargain is a bargain," but he referred the case to Burgin and me. After satisfying ourselves that the claim was just, we decided that the State should not deprive a poor man of his honest labor because God had given him a weak head.

Poor Mr. Burgin did not live long after his elevation to his office and was succeeded by Curtis H. Brogden, a good man of deficient education with a gift of flowery rhetoric, afterwards Governor on the removal of Holden. My relations with him were pleasant on the whole. Once he took offence at my writing to five or six counties for information which in the course of time would go into the Auditor's office. I was surprised by a letter from him accusing me of magnifying unduly the Treasurer's office. Seeing that he was under a misapprehension, I replied temperately that I needed the information in making a report on the pending revenue bill and could not wait until the sheriffs of those counties made their reports. He was mollified.

Here I must say that seldom is another man inflexibly bent on making you his enemy. Therefore, if language is used which you interpret as unfriendly, have an amicable chat with the offender on the subject. Generally it will be found that there was a mistake or misunderstanding and an explanation or apology will remove a soreness which otherwise might become permanent. And if you have been in the wrong, be truthful and admit it. I would not however recommend the apology my Uncle William Plummer made to a negro once. "Dunstan, I've found that you did not steal the tobacco I charged you with, and I am sorry I laid it on you. But the fact is, Dunstan, you are such a rogue generally that I always think you are guilty whenever anything is missing."

It is a great bore to be on non-speaking terms with anybody, no matter how sure you are that you are in the right. I had a memorable experience of this. Once I thought that an old acquaintance intentionally passed me without a salutation. My pride made me return the offence and so we were on non-speaking terms. It was remarkable how often I met that man. The constraint was so disagreeable that finally on meeting him suddenly at a street corner, I stretched out my hand saying, "How are you, John?" There was a friendly shake and we have been friends ever since, over fifty years. There was no explanation. None was needed. We both silently recognized that there had been a mutual misunderstanding.

Another time I made a jocular remark about an acquaintance's engagement to be married, such a remark as was common in my Chapel Hill circle. He said nothing but showed resentment by his manner. I felt provoked, but after reflection I remembered that he and I had been raised in a totally different environment. I sought him out and explained that I had been used to receive and return such teasing, as we called it, and meant no offence. Our friendship was unbroken but my teasing was never renewed. To me his taking offence was foolish but it was no reason for making an enemy.

My Report to the General Assembly, the first state paper I ever wrote, met with Governor Worth's approval, and was publicly praised by a man whose good opinion I greatly valued, ex-Governor

My Term as State Treasurer 207

William A. Graham. Being confident that the stupor in the public mind in regard to financial conditions would soon give place to confidence, I recommended that the coupons of the State's bonds whose validity was unquestioned, those issued during the war having been repudiated, should be funded into new six per cent bonds. I showed that in not many months the people of the State would be able to pay the interest on all her debt. My scheme was reasonable but was hindered from success by the wild legislation of the General Assembly of 1868-1869, elected under the Congressional Reconstruction acts which disfranchised for a time a numerous body of our most intelligent men and, still worse, gave all negro men the right of suffrage. There were so many new bonds authorized, called Special Tax bonds, that the payment of interest was beyond the power of the people.

The tax bill and the machinery bill, which I drew after an examination of all the past revenue laws of the State and many of those of other states, were passed with no material change. On the whole my intercourse with the members of the General Assembly was very pleasant, especially that with the Joint Finance Committee.

After adjournment of the General Assembly I found myself with three revenue laws to administer: the Act of 1859-1860, declared to be in force; the Tax Ordinance of the Convention of 1865-1866; and the new Revenue Act of 1866-1867. Many puzzling questions arose, and under the law I was vested with the duty of answering questions on tax subjects. There were so many inquiries that I found it convenient to publish a pamphlet of Decisions. Some questions were difficult to answer. The arguments pro and con nearly balanced. In one case I actually mailed a decision which further reflection made me conclude was inadvisable: the contrary would give greater general satisfaction. So I recalled my letter and reversed myself. I am glad to say that there was no appeal to the courts from any of my rulings. This duty of acting as judge had a lasting effect on my subsequent career. It drew my mind and tastes away from politics.

On one occasion the superintendent of the North Carolina Railroad, Edmund Wilkes, offered Governor Worth the use of a train for an excursion to Morehead City, the superintendent of the Atlantic and North Carolina Railroad joining in the invitation. The Governor had the liberty of asking others to join, and he included me. Ex-Governor Morehead, who might be called the father of both roads, as he was most prominent in procuring the charter of the North Carolina Railroad and was the contractor in building a large part of the Atlantic and North Carolina Railroad, was with us, in declining health but still with a fund of humor which made him a favorite in all circles. To my wonderment I saw him pick up an oyster from the shore of the sound, break the shell on a hard substance and swallow the animal with gusto. I was struck with the fact that along the coast the evergreen trees actually grew in a distorted shape from the force of the wind. Previously I had thought that those similarly swayed in pictures were bent by the wind then blowing and would resume their upright shape when the wind ceased or shifted.

A trip to Beaufort would be incomplete without a fish story. Governor Worth was excessively fond of fishing. So of course there was ample provision made for his benefit. A long schooner was provided and a good pole and tackle selected particularly for him. The boat being anchored, he was placed in the stern with no one near. Others including me were in the bow. We all had lines with Minié balls as sinkers. At our end of the boat we caught shiners as fast as we could pull them out but as they were about the size of one's hand and only about as heavy as the sinker I found no fun in it. By strange luck the Governor could not get a bite. I begged him to let us exchange places. He consented but no sooner did he cast in his bait in the bow than the fish, as if to tease him, deserted it. He caught nothing while I who took his place in the stern had more bites than I cared for.

Of course on a trip of this kind anecdotes were numerous. I recall one. John L. Morehead, the only son of the Governor, came to me with a gloomy face. "Have you heard of that dreadful murder on the coast of France?" "No, is it in the papers?" "No, but it certainly is true. About a dozen found hid in a box, dead! And the strange part of it is that they had been decapitated. Some think they are Americans from the name—all of one family—Deans —*Sardines*."

Before the beginning of the war the State had a small investment in the Albemarle and Chesapeake Canal. Governor Worth was invited to inspect it. By his invitation I went with the small party accompanying him. The weather was lovely and the still waters of the canal with the beautiful trees on the banks made a picture never to be forgotten. Nothing was done for many years towards finishing this work but it seems now probable that by the action of the Federal government it will form part of a great inland waterway from New England to Florida.

In order to pay the expenses of the State Government President Johnson, Secretary Seward drawing the proclamation, had authorized Governor Holden and Mr. Worth, then State Treasurer, to seize and sell cotton and other products which had been purchased for war purposes by Governor Vance. Among these products was rosin. In the process of making this rosin quantities often flowed over the ground and in ordinary times the price was too low to justify reclaiming it. After the war the price rose so high that it was profitable to dig it up, relieve it somewhat of its impurities, and send it to market. Treasurer Worth contracted with several citizens of Johnston County to do this work. It was called "resurrecting the rosin." When I became his successor, I continued the work until the price fell so low as to make it unprofitable.

This business was the cause of days of intense unhappiness to me. I started my term of office with only one clerk, though he was called Chief Clerk, an excellent, well intentioned man named Donald W. Bain. After a while, finding that it was impossible to do all the work with one clerk, I searched the Acts of Assembly and found a clause in one of them which the Attorney General decided gave me authority to employ another. But before this Mr. Bain had the laborious duty of settling with the rosin men and the sheriffs of over ninety counties, of copying my letters, and of handling routine matter. He was overworked and mistakes were bound to occur. On making up the final Report to the General Assembly, to my horror he informed me that his accounts would not balance and that I was some $7,000 behind.

I had had no experience in book-keeping and in the consternation caused by this news I failed to find the errors. If I had opened every voucher from the beginning and looked to see whether the amount had been properly entered, I should have found the trouble in an hour, but since I had faith in the accuracy of the clerk it did not occur to me to do this. I consulted the Governor but he was busy and only said he knew it was all right. Then I laid my trouble before Charles Dewey, who had been an officer of a bank since boyhood. His answer was comforting although he did not volunteer to make an investigation. He said, "Mr. Battle, rest satisfied that there is no fraud. Donald Bain is an honest man. You are excited now and as long as you are so you will not find the mistake. Dismiss the matter from your mind for a few days. Go to Chapel Hill to see your folks. It will all be right. Such errors are not at all uncommon. Only last week I was behind $500. I quit thinking about it for a few days and then found it without any trouble. A teller in New Bern once found himself in debt about $200. After much anxiety he found that in the addition of his debts he had included the year 1852. Be assured you will find the mistake." I took his advice and at Chapel Hill received a telegram from the Chief Clerk that he had found the error. It appears that he had from time to time with my approval made advances to the rosin resurrectionists to enable them to pay their laborers. Their final receipts on settlement were for the amount then due. The Chief Clerk had given me no credit on the books for those advances. He was excusable because he was overworked. He ought to have surrendered the receipts for partial payments and taken a voucher for the whole amount paid. However, all was serene. Not a question was ever asked about it by anyone.

My anxiety about this matter was intensified by the fact that the treasury safe, in which from time to time much money was deposited, had been left open for many days when the Northern army was in Raleigh and it would have been easy for an expert to fabricate a duplicate key. The possibility of robbery was therefore in my mind. I could have replaced the amount but money was scarce and interest twelve or eighteen per cent. Moreover, it would have been gall and wormwood to be an object of pity or suspicion to the State.

The next General Assembly was not materially different in character from those before the war, the voters being still of the same class. When my election came on a senator moved to postpone to next day, in order to inquire into the sale of State's holdings of stock in the Raleigh and Gaston Railroad Company, but it was pointed out that I had carried out the provisions of the act requiring the sale, the Governor approving, in fact, that I had no discretion in the matter. Postponement was refused and I received all the votes except those of the senator and one or two others.

I must describe an incident of the session in old times when whiskey drinking was fashionable, which was paralleled two years afterwards in the General Assembly of 1868-1869, but which I hope will never happen again.

The Convention of 1865-1866 repudiated all contracts tending to aid in carrying on the Civil War. Two men claimed that certain debts incurred during that time were in support of the Insane Asylum and other unwarlike objects. They applied to the General Assembly for payment. Being of the old school, on the morning when their bill was to be called up they caused tubs of intoxicating liquids to be placed in a portico of the Capitol on the same floor as the halls of the Senate and House, and invited all to partake—in other words, gave a free treat. I am grieved to say that at least two-thirds of each body accepted the invitation with the dire result that tongues were loosened and breaches of order and decorum so frequent that it became necessary to adjourn the session until next day.

When the General Assembly again met, the sober men were angry from disgust at the orgies and the drunken men were angry with themselves, and they united in promptly killing the bill for relief regardless of what merit it may have had.

When in 1867 Congress passed what are known as the Reconstruction acts, the states which had attempted secession were placed under military rule, the officers under the President Johnson Reconstruction being continued until the government provided for by Congressional action could be put in operation. I therefore was State Treasurer until July 1, 1868. The first general appointed over us under Congressional Reconstruction was Daniel E. Sickles of New York, the same who had killed Scott Key, the son of Francis, for seduction of his wife. It was in defence of Sickles that Stanton, afterwards Secretary of War, first came into public notice.

I had no dealing with Sickles and have no recollections of any actions of his materially interfering with the State authorities. I heard him in a public speech in front of the Yarborough House at Raleigh say emphatically that all history could not show greater courage in war or more good sense in defeat than the people of the South. He endeavored to carry out the spirit of our Stay Laws that were designed to defer the collection of debts by ordering a creditor who had obtained judgment for a debt in a United States Court to delay enforcing his judgment, but Chief Justice Chase nullified his order and Sickles' superior officer, General Grant, decided that Sickles could not control the Federal courts although his power was superior to the State courts.

In 1867 General Sickles attended our University Commencement with President Johnson, Secretary Seward, and other prominent men. He made a good impression on all, more so than Seward who was disposed to be critical. For example, when I with others called on him privately, Seward sneered at the Chapel Hill private buildings, saying that they were similar to the habitations of his town, Auburn, New York, sixty years ago. I was grieved that General Sickles was black-balled when proposed for election into the Dialectic Society as an honorary member. It required only five votes to do this. I understood that Robert and Augustus Graham, sons of ex-Governor Graham, labored to prevent this but the prejudices of half a dozen students could not be overcome. I never heard of the general's noticing the slight.

In 1826 an ex-Mason named William Morgan published a book against the Masonic Fraternity and divulged some of its secrets. Soon afterwards he was abducted and was never heard of again. Many thought that he was murdered and sunk in Lake Ontario. Naturally there was intense excitement aroused. Parties were formed on the issue, Masonic and Anti-Masonic. William H. Seward, a young lawyer then, became prominent as a leader of the Anti-Masonic party. Forty-one years afterwards on being initiated into the Philanthropic Society of our University, when the declaration was presented to him which honorary as well as active members are called on to sign containing a promise not to divulge anything to the detriment of the Society, he stopped proceedings until it was made clear that the Philanthropic Society was not one of the secret organizations he had fought so brilliantly in his youth.

On the day when President Johnson was to reach Weldon on the way to Chapel Hill Governor Worth asked me, as he was unwell, to meet him and make an address of welcome. I wrote off my effort and committed it to memory. As the train rolled into the town, the United States Marshal, Daniel R. Goodloe, who was Master of Ceremonies, informed me that Secretary Seward was in the President's party and asked me to welcome him too. I had not heard of his coming and had not thought out how to word a welcome to him. While my speech to the President was sufficiently appropriate, that to his Secretary of State was sufficiently lame. Goodloe comforted me, saying it was all that was needed, but I was mortified.

I was at Chapel Hill when President Johnson was escorted to the mansion of President Swain on his arrival from Durham. In reply to President Swain's address of welcome, he said among other things that before he reached maturity he passed along the street in front of President Swain's house, footsore and hungry, about

My Term as State Treasurer

sunset after his long walk from Raleigh, not knowing where to get a supper nor where to lay his head for the night. Upon making inquiry he was informed that about a mile beyond Chapel Hill lived a kindly and hospitable man named James Craig. He told Mr. Craig his plight, met with a warm welcome, was given bed, supper, and breakfast, and supplied with provisions to eat further on. With a lighter heart he went on his way to Tennessee, to return as the chief officer of the Republic.

James Craig, as his name implies, was a Scotch-Irishman, of excellent character and public spirited. He was with others a donor of the land on which the University is located. He was a victim of absent-mindedness. Once he attended church on horseback six miles from home, then walked back and did not recall until he entered his house that he had left his horse hitched in the woods near the church. His name has died out in this community but the house in which President Johnson slept is still standing, and I am told that his tailor's shop in Greenville, Tennessee, with his sign over the door still attests the lowliness of his early life. Although I knew the principal facts of his life, I was deeply impressed by his statement; he was in himself a concrete example of the rewards of energy, talent, and character in this glorious country of ours. For years our people regarded him as a violent and vindictive hater of his section, especially of the wealthier class. They dreaded his elevation. But he was so much more liberal than the majority in Congress that our feelings towards him became more kindly. We concluded that at heart he was our friend.

I had clear experience of the wish of General Canby, another of our military governors, to administer his difficult duties with good sense and freedom from arrogance. The General Assembly had by the carelessness of the draughtsman of the Revenue Act imposed a tax of fifty cents a gallon on spirituous and malt liquors. Of course malt liquors could not stand such a tax and a strong combination was formed to appeal to General Canby to forbid the carrying out of the act. I circumvented the movement by instructing the sheriffs not to collect the malt tax, and General Canby agreed to allow the spirits tax, a very considerable item, to be collected. There was no criticism of my action.

General Canby showed a thoughtful disposition also in a more important matter. Under the Congressional Reconstruction acts a Convention was to meet with power to levy a tax to pay its own expenses. As soon as it was organized, demands for money began to pour in on me. I was in a quandary. The states of Georgia and Mississippi had brought suit to have the Supreme Court of the United States declare the Reconstruction acts unconstitutional. If this movement should succeed, any payment by me to the new administration would be illegal. Even ex-Governor Graham, one of the most level-headed statesmen I knew, had faith that the Supreme Court would decide in favor of President Johnson's State Governments. I felt sure, however, that the decision would be in favor of the act of Congress, or else a decision in the case would in some way be avoided. I declined therefore to take ex-Governor Graham's advice to hide the money in a New York bank and await events. I determined to keep the money in its usual place of deposit, the vault of the Bank of North Carolina, and to refuse to honor the drafts of the new State Government, but, if General Canby should issue a military order to me to honor the drafts, I would yield. Governor Worth approved this and for greater protection to me called the Council of State together. They unanimously agreed that I could not fight the military power of the United States.

General Canby was very courteous. He called at my office in person and asked me to indicate the course I should like for him to take, but said that the members of the Convention and other creditors of the new administration should not be compelled to wait for the collection of taxes when there was already sufficient cash in the treasury. I told him that nothing but superior irresistible force could make me part with the funds. He issued a peremptory order and I yielded.

As this was the first occasion when my name could get into the New York papers, I was curious to see the next morning's telegram. It was my first opportunity to become known throughout this broad land. My ambition was not realized. The telegram was in these words, "We learn that the State Treasurer of North Carolina, Mr. Bottle, has refused to pay the delegates of the Reconstruction Convention. We presume that General Canby will speedily uncork that bottle."

Once with a few, a very few, other citizens I was invited to a reception in General Canby's honor. The affair was exceedingly stiff. There were no speeches and the conversation was cold and uninteresting. General Canby was a fine-looking man nearly seven feet tall but well-nigh as lifeless as a marble statue, beyond the usual handshaking and salutation.

I give another case which shows that the rule of the military was not altogether arbitrary or insulting. When Colonel Bomford was in charge of the Freedmen's Bureau at Raleigh, I hired a negro to work on a plantation in Edgecombe. He had a family in Wake and repeatedly applied for advances in order to visit them. Ignorant employees are apt to keep sure memory of what is promised them but a hazy memory of advances. After settling with my manager this negro, although he had given a receipt in full, became imbued with the idea that more was due him. He accordingly applied to Colonel Bomford for relief. Instead of citing me to appear before him as a judge, the colonel sent an orderly to my office to show me the complaint and ask my reply. I showed the orderly my receipt and assured him that my manager was a man of high character. The case was summarily dismissed. Of course this courtesy may have been because I was a State officer but I think not altogether. The general opinion was that the Federal officers were fair and not overbearing; certainly this was true at Raleigh and at Rocky Mount.

31. Northern Missionaries to the Negroes

IN 1867 REV. DR. J. BRINTON SMITH OF PHILADELphia was selected to inaugurate an Episcopal school for the colored at Raleigh, the principal subscriber being Rev. Mr. Avery of Pittsburgh, Pa., who gave $50,000. At Dr. Smith's request I accepted the office of treasurer without salary. The name of the school, which still flourishes, is The Saint Augustine Normal School and Collegiate Institute. It has a well managed hospital attached.

Dr. Smith showed a commendable energy in the endeavor to mitigate the hostile feelings between soldiers and citizens of the North and the South. Accordingly he gave a party, inviting those likely to meet in a friendly way. I was one of the guests, as was a young Massachusetts Major General then in command of the Federal garrison at Raleigh. In the course of the evening the game of Blind Man's Bluff was played and I had the honor of being in the same game with General Miles, who was afterwards Commanding General of the army. He was then a very handsome and agreeable man. No complaint was made of his conduct while in charge of Raleigh, but Southerners generally blamed him for his treatment of President Davis at Fortress Monroe. He claimed that he was acting under orders.

As my brother Richard and I were counsel in the case, I must give the subsequent history of Rev. Dr. J. Brinton Smith. He was a very able man and a forceful preacher, and skilled in the management of a school. But he had great defects—a quick, hot temper, impatience of opposition. He had such nervous energy that he could not be contented with his duties as school superintendent. When I was president of the North Carolina Agricultural Society, he was secretary, and as such the manager of all details. But he made so many enemies by his quarrelsome disposition that I was compelled to speak very plainly to him and he resigned. He bought land and went into raising cotton on borrowed capital. Soon he was in financial trouble and was accused of selling cotton which he had mortgaged. The neighbors said he made his only son expose himself in the southern sun working on his farm so that he was driven into fatal sickness.

One morning when half-sick Dr. Smith went early to his fields. When he returned for breakfast, he asked a married daughter who was visiting him to bring him a Seidlitz powder. The box containing it was on the mantelpiece of his bedroom. His daughter opened the box and brought to him the topmost paper. He swallowed the contents. They proved to be strychnine and in a half-hour he was dead. Upon becoming ill he had accused no one and expressed no surprise. The sheriff thought proper to arrest his wife. She chose my brother Richard and myself as her counsel. We procured at once a writ of *habeas corpus*, returnable before Judge Watts. We brought as a character witness Dr. Smith's brother, a captain in the merchant marine. The brother swore that Mrs. Smith's character was excellent, attributing to her "every Christian virtue."

My brother, acting in accordance with my request, took charge of the case and carried it through with his usual ability. He proved that there was no motive, that the room where the poison was obtained was, after the doctor and his wife had dressed, open to and entered by many people during the day, that Mrs. Smith was presiding at the breakfast table at the time when the powder was taken. The judge decided that there was not a scintilla of evidence against her and she was honorably discharged to the public satisfaction. The daughter who brought the poison was suspected by no one. Her father's asking her to bring the powder was accidental. She had a very high character and she and her father were on loving terms. The mystery was never solved. Some conjectured that he himself placed the poison in the topmost powder, designing to commit suicide on account of the financial difficulties then pressing heavily upon him, and that he adopted this plan so as not to be buried as a suicide. But this was a guess merely. The family soon afterwards removed to their old home in Philadelphia. There was no further attempt to discover the murderer. Dr. Smith was buried in Oakwood Cemetery, in sight of the house where he died. I have never known a more contradictory character than his. Well-read, big-brained, apparently religious, often agreeable, anger made him frantic—and he was easily angered.

His brother the captain told an anecdote on himself which I have not seen in print. In one of his voyages he dined with a mixed company of English and American officers. An Englishman engrossed much of the conversation speaking in a drawling style altogether on subjects relating to his own country. For example, "Did you ever hear of the last words of the great Admiral Nelson? When at Trafalgar he was lying in his last agony, his mind did not dwell on his victory. He said to the friend who was holding up his head as he was about to breathe his last, 'Kiss me, Hardy.' Was not that touching? It was subline."

Captain Smith became disgusted and took his revenge. "Did you ever hear of the last words of our great Washington?" "No, I would like much to hear the last words of one who was first in peace, first in war, and first in the hearts of his countrymen." "Well," said the captain, "as the immortal Washington was about to breathe his last he motioned to his wife to come to his bedside. With great difficulty came feebly his dying injunction, 'Martha, Martha, never trust a nigger with a gun.'"

As might be expected there was complaint among the Northerners that the Southerners did not receive them with social consideration. I think that if letters of introduction were brought from friends at the North those introduced had social recognition. Still, Southern people could not rapidly overcome their grief for the Lost Cause. Especially those who had lost loved ones in the fatal struggle could not readily put on a smiling face.

Their reluctance was considered as more than justified when they learned how they had been duped by a clever adventuress. She was bright, handsome, agreeable, the reputed wife of an officer of good appearance. She understood and performed well the roles of singer, actor in private theatricals, and the like, more rare here than at the North. She was not bashful. She sang and acted ravishingly the comic song then introduced into Raleigh, "I'm Captain Jinks of the Horse-Marines." She broke into our gay circles and behaved herself as a lady.

Alas, alas, her reputed husband was ordered away and then Mrs. Grundy discovered that they were not married and it was reported and believed that the wages of her shame had been so plentiful that she was able to be the mistress of a bagnio in Chicago. Can our people be blamed for extreme caution afterwards?

It seems strange that many at the North could not understand the sentiments of our people in regard to mixing socially with negroes. They complained that white ladies who came South to teach the colored were not received into society while Southern ladies who accepted positions in the schools did not lose their status, although a few hotheads resented even this. But it must be remembered that abolitionists at the North were peculiarly hated because they were regarded as having brought on the Civil War. The teachers who first came out were regarded as creatures of these abolitionists and shared their odium. In the course of time a better

Northern Missionaries

feeling prevailed with the less bitter part of the community. But some made a boast of never being reconciled.

One teacher, Rev. Fisk P. Brewer, soon after the war ended brought letters showing his good character and social position. He was a graduate of Yale with high distinction, then a student of Greek in Athens, a brother of the Brewer who was later a member of the Supreme Court of the United States, and son or grandson of the Rev. Dr. Brewer who was an eminent professor in the American College in Turkey. Later he was made a professor in the University by the Reconstruction régime, but he came to Raleigh as principal of a colored school endowed by a wealthy man in Connecticut. His duties, as he believed, required him to receive in his home visits from colored people. He and his wife may possibly have been socially recognized by friends of Governor Holden but by no others. He had my sympathy and I met him courteously but did not think it my duty to call on him.

32. The Special Tax Bonds

WHEN THE GENERAL ASSEMBLY OF 1868-1869 under the Reconstruction acts was convened, I was attorney of the Raleigh and Gaston, the Raleigh, Columbia, and Augusta Airline, and the Williamston and Tarborough Railroad companies. My duties as State Treasurer had made it necessary for me to become acquainted with the bonded indebtedness and history of all the railroad companies of the State. Moreover, the new Republican Treasurer, David A. Jenkins, retained me as counsel to aid him in his duties. Such was his caution that he also retained my Democratic chief clerk. I am glad to say that, although the leaders of his party attained such notoriety for wild appropriations for railroads, Treasurer Jenkins managed his office without being charged with evil conduct. A former senator, Mason L. Wiggins, sent me two ante-bellum bonds asking me to endeavor to secure payment of the interest. On my consulting the Finance Committee about them, one of the committee, Mr. Respass, took me aside and said, "I think I ought to tell you that a ring has been formed and nothing will be done without their getting a large share of the proceeds." Whereupon I returned the bonds, having no mind to deal with a clique of this kind.

This clique was said to have been organized by a man of singular courtesy and intelligence, not a member of the General Assembly, known as General Littlefield. At first the majority of the General Assembly seemed desirous to begin by proper legislation the payment of the interest on the old debt of the State and to finish the railroads already begun. But much more was to follow. Under the new constitution bonds issued for the unfinished roads need not be submitted to the vote of the people; bonds for new railroads must have in the the act authorizing their issue a special tax for interest and sinking fund. There ensued wild legislation running the State into debt for new enterprises and entailing taxes far beyond the ability of the State to pay. To make matters worse the bonds went into the hands of presidents and treasurers who, as was generally believed, were not faithful agents. So much odium was aroused that the very General Assembly which authorized the issues for new roads passed an act repealing all of them.

Such able lawyers as B. F. Moore, S. F. Phillips, Thomas Bragg, and Joseph B. Batchelor agreed with me as attorney of the company in the opinion that if the State subscribed for stock in the Raleigh, Columbia, and Augusta Airline and paid for it with her bonds at par, this would be constitutional. An act was procured authorizing the exchange of bonds of the State for a similar amount of stock in the company for the purpose of building the road to Columbia and Augusta. One Galloway at the instance of the Wilmington and Weldon Railroad brought suit to prevent this. Notwithstanding the opinions of the above-mentioned lawyers the Supreme Court decided that the act was unconstitutional because it was not to be submitted to the popular vote.

An effort was made by another act to issue bonds to the amount of $300,000 to build a railroad to Chapel Hill, the State doing all the work and owning all the road. Inasmuch as the directors appointed by Governor Holden refused to elect as president the man whom he favored, Colonel Argo, he refused to sign the bonds. Whereupon suit was brought by the University Railroad Company to force him to do so. The court decided that the University Railroad bonds also were unconstitutional. Then the great question was raised which of the Special Tax Bond acts were constitutional and which were void.

I had the fortune to appear in other important cases besides Galloway *vs.* Jenkins, the one that involved the constitutionality of the bonds issued in exchange for stock in the Raleigh, Columbia, and Augusta Airline. A tax had been levied and partly collected for the payment of interest on certain bonds afterwards repudiated. The holders of coupons of these bonds sued Treasurer Jenkins for payment out of the taxes collected for this purpose before the repudiation. The defendant contended that the suit against the Treasurer, a State officer, was really against the State and that the State cannot be sued by an individual without its consent. Chief Justice Waite and Judge Bond of the Circuit Court of the United States decided in favor of the State officers for whom I appeared.

I also appeared in a branch of the *habeas corpus* case brought by Sheriff Wiley and others who were under arrest by order of Governor Holden declaring martial law in Alamance and Caswell Counties. They applied for release from the custody of the State military officers. The application was before Judge Brooks of the United States District Court under the Fourteenth Amendment to the Federal Constitution. The suit was at first before a State court and I was employed to obtain permission to withdraw it so as to give Judge Brooks exclusive jurisdiction. He released the prisoners, the grand jury of Caswell refused to find a true bill against the accused, and Governor Holden was impeached and removed from office for declaring martial law and for other arbitrary acts.

The State in 1848 and 1852 subscribed for stock in the North Carolina Railroad Company and issued three million dollars of bonds to pay for the same. The company was paying six per cent interest on the stock and the General Assembly ordered that the State dividends should be paid into the treasury and the holders of the bonds should receive none of the fund. The holders of the coupons brought suit asking the court to order the company to pay their share to a receiver, appointed by the court, who should pay it to the coupon holders. I was employed with my father and brother, B. F. Moore, S. F. Phillips, and perhaps others, on behalf of the State. The court decided against us. S. F. Phillips was appointed Receiver and I was one of his bondsmen. Having been State Treasurer I was credited with being an expert in ascertaining which coupons came from the bonds of the North Carolina Railroad issue. I made some good fees in collecting for brokers who dealt in such securities.

The fact that I was attorney for the Raleigh and Gaston, and the Raleigh, Columbia, and Augusta Airline Railroad Companies, and that members of the General Assembly came to me for information about the history of State institutions and some legal matters, made some people conjecture that I aided the clique in league with General Littlefield who procured the issue of the Special Tax bonds afterwards repudiated. I was therefore summoned before the Fraud Commission, ex-Governor Bragg, S. F. Phillips, and Joseph B. Batchelor. I told them that I had no connection whatever with anyone in regard to the Special Tax bonds, was not an attorney in connection with them, and knew nothing about their issue except from hearsay. Moreover, when the constitutionality of the Special Tax bonds was before the Supreme Court, I was not one of the lawyers engaged by the bond-holders.

The Fraud Commission also asked me to explain my sending a telegram to Mr. Porter, of the firm of Soutter and Company telling the decision of the Supreme Court in regard to the unconstitutionality of some of the Special Tax bonds. My answer was that Mr. Porter requested me to do this and I complied with his request, as soon as I learned the facts. I was not at all interested in the sale of any of the bonds. I conjecture that there existed a suspicion that a member of the court had sent advance information of the decision. Otherwise I cannot conceive why I should have been examined on the subject.

In the purchase of land for the new penitentiary there were two distinct steps. One was the gift to the State of twenty-five acres of land adjacent to the Lockville dam on Deep River provided the penitentiary should be located thereon. This was not a fantastic scheme. Lockville would have had advantages not to be despised.

The second step was the sale by the Deep River Manufacturing Company of 8,000 acres of land, mostly piney woods, several miles from Lockville to one Pruyn for $56,000 in state bonds and the transfer thereof by him to the Legislative Committee charged with the location of the penitentiary, the deed being made to the State. The land was said to be of value in the way of building material and fuel. I drew the deed to Pruyn for the lands in question and Judge Merrimon drew Pruyn's deed of the same lands to the State. I had no dealings whatever with the Legislative Committee. This transaction was regarded by the public as fraudulent and the General Assembly repudiated the bonds and refused to accept the deed to the lands. I knew nothing about it except as an attorney preparing the deed to Pruyn.

I make these explanations because some men, since I was attorney for several railroad companies and also was consulted as attorney by some connected with the General Assembly, imagined that I was connected with the schemes for fleecing the State. This is absolutely false. I never did anything which any other lawyer in the State would not have done. If I had aided the perpetration of any fraud, certainly such men as ex-Governor Graham, Paul C. Cameron, Thomas S. Kenan, John Manning, Walter L. Steele, and the other trustees of the University would not have chosen me to be the President of the University, a position to which no man with any stain whatever on his character should be elevated.

33. Revival of the State Fair

BY 1869 OUR PEOPLE HAD IN SOME DEGREE RE-covered their equanimity lost by the outcome of the war. There arose a demand for the revival of the State Agricultural Society. Starting with an old appropriation by the State of $1,500 per annum for the support of a fair, a number of us Raleigh men resolved in spite of all obstacles to hold one in the following October. One of the most active in the movement was Rev. Dr. J. Brinton Smith, of whom I have already written. He was elected secretary and to my surprise the office of president was conferred on me.

Although I had no experience in such matters, the secretary and I entered into the work with such industry that we succeeded in replacing the buildings which had been burned during the war and in obtaining respectable exhibits. We secured an exhibition which gained the plaudits of the newspapers and people generally. But it was a herculean task. Our chief-marshal was Gen. William Gaston Lewis, one of General Lee's best brigadiers. His war experience enabled him to manage the crowd that attended easily and efficiently. I made an address at the opening of the fair which was printed and was well received by the public.

I was elected a second and third time. After the second fair I begged the Agricultural Society to allow me to retire. But the members had not picked out my successor and I was pressed to continue in office. I consented reluctantly and made a mistake in doing so. The old fair-grounds were only a few acres in the eastern part of Raleigh and the buildings were too small for the exhibits. The site was a mile or two from a railroad and I could not arouse enough enthusiasm to make much improvement. My task was more difficult because James J. Litchford, who succeeded Dr. Smith as secretary, although excellent in most respects, lacked energy and skill in getting exhibits and drawing crowds to see them.

I think that the third fair detracted from what reputation I had gained by building up a respectable exhibition out of nothing. It became manifest that enthusiasm must be aroused by purchase of a larger area on the line of the North Carolina Railroad and the Raleigh, Columbia, and Augusta Airline, which ran side by side from Raleigh for eight miles. My business engagements did not allow the time nor did I have the inclination to undertake the new

Revival of the State Fair

task. So, after my peremptory resignation, the Society concluded to elect as president Col. Thomas M. Holt, a wealthy manufacturer, afterwards Governor, liberal with his money. By selling the old grounds, procuring subscriptions, and making a liberal mortgage the Society bought larger lands with the advantage of railroad connections.

Notwithstanding that I was not active in starting the fair on its new site, I had the credit of bringing it into life from its ruined state. And it happened that by being fair to men of both political parties I gained popularity of decided advantage to me afterwards in the struggle to revive the University. I was so impartial in appointing judges for the horse races and for awarding prizes that hot-headed Democrats accused me of betraying my party. Once, when a Raleigh colored fire company gained a victory over its white competitor and the award was read out by the secretary in favor of the defeated company, I corrected the mistake promptly. When the prize—a silver trumpet—came from the maker, I had a public presentation with a short speech testifying to the gallantry shown by colored men in fighting fires—how once at a great conflagration two men were seen on top of a burning building in a perilous situation successfully extinguishing the flames. One was white and the other colored. When votes were needed in the General Assembly for the University, my action was remembered by colored as well as white Republican members.

I never regretted my labors for the Agricultural Society. They certainly aided in giving a new life to our people.

34. Commissioner of the City of Raleigh

THE INCIDENT OF THE FIRE COMPANY PRIZE led me to another office. Raleigh was in the hands of the Republicans owing to the large negro vote, there being then no check on their freedom in exercising their franchise. The majority of the commissioners (now called aldermen) was Republican. In this majority were two negroes, Stewart Ellison and Norfleet Dunston. Mr. Lougee of the Middle Ward, in which I was resident, resigned from the board. The two negroes united with the Democrats and elected me in his place.

I accepted. On examination I found the finances of the city in disorder. The treasury was empty. The officers were paid in scrip worth only ninety cents on the dollar. There was confusion in the accounts. The books did not show the amount of bonds which had been issued nor the indebtedness for current expenses. On my motion a committee was appointed to straighten the city finances. I was made chairman and advertised for all holders of bonds and other creditors to bring in their evidences of indebtedness. I found some suspicious items but the aggregate did not show any fraud worth considering. There was a general belief that the former Board of Commissioners had committed frauds and I had the power to institute litigation which would have brought me praise from angry tax-payers, but I could not find clear evidence against anyone, albeit there was bad book-keeping and general carelessness. I concluded that it was best to overlook the mistakes of the past and manage in the future on sound business principles. The committee adopted my views and the taxes soon were sufficient to pay expenses and interest. A Commissioner of Sinking Fund was appointed, and the office conferred on me. Before many months the treasury was on a par basis.

Adverse criticism was hurled at me for one vote. It did not irritate me because I was sure I was in the right path. I voted to increase by ten per cent the salaries of the officers. They were paid in scrip worth only ninety per cent. The city had promised to pay par. It was honest to pay according to promise especially as the salaries afforded only a decent style of living. The adverse criticisms soon ceased and I was elected without opposition to a second term by the voters of the Middle Ward.

I believe that it is best for public officers to explain in detail to their constituents the matters under their charge and the reasons for their acts. I accordingly published in the city papers without any concealment the state of the accounts and the measures adopted to remedy defects. This had a good effect in silencing complaints and allaying suspicions.

It was my habit for years to take an hour's walk before supper through various sections of Raleigh. After marriage I kept a horse and buggy and my wife and I often pleasantly explored the streets and the roads adjacent. I was thus familiar with the secluded places of the city usually unnoticed. When I became commissioner, I persuaded my colleagues to run cross streets in many places where they were necessary for the convenience of the inhabitants. Every new street thus opened made four cornered lots attractive for residences. Once, when I was in my pew in Christ Church before service began, Tom Devereux at the door said to a companion, "See Kemp Battle sitting yonder looking sanctified. He is studying how he can open up another pew in the church." If the commissioners of Chapel Hill had been similarly farsighted, convenient streets through long blocks would have vastly improved the village.

Having done my best to rehabilitate the finances of the city and to improve the congested conditions by opening new streets, I declined to offer myself for another term, although I continued to be Commissioner of the Sinking Fund until I left Raleigh in 1876.

35. Oakwood Cemetery, Raleigh

I AM PROUD OF MY PART IN THE ESTABLISHMENT of Oakwood Cemetery in Raleigh. The city cemetery comprised two squares in the eastern part of the city, originally outside the corporate limits but afterwards, when the limits were extended in 1813, made a part of the city. There were many worthy citizens buried in it but it was not properly laid out with paths and shrubbery and evidently would in a few years have no space left for other burials. And perhaps in the course of time there would be a successful demand for removal to a place distant from habitation. An acre of ground had been purchased by a patriotic company for burial of soldiers in the recent war. It was northeast of the city about half a mile and was called the Confederate Cemetery. Colonel William E. Anderson, whose brother General George B. Anderson was buried just outside its limits, conceived the idea of establishing a public cemetery adjoining that of the Confederates. In 1869 he consulted George W. Mordecai and me about it. We entered warmly into the project. We purchased from Henry Mordecai a beautiful grove of thirty-five acres adjoining the Confederate Cemetery, and obtained corporate privileges, the shares to be one hundred dollars each. Mr. Mordecai and I subscribed for five shares each. Subsequently an agreement was made with the St. Augustine Normal School, by which it obtained a longer front on North Street in exchange for a much larger addition to the cemetery land on the north.

At this time people were despondent about business and reluctant to part with money. It seemed almost a hopeless task to raise the funds necessary to put the grounds in such order as to attract public attention. At a meeting of directors I moved that a share of stock should be offered with the privilege of selecting a burial lot. This was agreed to and we appointed two successful insurance agents to canvass the city for subscriptions. In a few weeks they reported that nothing could be done. Satisfied that they had not been diligent or tactful, I asked the directors to add me as a solicitor, which was readily done. By personal interviews with men when they were not too busy to discuss the matter I procured in a fortnight $4,000 from individuals and from the commissioners of the city $2,000 for a suitable plot for the burial of paupers. This enabled us to start under favorable conditions. We named the new home for the dead Oakwood Cemetery, Sleeping Place among the Oaks. The name was suggested by Mr. Mordecai and is peculiarly appropriate, as the tract was part of an oak forest and Raleigh is known as the City of Oaks. The rapidity with which it has been covered in large part by monuments, many very handsome, is a visible demonstration of the swift changes of the population of even a healthy town. Mr. Mordecai was the first president. I succeeded him in 1871 and served till I removed to Chapel Hill in 1876. My brother Richard was elected president in 1882 and held the office until his death in 1912.

My father, who now was again living in Raleigh, took as much interest in the new cemetery as I did. There he buried the body of my mother in 1874 and thither he removed the bodies of other members of his family from Chapel Hill and Edgecombe. In 1879 his own body was carried from Chapel Hill to rest among his loved ones.

It has been my duty to watch at the deathbeds of a number of people. I never saw one afraid of dying. Physical suffering was seldom present. The thinking functions seemed to decay with the body. In my opinion deathbed changes of religion, dispositions of property, last messages, should be viewed with grave suspicion.

Sometimes, however, deathbed scenes are thrillingly interesting and instructive. Of this kind was that of a most worthy man, Dr. William H. McKee of Raleigh, who married first my Aunt Susan Battle, second Eliza O. Nixon of Wilmington. There were present by his dying bed my brother Richard and I, James, the son of his first wife, Eliza, daughter of the second wife, his sister Priscilla, and two nieces. Shortly before he breathed his last about ten o'clock at night, he said, "There is no danger of dissolution before sunrise. It is not worth while for all of you to sit up. Some go to bed and rest." After a few minutes he said, "I want all to go out except Kemp, Richard, and James." After these were left with him, he said with perfect clearness, "James, I have left you my executor. I have some money in the bank and $2,000 insurance. You will have enough money to settle my estate without selling anything. I wish you to act under the advice of Richard in law matters. Kemp, I have left you as guardian of Eliza, and I have directed that you are not to give bond. Now let the others come in." But he mistook the time of his departure. In less than a half-hour he breathed his last.

Dr. McKee was one of the best of men in word and deed, always ready to attend to calls of the poor in city and country, in good weather and bad. Although he attended the Episcopal Church whenever his practise allowed, he had not connected himself with the church as a member. His sister was a warm Methodist. He seemed to think that for her sake he ought to give his religious conviction. It was in these words, "I have tried to do my duty in life. God will do what is right."

The penitent thief on the cross was not dying from disease when he spoke to the Saviour. Crucified men have been known to live three days with the nails piercing hands and feet. As they approached death, they experienced delirium and then coma but in the early hours of their punishment their mind was clear. Undoubtedly, too, wounded men often retain their faculties to the end.

I do not deny the possibility of deathbed repentance, but trusting to it is the extreme of danger and of folly. It is by right living that Heaven is won.

36. Visits to Lenoir, Boone, and Three Summer Resorts

IN 1872 THE STATE OF MY WIFE'S HEALTH REquired recreation and absence from household cares. We concluded to spend some weeks in the piedmont and mountain country. With Herbert and William (the baby) we journeyed to Lenoir in Caldwell County. There we stayed three weeks at the home of Mrs. Lanier. On the way we took dinner at a private boarding house in Hickory. I had on a pair of old-fashioned high-heeled boots. As I descended from the bottom step of the front porch, I turned the same ankle that had met a similar disaster at Burnsville long before. We had a four hours' ride to our destination. The discomfort of the pain was increased by a rain so heavy that I was compelled to hold an umbrella over my wife and the baby inside the hack. On arrival at our temporary home it was with extreme difficulty that the boot could be removed. The leg was discolored even to the knee on account of a broken blood-vessel. And yet to my surprise I had no further pain, not even when walking, although for some days I could take only short walks. The baby was not injured at all by the journey. Although from birth he was fed on the milk of a cow, such was the judicious management of his mother in keeping the cow in the stable and feeding her on dry selected fodder and on corn meal that he was perfectly healthy for a year and a half. He never had an ache or a stopped-up nose until our visit to Lenoir. Like all children he kicked off his cover after going to sleep at night and the mornings being colder at Lenoir than at Raleigh it caused him to have his first chill and fever.

Our other two boys followed us in our phaeton, drawn by a powerful horse, gentle except when near a railroad train. As I was unacquainted in Lenoir and it is not the habit of men in North Carolina to visit strangers, I spent nearly all my time with my wife and children. Hoping to give the boys a small swimming pond, I hired the laziest negro I've known to make a dam across a brooklet near by but I mistook the nature of the soil. The water rose a foot or two and refused to go higher, seeping through the neighboring earth.

At Lenoir and other mountain towns I was disappointed at finding the forests so far off. I had anticipated pleasant rambles in the wild woods. I found that I should be compelled to go a mile or more before passing beyond cultivated fields. Chapel Hill is the only village I know where the forest adjoins the dwellings and gardens. This is because the University owns the woodland.

I had several fine outings with my boys. One day, hiring a wagon, driver, and horses, and borrowing blankets and spreads from our landlady, we went to the top of Hibriten, a beautiful peak overlooking Lenoir. We spent the night there in the open. I noticed that the driver made his couch under the wagon. The rest of us preferred to sleep under the silent stars. I was pleased with the experience, especially as I was on the outside of the recumbent boys. There was no trouble in rising before the sun. We had a rare view of a thick fog covering the town and valleys of the streams as far as the eye could see and almost suddenly rolling away and vanishing when the rays of the great hot sun shot down from over the eastern hills.

We had as a fellow-boarder Governor Vance's first wife, daughter of Mr. Espy, a Presbyterian preacher at Morganton. A mountaineer said to the Governor, "Zeb, who did you marry?" "Why, the daughter of Parson Espy." "You did? I heerd him preach oncet. I heerd him give the devil hell." Mrs. Vance left her son Zebby at a school whose principal was a teacher of note. There was also in the village the Davenport Female School whose principal refused to allow the boys to visit the girls. Whereupon his horse's mane and tail were cut off. There was a storm of indignation among the elderly people. Governor Vance told me that he felt sure that his son was one of the guilty party, for Zebby had written his mother a long affectionate letter, at the close saying, "Somebody has cut off Mr. Espy's horse's mane and tail. You needn't be troubled. They can't prove anything on me." Mrs. Vance was delighted, "Didn't I tell you Zebby had nothing to do with it? He always tells the truth." Her husband did not enlighten her.

The Governor was not averse to taking a dram occasionally. Once a wagon stopped at his door and the driver delivered a keg with the brand "Zeb Vance Whiskey." Mrs. Vance was furious. "They have named horses, dogs, hogs, chicken-cocks after you! They shall not couple Vance with ardent spirits. I will have the keg rolled into the gutter." Vance said, "My dear, you'd better not do that. Some boys might drink it and do mischief. Suppose you hide it in the cellar." She caught at the idea, and the Governor says he got many a good drink from it. I am making a digression but the mention of that very able man and incorrigible humorist invariably brings to my mind some of his amusing sayings or actions.

While at Lenoir, General Samuel Finley Patterson, the father of Rufus L. Patterson, my friend and deskmate at school, called on us. He lived a few miles away at Palmyra in the region known as the Happy Valley. I was grieved to see that he was evidently slowly going down the hill of life. I always looked up to him with a kind of awe as he was tall of stature and very grave in his manners, but despite his dignity, kindly and courteous always. As he lived much of his time in Raleigh, I often met him. He gave his son and a party of us boys our first ride on the railroad, to Crabtree Creek for a fishing and swimming frolic.

General Patterson came out from Pennsylvania when young and started as a merchant. He married a daughter of Col. Edward Jones, granddaughter of Col. William Lenoir of Revolutionary fame. As she inherited a valuable farm, her husband was compelled to exchange the business of a merchant for that of a farmer. The people sent him to Raleigh, sometimes as senator sometimes as commoner, and thus he was made State Treasurer and then President of the Raleigh and Gaston Railroad Company. He was a trustee of the University and as such procured a settlement of the burning question of student attendance in the University Chapel at the Sunday morning services. On his motion communicants and those whose parents requested the privilege were allowed to worship in the village churches. The general had his military title from the militia. There never was a more high-toned, honorable man in any age or country. I recall his expression of deep regret that his old friend and neighbor, Col. J. C. Harper, voted for the increase of the salaries of members of Congress from $5,000 to $7,500 and accepted the increase. He said he could not understand how so honorable a man could vote for and take his back-pay. I was often thrown with Colonel Harper too, as he was chairman of the legislative Joint Committee of Finance when I was State Treasurer, and I thought he was on the same high plane as General Patterson. Those members of Congress who acted as he did excused themselves on the ground that the first Congressmen of 1789 voted that their compensation should begin prior to the passage of the law. Not--withstanding this precedent the measure was unpopular and many members failed to be re-elected, Colonel Harper among them.

General James Madison Leach was another who voted for and received back-pay. He was a plucky man and ran again for Congress. I give a specimen of his defence. "Fellow citizens, the early Congressmen took back-pay. The great General Washington, first in peace, first in war, and first in the hearts of his countrymen, took back-pay, and before General James Madison Leach will go back on G. Washington, may his tongue cleave to the roof of his mouth." This he uttered with stentorian voice and sweeping gestures but the disapproval of his course could not be overcome. He was left at home and the fine house he started to build at Greensborough was not finished by him. Selling his place he returned to his old home in Lexington. Leach was a strange man, of limitless self-confidence, no student, but of much power to appeal to the prejudices of the people. I met him once as he emerged from the Capitol indignant at a vote cast by William A. Graham of Lincoln against some appropriation. "I sometimes demagogue it," he said, "on the stump. I enjoy it. But you will find no demagoguery in my votes. To see a son of the great high-minded Governor Graham, with the same name, guilty of this vile subterranean demagoguery is disgusting." As he pronounced the word subterranean, he made a sweeping gesture nearly touching the earth.

The only man who ever got the laugh on him was Governor Vance. Leach was in the habit of speaking to juries in a rambling way, bringing in personalities, anecdotes, and the like, often without relation to the facts or the law of the case. Vance did not usually practise in Davidson but was called there in a special case. Leach replied to him and told the jury that the great war Governor had treated them with contempt. "It is known that he is fond of telling jokes. Yet he came all the way from Charlotte, made a long speech, and did not, as he always does for a Mecklenburg jury, relieve the tiresomeness of his harangue by injecting a little fun. Gentlemen, it is an outrage. It shows that his case is so bad that it makes him melancholy. If he had a good case, he would boil over with fun." Vance interrupted him, "Will the gentleman allow me to tell just one anecdote to keep the jury from going to sleep?" "Certainly," said Leach. "I will give way for one only." "Well," said Vance, "a Presbyterian minister was lecturing to a class of boys on the omnipotence of God, 'He can do everything.' A little red-headed boy jumped up. 'I know something He can't do.' 'What is it?' 'He can't make Bill Jones' mouth no bigger 'thout he sets his ears back.' Gentlemen of the jury, the Almighty with all His Omnipotence can't make General Leach's mouth any bigger unless he sets his ears back." For once Leach met his match.

From Lenoir we journeyed to Boone, the county seat of Watauga. We made an easy journey, spending the night at the home of a man named Nelson, I think. It was in a gorge where the sun did not appear above the horizon until about nine o'clock and disappeared not far from three o'clock in the afternoon. A mountain creek ran within a few yards, rippling merrily.

Our nurse applied for a vessel to meet the needs of our baby. The landlady replied, "We never had such a thing in the house." "What am I to do with my child?" "Take him out into the laurel." This was not difficult as laurel on the mountain sides could be touched from our back door. It was amusing to see the horror of the nurse, an elderly woman of uncommon faithfulness, Margaret by name. We had with all our children only two nurses, both named Margaret. It means pearl and they were pearls of the nursery.

Boone consisted of a few houses strung along one street. The hotel was of white pine, the ceiling of the same material. It was kept by Mr. Coffey, and was very comfortable, except that conversation and other sounds were more audible than in plastered houses. I enjoyed the time in company with my wife and children and reading *Middlemarch*, very indignant at the conduct of Rosamond and Dr. Lydgate.

One day we hired a wagon and had a pleasant picnic in a deep forest but were frightened when we found that our son Thomas, about twelve years old, had wandered into the forest and was lost. I borrowed a horse and endeavored to find him but in vain. As the forest extended in two directions many miles, I returned to the hotel with the intention to organize a party for a thorough search. He soon came in, however, having reached an open field where was a laborer who showed him the way to the village.

Another time, likewise by wagon, a trusty driver in charge, we paid a visit to a mountain peak known as Elk Knob. Sitting in chairs we found the jolting over the rocks not unpleasant and the road for much of the distance had on both sides a great wealth of rhododendrons, wrongly called laurels. The countless blossoms were mostly pink but in deep ravines a lovely white. We spent the night at the house of a gentlemanly man, an emigrant from Wake County named Blackburn, father of Spencer Blackburn. He told us that nearly all the food and other comforts he supplied came from his own farm. The sugar was from maple trees, the blankets from his sheep, and so on. After a well prepared breakfast we spent the morning most pleasantly on the Knob. I know no more delightful place. The road to within a quarter of a mile of the summit is of easy ascent. We stopped at a spring of water almost as cold as if of melted ice, about 40° F. Ascending on foot we passed through what resembled apple trees, but were really dwarf beeches. On the summit, several acres in extent, grass was abundant, interspersed with flowers. I counted twenty-seven varieties in bloom. We voted that Elk Knob with its fine view of forests and mountains was one of the most attractive spots we had found.

This trip reminds me of a balsam cane that Frank Dancy added to my collection, now eighty-five in number. It has a history. A mountain man shot a neighbor's ox for trespassing. Being sued, he contended that he had only peas in his gun and fired only to scare the ox. The ox-owner replied that the wounds were from lead. The Justice of the Peace trying the case became appalled at its magnitude and adjourned the trial to Boone, about eight miles off, in order to associate another justice with him. So all trooped to the county seat. On the road one of the witnesses found a beautiful cane in the rough. It struck Dancy's fancy so that he purchased it for me. He accompanied the gift with a four-page foolscap humorous story, told in grandiloquent style.

We were so pleased with the mountain corn-bread that after reaching home I wrote Mr. Coffey asking the cost of five bushels of the grain. He replied that it was worth in Watauga two dollars a bushel. Adding charges for freight by wagon to Hickory and thence by rail to Raleigh, I found the total cost would be greater than I wanted to pay and gave up the purchase.

On our way back to Lenoir we spent the night in the only habitation in Blowing Rock, Mr. Sherrill being the owner. There were several gentlemen in the waiting-room. Our bedroom adjoined the waiting-room, with a bedquilt hung over the opening instead of a door. However, the food was good. We visited the precipice which gives the name to the place, the wind usually being strong enough to blow back a hat or other light object thrown over the edge of the rock. The view was extensive, over a wide area of piedmont land. Since our visit a good-sized village has grown up, with spacious hotels and boarding-houses for summer visitors. The air is delightful and excursions can be had over well-made roads to Valle Crucis, where is a school under the charge of the Episcopal

Church, to Linville Falls, and to the lofty summit of Grandfather Mountain. Back at Lenoir we were served dinner in the leading hotel on a round table with a revolving center that brought us our food without the intervention of waiters.

Our next visit was to the Sparkling Catawba Springs about six miles from Hickory. Here we had a cottage to ourselves. Accommodations were plain but sufficient, the company well-bred and agreeable. We had such a good time that, when we left, mine host said he had never had guests that he liked as well as our family.

Among the company was a most intelligent elderly high-toned South Carolina lawyer, Mr. Hemphill. He had religious services on Sundays, reading a fine sermon. I recall an anecdote which Mr. Hemphill declared to be true of his own knowledge. A country preacher in his neighborhood gave a sermon on the text, "There was gross darkness on the face of the land." "My brethren, as you may perhaps know, a gross is twelve times twelve and the meaning of the Scriptures is that the darkness was one hundred and forty-four times common darkness. What awful punishment those people suffered!" The village newspaper ridiculed this explanation, whereupon the following Sunday the preacher said, "Some ignorant men have made fun of my understanding of the Holy Scriptures. I have studied over it for a week and I am certain I am right. If the text does not have the meaning I gave it, then it means nothing, and the prophet never would have talked nonsense."

Rev. Dr. George B. Wetmore, a first-honor University man, long labored as an itinerant preacher in our mountain lands. He told me that there was an uneducated Baptist preacher in his section who preached on the text, "Beware of the leaven of the Pharisees and Sadducees." "My brethren, you will notice how fortunate it was that there were only eleven of these enemies of Jesus, whereas He had twelve apostles to oppose them. If there had been more, the followers of Christ might have been whipped and perhaps destroyed."

Such uneducated preachers were common when I was a boy. There was one in Nash County, a man of much influence, named Elzey Taylor. His church was called Sapona, an Indian name. "My brethren, as I was coming to Sapona to preach to the Saponians, I met the devil. He said, 'Where are you going, Elzey?' 'I am going to Sapona to preach to the Saponians.' 'Elzey, you can't preach.' Said I, 'You are a liar and the father of it.'" Elzey Taylor was a Primitive or Ironside Baptist. He taught predestination. "My brethren, if the Lord wills that a soul shall go to the place of torment, he cannot go to Heaven any more than my horse hitched under that tree can come to me, when I call him 'Cu-boy, Cu-boy.'" He taught also that God directs all actions; for example, that when the Bible is opened at random, the preacher should expound the text on which his eye first lights and the chapter accidentally turned to should be read. Once he opened to a chapter of genealogies in First Chronicles, "Attai begat Nathan, and Nathan begat Zabad, and Zabad begat Ephlal, and Ephlal begat Obed." Here his heart failed him, "And so, my brethren, they went on begetting one another to the end of the chapter."

I had a peculiar disappointment at Sparkling Catawba Springs. For the first time in my life I played tenpins and to my surprise won the reputation of being an expert. But a match was made, my friend Thomas W. Steele of Arkansas being captain of one side. He chose me as one of his best. I was mortified at my many misses. I found out afterwards that not being used to the sport my right hip had become "painified," as the negroes say, and therefore my throws were not accurate.

Afterwards I played whist with Steele as partner. Just as I was to play the last round, I saw the mail coming in. I was expecting an important letter and in my hurry to get it I played the wrong card. My friend Steele, who took deep interest in the game, threw down his cards and exclaimed, "I don't know why the Lord has given me such sorry partners this summer." All in good humor, of course.

I must tell of Steele's winning fame in the Dialectic Society, of which he was a member during his short course in the University. His turn came to read a composition. Tall and grave in his manner, he read without a trace of humor in his countenance a story about a horseback ride of two lovers. They came to a swollen stream. In crossing it the water reached so high that the lady had difficulty in keeping her feet dry. The lover tenderly said, "Let me put my arm around your waist and support you." With flashing eyes the fair one replied, "You be d——d." By the laws of the Society there was a fine for each laugh heard by the *Censor Morum* or a monitor. There was a rich harvest of dimes at this unexpected end of the composition.

Afterwards Steele visited us at Chapel Hill with his brother, Col. Walter L. Steele, one of our best University trustees. Tom was fond of hunting in the mountains of Colorado. He sent my wife the very large antlers of a wapiti or American stag, probably not killed by himself, that now hang over our dining-room mantel.

Mr. Elliott, the owner and manager of the Sparkling Catawba Springs, was a good man but not skilled as a major-domo. We had sufficient food but not in modern style. It was an interesting spectacle when the servants aided by the boy visitors, in the presence of the ladies and gentlemen sitting on the porches, pursued over the hills the sheep destined for our dinner. Old Mr. Edwin Holt, a prosperous farmer and manufacturer, father of Governor Thomas M. Holt, feelingly expressed his indignation, "It is horrible. They ought to have the sheep in an enclosure, with the fences converging to a corner. Then the animals should be slowly driven into this corner and gently caught and slaughtered. In this way the peculiar odor would not be driven into the flesh." He accompanied this advice with a soothing motion of his hands as if he were caressing a grandchild.

The next year we spent a few weeks at the Yellow Sulphur Springs, in Virginia. On the way we spent the night at Christiansburg. Our bedroom there was over a rippling stream, the music of which lulled us pleasantly to sleep. I greatly admired the location of this room. Next year I changed my mind when the rains swelled the brook into a torrent and stocked the room with craw-fish.

At the Springs, three or four miles from Christiansburg, I had the good fortune to secure a cottage convenient to the dining-house. We had good books and papers to read and were so much alone that we were mistaken for a middle-aged bride and groom, happy in our honeymoon. The most valued friends we made were a family of Reids from Savannah. I made spasmodic efforts to be interested in the tenpin alley but I found my antagonists so expert from constant playing that I was easily beaten. One of my weaknesses is to be unhappy in defeat; so I paid the cost of the game, sixty cents, a few times, and gave up the sport. When not with my wife, I strolled through the lovely forest near by. There were interesting informal dances every night except Sundays and we occasionally found pleasure in looking on. On the whole we found the place, while not what is called a fashionable resort, very suitable for those loving quiet and rest.

From the Yellow Sulphur we went to Buffalo Springs near the Virginia line, reached from the railroad by an uninteresting carriage ride of fifteen miles. Its chief boast is its Lithia Spring. There were North Carolina people present, some of them akin to us. The chief food was lamb and one of our friends reported that he had eaten so much lamb that he was ashamed to look a sheep in the face. I recall little of our sojourn there. An amusing joke was played on our son, William, not three years old. I found him in a towering rage, "That colored boy says there is a hole in my new hat." I saw from the colored boy's face that the teasing was jocular. He drawled out, "Ef there ain't a hole in your hat, how kin you git it on yer head?"

Election day, then the first Thursday in August, came on. My friend Charles M. Busbee was a candidate for the General Assembly and I decided to go home by way of Henderson to vote. So I hired the only conveyance at the Springs, a carriage and two horses, to take me to Henderson, where I could take the train to Raleigh. But the strength of one of the horses gave out and I failed to make connection, and thus lost my vote. Not long after this I concluded to quit politics and never sought office again. It was a fortunate resolution because naturally a non-party man was needed to lead in the revival of the University, and its presidency was a more honorable office than any which I could have secured in the political field.

37. Revival of the University

MY CONNECTION WITH THE UNIVERSITY OF North Carolina as student, 1845-1849; Assistant in Latin, 1849-1850; President of the Dialectic Society in 1848; Tutor in Mathematics, 1850-1854; member of the Board of Trustees, 1862-1868; had inspired me with a strong attachment to the institution. Besides affection for the University I had a similar love of Chapel Hill and the forests, streams, hills, and valleys of the neighborhood. It was with deep regret that I saw under Reconstruction the faculty and trustees lose their places and new men who did not have the confidence of the people succeed them. The General Assembly could not be induced to supply an income and after one year's experiment the doors were closed in 1870. The true friends of the institution anxiously looked for an opportunity of reopening its doors.

Superintendent of Public Instruction McIver was a warm friend of the University, of which he was a first-honor man in 1853. He made a praiseworthy effort to revive the exercises. He called a meeting of friends of the institution, with a view to procuring the resignation of the members of the 1868 board and filling the vacancies with active supporters of the movement. I attended of course. My father was made chairman. An excellent spirit was shown but the movement failed because the resignations could not be procured. The existing trustees, though doing nothing to restore the University to active work, were unwilling to make a public confession of inferiority to others.

Obviously it was necessary to secure an amendment to the State Constitution displacing the 1868 Board of Trustees which was ruled by Governor Holden, and giving the choice of a new board to the General Assembly. In 1871 this body had a majority of anti-Republicans. A suitable amendment was approved by the General Assembly, submitted to the people, and became in 1873 a part of the Constitution.

The new board provided for by the Constitutional Amendment of 1873 was elected in the winter of 1874, the term of office not for life, as was the law prior to 1868, but for eight years. I was a member. Governor Caldwell refused to recognize the election as valid, contending that he had the right to appoint subject to confirmation by the Senate. The board refused to assent to his claim, elected ex-Governor Graham Chairman and me Secretary and Treasurer. They instructed me to take steps to have a decision by the Supreme Court of the State as soon as possible. Former Secretary and Treasurer R. W. Lassiter did not wish to make resistance and deposited his official books and the University seal in the office of the Superintendent of Public Instruction. Superintendent McIver agreed to expedite the suit to decide the question and the Supreme Court in *Trustees of the University* vs. *McIver* sustained the legality of the action of the General Assembly.

The next important question to be decided was as to the extent of the ownership of the property of the University. Prior to the Civil War the institution had as part of its endowment one hundred thousand dollars of stock in the Bank of the State of North Carolina. This bank was wound up and the General Assembly allowed the University to invest the proceeds of its stock in the same amount of stock in the new bank, the Bank of North Carolina. As a favor the University was allowed to subscribe for an additional one hundred thousand dollars of stock. This seemed a good operation as the stock of the old bank usually paid eight per cent dividends and the University as then conducted had a surplus each year, which could be used to pay for the new stock. Ten thousand dollars was actually paid, leaving a debt of ninety thousand dollars. There were other minor debts.

But the best laid schemes of mice and men gang aft agley. By the losses of the war the stock became worthless but the debts remained. The University became bankrupt. Eventually the Circuit Court of the United States decided that as the University was a State institution, such part of its property as was necessary to its life could not be alienated, and George H. Snow was appointed Commissioner to report to the court the items of such necessary property. His report was liberal and Judge Hugh L. Bond of the Circuit Court allotted to the University all its land from Franklin Street and the Durham road to the Pittsborough road except the seventy acres which included Piney Prospect. The court decree included also the four faculty residences and all books, apparatus, paintings, and other items useful in teaching. Including the campus the land comprised about six hundred acres, nearly all in forest. Paul C. Cameron became purchaser of the land ordered to be sold, as he wished to save a debt due his sister.

The buildings sadly needed repairs. Some of the trustees signed a five-thousand note as sureties to the University for raising funds

Revival of the University

to secure these repairs but it was not used. I moved in the board that a committee should be appointed to procure subscriptions for the purpose. I was made chairman. As might have been foreseen, the other committeemen left the work to me. I met with unexpected success. First I applied to those most likely to give. My father and B. F. Moore gave one thousand dollars each, my brother Richard and I, Col. D. M. Carter, William Grimes, Professor W. C. Kerr, Gen. J. S. Carr, five hundred dollars each, and others varying amounts. I adopted a new plan for appeals by mail. I employed a clerk and had a number of appeals written, not printed. On each paper were copied the names and amounts of those who had already subscribed. Those receiving these papers could thus be stirred by the examples of others. The plan worked well. The subscriptions were payable in five equal annual instalments. I reported to the next meeting of the trustees about twenty thousand dollars promised. Of this eighteen thousand dollars in due time was collected. Mr. Cameron, who gave an eight per cent bond for one thousand dollars subject to three scholarships after several years, was made chairman of the Building Committee and generously at his own expense supervised the repairs, residing in Chapel Hill and securing the strictest economy. His subscription counting interest on the bond netted the University $540.

The next step was to secure an appropriation from the General Assembly which with tuition money would enable the University to run. Congress had by the Morrill Act of 1862 donated to the several states land scrip to be used for teaching, in addition to the studies usually taught in universities, such branches of learning as are related to agriculture and the mechanic arts. The share of North Carolina was 270,000 acres. The General Assembly in 1867 granted it to the University. A former Board of Trustees sold this scrip at the then market rate of fifty cents per acre, realizing $135,000. Ten thousand dollars of this was used, leaving $125,000, which was invested by the trustees in 1868, one-half in ante-bellum State bonds and the other half in Special Tax bonds. The State was not paying interest on any part of its debt. The act of Congress contained a provision that the State should replace any deficiency in the funds donated. I called the attention of ex-Governor Graham to this obligation and on his motion a committee of trustees was appointed to ask the General Assembly of 1875 for the annual payment of $7,500, being six per cent interest on the $125,000 which had been invested as above stated. I was made chairman of the committee.

Col. D. M. Carter and I appeared before the Joint Committee on Education in advocacy of the appropriation but Colonel Carter left the subsequent lobbying to me.

There was much opposition. Many members were opposed to aiding any university or college, calling it a rich man's school. Others were hostile to the bill because they said it was a precedent for paying interest on the state debt and the people were too much impoverished to do this. Others hated Special Tax bonds so virulently that they felt bound to vote against the bill because it seemed to recognize the duty of the State to give a partial recognition to the repudiated bonds. They were afraid of making a dangerous precedent. The bill as first drawn required these bonds to be delivered to the State Treasurer to be burnt. Even liberal members like Alfred Erwin of McDowell County thought that the delivery to a state officer could be held a recognition. At my suggestion the wording was changed to read, "The said Special Tax bonds, being unconstitutional and void, shall be burnt by the trustees of the University." This satisfied Erwin; he voted for the bill and it passed the House by one vote. The majority for it in the Senate was larger.

The trustees determined to open the doors of the University on this slender income, supplemented by about five thousand dollars of the subscriptions not needed for repairs and by tuition money hoped for. I was appointed chairman of a committee to report a program of studies. In addition to the usual classical and scientific departments we recommended a professorship of the branches relating to agriculture. The election of professors was held in June, 1875. Rev. Dr. Charles Phillips was chosen Professor of Mathematics and Chairman of the Faculty. The slenderness of our income prevented us from going far afield in filling our faculty but we started with six professors and one assistant professor.

[In June, 1876, the trustees elected Kemp Plummer Battle President of the University of North Carolina, and he remained its president for fifteen years.—EDITOR.]

38. Back at the Old Home in Chapel Hill

AFTER ACCEPTING THE PRESIDENCY OF THE University I was unwilling to occupy a residence belonging to the institution because I was greatly attached to the home where I lived from 1843 to 1854. I accordingly bought it from my father for $2,500, a full price at that day. It was painful to me to ask my wife to exchange our Raleigh house for the uncomfortable habitation at Chapel Hill; so I resolved to have it repaired and enlarged so that it might be equal to that at Raleigh. The additions were planned by Mr. Keith, a skilled architect, the chief changes being the addition of a long front porch and two one-story wings, one our bedroom, the other for some years the parlor but now a bedroom. The southeast porch is also new and changes were made near the dining room. My father had never given the place a name but it seemed to me that it ought to have one. On reflection I decided to call it Senlac after the hill on which William of Normandy defeated Harold the Saxon and made himself King of England. That name it still bears.

On the whole my wife was well pleased with her new home and she became eager in all ways to assist me in advancing the interests of the University. The demands on the faculty for entertaining visitors at Commencement were much greater than after the finishing of the railroad to Chapel Hill. Visitors often stayed from Saturday evening to Friday morning. In addition to having all the sleeping apartments full of guests, it was customary to have full tables of invited strangers. Once at my house there were twenty-five guests at dinner. When President Buchanan with a suite attended the Commencement of 1859, President Swain solved the problem of neglecting no one worthy of notice by a grand dinner on his lawn, to which the members of the senior class were also invited. The necessity of providing for so many visitors was a serious burden.

To my surprise my father's slaves refrained from coming near us. They not only did not offer their services but I learned afterwards that they discouraged others, alleging that Miss Patty was hard to please, an arrant falsehood, because she was conspicuous for keeping her servants for long periods. I think the chief reason was that they were afraid that in working for their old master they would appear to other negroes to be like slaves. I heard of others who took the same position. Their attitude caused trouble for a while in procuring permanent help. The mildness of my wife's rule was discovered. The cooks she hired, Silvy and Jane, for example, stayed with her for years. The last, Easter Snipes, has served us most faithfully and efficiently more than twenty years. I was so indignant at the behavior of our old darkies that when one who had not been near us for several years applied to me for a loan to lift a mortgage on her furniture, I promptly refused.

My mother's old cook, Aunt Jinny, who had always been kind to us boys in advancing niblets of forthcoming meals when we were hungry, was an exception to the rule of aloofness. I gave an instance of her devotion in the second volume of my History of the University. She walked a long way one night through the rain to inform me that officers of the law intended to search the University buildings for proof that some of our students had robbed a grave for dissecting purposes. I was so pleased with her general behavior towards us that I told her to call on me if she should have need. It is creditable to her children and grandchildren that they supported her and her aged husband, Uncle Ben, and my help was not asked for. Her mind was superior to his. Her daughter in slave times was married with the Episcopal service by Rev. William M. Green at the request of the white family. The parties were carefully coached beforehand. When the preacher asked if any objected to the marriage, Uncle Ben moved forward and said, "I, sir!" Aunt Jinny pulled him back, "Stop, Ben, stop. Your time hasn't come." So he stepped back and waited till the bride was to be given away, then came forward and performed his part creditably. After Mr. Green became Bishop of Mississippi, he told me that the announcement in a prominent newspaper that he had married a negro woman convinced him that the proper word was "marrify," as not asserting that he had taken the negress as a spouse.

The groom in Aunt Jinny's daughter's marriage, although a decent quiet man, happened to incur the enmity of a negro named Asgill, who murdered him by stabbing not far from our front gate, The murderer was duly convicted and hung at Hillsborough. The body was delivered to his negro friends, who brought him away for burial on the farm of his master, Jones Morgan, near Chapel Hill. There was no prohibition in those days. My brother Richard met a jolly, riotous company on the road and inquired the cause. The answer was given in a tone of triumph, "It's Uncle Asgill. We've been to the hanging. We've got him here in a kyart!"

39. The University Loses the Land Grant Money

IN APPLYING TO THE GENERAL ASSEMBLY FOR payment of interest on the Morrill Land Grant already in 1867 given to the University the trustees were fully aware of the provisions of the act and they sought to carry them out as far as they could. According to the act it was necessary for the University, "without excluding other scientific and classical studies, and including military tactics, to teach such branches of learning as are related to agriculture and the mechanic arts, in such manner as the legislature may prescribe, in order to promote the liberal and practical education of the industrial classes in the several pursuits and professions of life." These are the words of the Act of Congress of 1862.

In order to ascertain the duty of the University in this regard, the trustees authorized me in 1876 to visit such colleges as I should see fit and report the best plan for carrying out such duty. Professor Kerr, the State Geologist, volunteered to go with me and we visited the Massachusetts Institute of Technology, the Massachusetts Agricultural College at Amherst, the Bussey Institute at Boston, the Sheffield Scientific School at Yale, the Connecticut State Experiment Station, the State Fair at Northampton, Williams College, and Rutgers College with the New Jersey State Experiment Station there.

I reported that as neither the State nor others had given the University any funds for working farms, buying machinery, etc., as other states had done, and as the Act of Congress did not allow the use of the Land Grant fund for such purposes, the only thing possible for us was theoretical teaching, combined with laboratory work. This we did until the Land Grant money was taken away from us in 1887.

On this same visit in 1876 to the Agricultural Experiment Stations of Massachusetts, Connecticut, and New Jersey, I became convinced that a similar institution would be helpful also in North Carolina and I determined to advocate the establishment of one as a part of the University's agricultural work. The State's agricultural interests obviously needed it. I thought also that our students might help in the chemistry and other branches and thus help to satisfy the demand for practical instruction. Accordingly I prepared an address and delivered it at fairs and before schools, etc., in eighteen counties. I also wrote abstracts of the address for the papers. This address was the introduction of the subject into North Carolina. Then I invited the president of the State Grange, Dr. Columbus Mills, and the presidents of the State Agricultural Society and the local agricultural societies (I recall at least New Hanover, Cumberland, Roanoke and Tar River, Rowan) to a meeting in Raleigh to memorialize the General Assembly about the matter. Dr. Mills was chairman. At his request I wrote a petition in his name to establish the station. The General Assembly approved the idea and created an Agricultural Experiment and Fertilizer Control Station as part of a new Agricultural Department headed by a Commissioner of Agriculture and controlled by a board of which the President of the University as head of the State's Agricultural College should be *ex-officio* a member. In recognition of my labors the chemical work of the station was located in one of our University buildings. Here the station was inaugurated in 1877, Dr. Albert R. Ledoux being the first State Chemist. He resided in Chapel Hill as also did Dr. Charles W. Dabney who succeeded him in 1880. Later it was found more convenient to have the station in Raleigh, where the State could supply quarters much superior to those at Chapel Hill. The analyses and all reports were issued from Chapel Hill till the removal of the station to Raleigh in 1881. It is certainly true that the Experiment and Fertilizer Control Station was the largest and most popular part of the Agricultural Department. Dr. Ledoux told me that, while the removal to Raleigh had to come, yet its early connection with the University was of incalculable advantage. He was good enough to say that my knowledge of the State and great prudence were essential parts of its success.

Col. L. L. Polk as Commissioner of Agriculture was a visionary, unpractical man, and I could not always vote for his proposals. Moreover he tried to boss the Director, Dr. Ledoux, and I took Ledoux's part. He got up a plan for getting rich by selling agricultural machinery and resigned. After he failed at this, he went to Boston to push his diphtheria cure, which he got from an old woman, and failed. Then he became an editor and sought popularity by accusing me and the University of perverting the Land Grant Act.

As the years passed the demand increased that the State should give practical teaching in agriculture and the industries. In 1887 the General Assembly passed an act to inaugurate an industrial school to be partially supported by the State. The Board of Agriculture was to advertise for proposals by the towns of the State, and if any town should agree to appropriate an amount sufficient to establish the school, the State would pay five thousand dollars a year for its support. Raleigh offered to contribute, besides a site, what amounted to about seven thousand dollors, not annually, but in a single sum. The responses of other towns were even more unsatisfactory. Some members of the Board voted that Raleigh had properly complied with the law, but Governor Scales and I and enough other members to make a majority thought that the law was by no means complied with—that it would be a fraud on the General Assembly to accept Raleigh's proposal. So the matter was postponed. Afterwards a majority voted in favor of Raleigh but an Agricultural and Mechanical College law was passed, the Industrial School being merged into the College, and the $7,500 income of the Morrill Land Grant was transferred from the University to the new college.

It pleased certain Raleigh men to assail me in the papers, passing by Governor Scales, for the position I took, doubtless thinking that I was afraid of a possible injury to the University. Two of them I ascertained to be Judge E. G. Reade and John Gatling. My answers were pronounced to be entirely satisfactory by all disinterested people. That I did not incur any permanent odium among the people of Raleigh is proved by the fact that I was selected to deliver a second address on the history of the city at the celebration of the centennial of its foundation to be held July 4, 1892. The other address was delivered July 4, 1876. This had been printed but was forgotten by most of those who had heard or read it and I was tempted to repeat it in 1892. But on reflection I concluded to chronicle new matter. The two addresses together are a tolerably complete history of the first hundred years of the city's life. On both occasions I had large and appreciative audiences.

40. Speech at a Banquet in Honor of Col. L. L. Polk:

THE UNIVERSITY, THE FARMERS, AND THE AGRICULTURAL AND MECHANICAL COLLEGE

IT HAS GIVEN ME GREAT PLEASURE TO LEAVE MY boys wrestling with their various winter examinations and come down to my old home to bid God Speed to our distinguished townsman, Colonel Polk, on his departure to his great work. I have for years longed for and predicted a union between the farmers and workmen of the Northwest and the farmers and workmen of the South. My dreams seem now in process of realization as I see a North Carolina Confederate soldier elected by the joint votes of men of the two sections to the headship of this powerful organization.* Prejudice and passion seem to be giving way to reason and self interest.

But I must not depart from the subject assigned to me.

The University of North Carolina is what the farmers of North Carolina have willed it to be. They control our State and all its institutions. Under our first constitution, which lasted unchanged for nearly sixty years, the General Assembly was all powerful, elected all the officers of the executive and individual branches, and controlled them by their power, even their salaries. This powerful body was in its organization the representative of the landholders. No one could sit in either branch without being a landholder. No one could vote for a senator without being a landholder.

This body of farmers founded the University and elected its managers. The farmers have therefore always dominated the University and appointed its professors and controlled all its operations. This may sound strange but it is true. If you ask why studies usually looking to what are called the professions have been dominant, the answer is plain. The farmers of old times did not believe in special farming education. Those who were able gave all their sons a general training. Those who could not send all of their sons for higher education sent those who were not expected to be farmers but were to adopt a profession. Farming requires capital and the son

---

* The National Farmers' Alliance. Colonel Polk was elected president of the National Alliance in 1889.

who was not destined to inherit the paternal acres had his capital invested in an education. No farmer should therefore throw it up as a reproach to the old University that it was a training school for divines, physicians, lawyers. Nearly all of these professional men were the sons of farmers and were educated in the way farmers prescribed and preferred. There were many farmers likewise trained, but their fathers chose that they should receive the same education as others. They went home with disciplined minds and, as a rule, became successful at their calling.

I have not time to name a hundredth part of those whose talents have advanced this greatest of all our interests. I will mention only a few. Who was the chief man of your State Alliance last year? The eminent agriculturist of Mecklenburg, S. B. Alexander, a University man, the father of good roads in his county and one of the fathers of the no-fence law. Who is the captain of the Alliance now? Elias Carr, another University boy, whose farm is one of the model cotton farms of eastern North Carolina. Who is the owner of the broadest clover fields in the State but Col. Thomas M. Holt, your Lieutenant Governor, the energetic and wise president of the State Agricultural Society, a University boy? Who turned the barren Camp Mangum field, trodden down by the feet of our gallant Confederate soldiers, into a cotton field of a bale to the acre? R. S. Tucker, a University boy. Who imported the first cream separator into the State? Dr. Richard H. Lewis, a University boy. Who was the first president of the North Carolina Agricultural Society, an institution which has conferred such vast benefits on the State by arousing the spirit of emulation and by teaching the ignorant through the object lessons of fine breeds of cattle and horses, agricultural implements, etc.? Capt. John S. Dancy, of Edgecombe, a University boy. Who was its second president? That noble farmer, Richard H. Smith, of Halifax. Who was its fourth president? That pioneer of fine cattle breeding and clover culture, Dr. William R. Holt, of Davidson, a University boy. And when the war had ruined the society and left only a desolate ground for its property, who was selected to bring it into life and help rouse the people from the lethargy of despair into which it had fallen? A University boy, your humble speaker. And when there was demand for larger grounds and greater buildings, who was the energetic and large-souled president chosen to carry out this great work? Thomas M. Holt, your Lieutenant Governor, another University boy. Five of the seven presidents were University boys and the sixth, Chief Justice Ruffin, was for many years one of our University trustees, while the present able and efficient head is not only a friend but in one of our darkest hours was a pecuniary benefactor.

Again, the first department of the State Government for the benefit of the agricultural interests was that for the geological and agricultural survey of the State. Professor Olmsted of our University and his successor Dr. Mitchell inaugurated this the first of the kind under state authority in all the Union. Great financial pressure put a stop to this but it was revived in 1850. The champion of the measure was a University man, John Gray Bynum, the elder, and afterwards, when it was assailed and about to be destroyed, I well remember how another University boy, that great statesman, lawyer, manufacturer and farmer, Governor Morehead, came forward in its defence and saved it from an adverse vote in the House of Commons. Professor Kerr, the State Geologist for so many years, was likewise a University boy. It was the University which sent its president to visit the Agricultural Colleges and Experiment Stations at the North in 1876, which first brought to the public attention the need of a State Chemist for the analysis of fertilizers. The president of the University made speeches on the subject in eighteen counties and before the General Assembly and aided in the establishment of the Board of Agriculture. And when it was found that other states outbid us and carried off our first two chemists, the University supplied Dr. H. B. Battle, the present occupant of the post. In the Board of Agriculture itself one of its commissioners, Mr. McGehee, two of its secretaries, Messrs. Robinson and Wilson, and eight of the assistants in the laboratory have come from the University. For several years we gave the Fertilizer Control Station its laboratory free of charge.

"Oh," but some may say, "your University opposed the Industrial School, now the Agricultural College!" Mr. Chairman, this is a great mistake. All that was ever done was done by myself as a member of the Board of Agriculture. The University had nothing to do with my action. On the contrary our professors and such trustees as I talked with advised me to vote for and advocate it too. My trouble was that I did not think the offer of Raleigh large enough, and I contend that Durham's generosity to Trinity College shows that I was right in demanding that Raleigh should offer more. As it was, my vote only aided in postponing the matter three months. The postponement did no harm, rather it did good. It gave time to that noble benefactor of Raleigh, Stanhope Pullen, to mature his plans and to donate the grand site where the College now stands.

But some say the University did not use the Land Scrip Fund for the benefit of the farmers and mechanics. We did all that was possible. We were charged by the General Assembly with carrying on the work of the University and of the Agricultural College also. Who could have done better than we did with only $7,500 a year? As no money for workshops and steam engines and mules and wagons and barns was given, nothing remained for us but to give theoretical instruction, supplemented of course by laboratory work. And we gave it faithfully. We taught more hours of the branches relating to agriculture and the mechanic arts than the Agricultural College of Mississippi. But when the farmers of North Carolina concluded to have practical work in the field and decided that it was best to have it separate from the general University work, we surrendered the fund with as much cheerfulness as any mortals ever did. Mr. Chairman, this giving up $125,000 which you have had for nearly twenty years is not an agreeable process. No one who has never tried it can imagine how unconstitutional and against nature it feels. Old Colonel Harrison Waugh of Surry described the sensation. After our second State Reconstruction he awoke groaning once while he was a member of the General Assembly. His room-mate, Colonel Cowles, said, "What is the matter, Waugh?" He replied, "I'm sick, Cowles! Andy Johnson said, 'Eat this dirt, Waugh.' And I ate it. 'Swear it is good, Waugh.' I felt bad, but I said, 'Mr. President, I swear it is good!' Then Congress came along and said, 'Here's a pile of filthy mud. Eat it, Waugh.' My stomach was all crammed with Johnson's dirt, but I crammed that down too. 'Now swear it is good, Waugh.' Then I jumped up and said, 'I'll be d——d if I do!'" We were something like Colonel Waugh. The General Assembly gave the University an emetic and said, "Disgorge." And we promptly, with the usual wry face, did disgorge. But we could not right at once swear it was good. The bile would come up a little with the mess—and bile is bitter you know. But I am going to make a confession. ("Honest confessions are good for the soul.") Now the matter is all settled, we feel better. It was not pleasant to be charged with perverting a trust. And it was not pleasant to be perpetually defending ourselves from the charge. I think I have at least one hundred times proved to my own satisfaction, but to few besides myself, that theoretical teaching was all the law required. Let it go! We welcomed the coming. We speed the parting guest. We claim the credit that without the powerful aid of University boys, Strong and Mebane and others, in the General Assembly of 1875 the fund, which had become much dilapidated, would not have been restored. Let the farmers have it and use it as they wish. The University to the College, and to all other measures designed for the benefit of agriculture, bids God Speed. Its alumni and its officers will always be active supporters. We still do our part by giving higher theoretical instruction in all the branches useful to farmers. And all our endeavors shall be exerted to spread enlightenment among all our people until every arable acre in our beloved State shall pour forth its bale of cotton or forty bushels of wheat or the equivalent in other crops, until North Carolina breeds of horses and cattle shall win the prizes at all the fairs of the Union, and sleepy Rip Van Winkleism shall be forever imprisoned in the deepest cave of old Bald Mountain.

41. Unpleasant University Duties

I WILL NOT REPEAT THE DETAILS OF MY PRESIdency of the University. They are recorded in the second volume of my History of the University. I will only record some incidents not therein contained.

In the spring of 1876 I was chairman of the first Visiting Committee after the revival of the University. The others were Rev. Dr. Neill McKay and John Manning. John Kimberly had been elected Professor of Agriculture. It was a mistake. He was an expert in chemistry but not in botany, physiology, and other similar branches which had to be taught. Professor Redd had charge of chemistry. Instead of paying the full salary of $2,000 a year to Professor Kimberly the Visiting Committee reported that a young graduate from a Land Grant college could be secured for about half the money, specially trained in the branches relating to agriculture. The trustees, at a meeting in the South Building in the Mathematics Room once called the Philosophical Chamber, adopted our views. As no one else would move, I asked that a committee be appointed to interview Professor Kimberly and procure his resignation. The motion was carried and Col. W. L. Saunders and Col. David M. Carter were appointed with me as chairman. We sent for Professor Kimberly and after I had explained the matter to him he made no opposition and wrote his resignation without a word of either protest or acquiescence. As the committee walked back to the trustees, I noticed that Colonel Carter, who was a rough-looking man but tenderhearted, had a teary look out of the eyes. I said, "Colonel, that man is evidently not satisfied." He replied, "Satisfied the dickens, Kemp! You spent a half-hour trying to persuade him that he is a d——d fool, and no man will admit that." The colonel exaggerated, for while I pointed out to Professor Kimberly that he was not an expert in botany, zoology, etc., which he could not deny, I gave him full credit for his attainments as a chemist. He owned a good farm in Buncombe and his family resided there. He could have returned home with unstained reputation. But he chose to complain of his treatment. I am satisfied that he convinced no one that the trustees did wrong. He retired to his farm and shortly afterwards was found dead in bed.

Considering that I am inclined to be tenderhearted myself, I have had some rough experiences. A professor from Michigan was reported to have been too intimate with a fat negro cook. I called on him and stated what I had heard and added, "Mr. Blank, if this story is not true, I will stand up to you and our trustees will also, but if you are guilty, you must resign. It would be impossible for you to remain. The students themselves would make your chair too hot for you." He made no denial. Somebody suggested an apt name for the fruit of his amour—Ann Arbor, after his alma mater. He was a good teacher, well equipped, and in his manners a gentleman. I made no official report of the case, merely stating that he had resigned.

I was badly treated by a committee of the trustees shortly afterwards *in re* another professor. I felt bound to report to the board that this man's colleagues had lost faith in him, and I believed that the students had also. I asked that the Visiting Committee look into the matter. Three committeemen, one preacher and two lawyers, Rev. Dr. Calvin H. Wiley, A. M. Lewis, and James A. Graham, summoned the members of the faculty, one by one, assured them that their communications would be kept entirely secret. On this assurance the professors gave unreservedly their opinions of the man under investigation. Without impeaching his character their opinions as to his carelessness in keeping promises, his inefficiency in his department, and his want of harmonious cooperation with the faculty were very unfavorable. These opinions were put in writing and contrary to promise were carried to Raleigh and delivered to the Executive Committee of the trustees, who showed them to the accused. Of course he made complaint of Star Chamber proceedings, violation of the Bill of Rights, and the like. Many of the students, even though they agreed with the faculty, thought he had not had a fair opportunity for defence. If I had not seen the leaders and explained matters, there might have been an open attack on the authorities of the institution. One of the most effective in calming the excitement was Charles B. Aycock, afterwards a most popular Governor.

I give an example of the professor's carelessness. He had managed to have himself called to court as an expert in cases of strychnine poisoning. He testified to so large a quantity of the drug in a certain woman's stomach that, as stated by one of the ablest and most reliable chemists I have known, she must have swallowed two gallons of the whiskey containing the strychnine. The professor also testified that the viscera of those who were alleged to be poisoned were kept by him so closely that it was impossible for anyone to approach them. The fact was that they were in a part of a lecture room separated from the seats of the students by a partition so low that it could easily be leaped over. At least five students were ready to testify that in the professor's absence they had been over the partition to see what he was doing. The trustees did not hesitate to demand the professor's resignation. Personally I liked the man but was much relieved when he left us. He had brains but disliked continuous labor.

While my mind is on this subject of the occasional necessity to give pain to others, I will chronicle two other cases of an unpleasant kind.

A newspaper editor belonging to the Christian Methodist Church favored for a professorship a man of his denomination who was not elected by the board. Thereupon he accused me of being prejudiced in two appointments, in one case by my friendship for Mrs. C. P. Spencer, in the other by my kinship to the man appointed. I answered the querulous critic without any exhibition of temper by showing that if the board had not voted as they did, they would have subordinated the interests of the University to a desire to please the leaders of an ecclesiastical body in the first case, and chosen an inferior candidate in the other for fear that I would be charged with nepotism.

The first charge concerned the election of James Lee Love as Assistant Professor of Mathematics. He had been selected by Professor R. H. Graves, the head of that department, and had the reputation of being the best mathematician the University had turned out since the graduation of General Pettigrew. I was accused of subordinating the interests of the University to personal friendship because the wife of Mr. Love was connected with our family by social ties. This charge came to nothing because the opposing candidate was plainly inferior to Mr. Love. The second charge was that I recommended Dr. William B. Phillips as Professor of Metallurgy because he was my cousin. The truth was that Dr. Phillips was a man of so much reputation for ability, personality, and experience that nobody took the editor's charge seriously.

The Love episode had another chapter, two in fact.

Mrs. Spencer, the mother of Mrs. Love, was a free-speaking woman and had offended two of our most active trustees. When the General Assembly took from us the $7,500 per annum of the Land Grant money, it became necessary to diminish our faculty. The trustees aforesaid thought this a good opportunity to get rid of Mr. Love. The Visiting Committee was induced, one of the two offended trustees being a member, to report in favor of the abolition of Mr. Love's assistant-professorship. I opposed this but could not move the committee. Governor Scales stayed at my house the ensuing Commencement and I stated the facts to him. He was indignant and the next day induced a majority of the board to vote down the item of the committee's report abolishing Mr. Love's chair.

Two years afterwards, the professorship of mathematics being made vacant by the death of Professor Graves, Mr. Love was a candidate. His qualifications as a mathematician were undoubted but unfortunately for his aspirations another applicant, Major William Cain, possessed of similar qualifications as a mathematician and teacher, had the additional advantage of thirteen years' experience as a railroad engineer, had some excellent publications to his credit, and was widely known in this and adjoining states. I had no hesitation in recommending him and he was chosen. I thus had the ill-fortune of displeasing the opponents of Mr. Love at one time and his friends at another. If I had supported him at the second election, it would have been impossible for me to answer the charge that I subordinated the interests of the University to my attachment to my friends. Moreover, I should not have changed the result. The advocates of Major Cain were a majority of the Board of Trustees. Col. R. R. Bridgers, the able and influential president of the Coast Line Railroad Company, a trustee of the University, was present at the election and testified that Major Cain was the best locating engineer he had ever known. For the time being, however, I lost the friendship of Mrs. Spencer and Mrs. Love. They found it hard to forgive me for not recommending Mr. Love. Mr. Love secured a position in Harvard University. Mrs. Love of course went with him and Mrs. Spencer presently followed them. Time is a great softener and our old friendship was renewed. I am persuaded that Mrs. Spencer died with no angry feelings towards me.

42. Visits to My Brother William at Lilesville

FOR SEVENTEEN YEARS, BEGINNING IN 1876 AND continuing through 1892, I spent my yearly vacation of two or three weeks with my brother William in Lilesville, Anson County. These visits were of inestimable benefit to me, periods of rest for mind and body, periods of recreation in the early meaning of the word, re-creation.

After breakfast the morning was spent driving with my brother, who was a physician with a country practice. Lilesville is on the upland west of the valley of the Pee Dee, called Yadkin above the junction with the Uwharrie flowing into it from the east through Montgomery County. The scenery is in many parts lovely, there being hills and dales and perennial streams and numerous species of trees from oaks to long-leaved pines, the soils rocky, clay, or deep sand. I was much interested in my brother's patients and their friends. The settlers of the Yadkin, as their families increased, gradually descended the river, and as they approached South Carolina they met colonies of Huguenots ascending the Pee Dee. The intermingling of these people, English, Scotch, and French has given rise to strange-sounding names. For example we have Seago, Livingston (pronounced Leveson), Boggan (Bogan), Bivens, Ledbetter, Gulledge, Dabbs, Trexler, Dittle, Redfern, Niven, Chewning—very entertaining to one fond of the study of names. I met a farmer named Angus Livingston who was universally called Anguish Leverson.

My brother had many stories to tell me, some tragic, some amusing. A specimen of the former is this. A young man killed another under circumstances strongly savoring of self-defence. Being ignorant of the law he ran away in a panic to Georgia and was not pursued. After many months he resolved to return home and being without money walked all the way. He arrived about sunset and hearing neighbors talking in the house waited in an outhouse until it was dark and they had gone. Unfortunately during the preceding night chickens had been stolen and his brother with loaded gun was watching for the thief. When the wretched wanderer emerged from his hiding-place to make himself known, instead of the welcome he expected he received a load of buckshot in the **breast** and fell dead. If he had stood his trial he would have been **acquitted**.

Here is a story of a different character. A neighbor of my brother was a rigid Sunday-observing Baptist. He had a stuttering son who did not believe in this strictness. One Sunday he left his son at home and went to meeting. On his return he was horrified to hear a gun fire and saw a large hawk drop from a tree. The son was the murderer. With tears in his voice the father said, "Oh, John, you have broken the Sabbath. Surely the devil tempted you by sending that hawk." "Yes, sir, and if the dev-dev-il sends hawks to tempt me, he-he-he'll soon git out er hawks!"

Another farmer, if he saw a cloud in time of drought, would go out and implore it to come over to his land, crying, "Here's where you are needed. Come over here, *over here*." If the cloud passed by without rain, he would cry, "Yes, you can go to Ingram's, to Ben Sanders', to Ed Liles's, where you are not needed, but dog gone you, you won't come here where I am burning up."

Another farmer, who imagined that brandy taken repeatedly during the day was necessary to his health or comfort, fabricated for himself a hollow walking stick, the handle being a convenient stopper. Filling his cane with the liquor, he had convenient access to his favorite drink. He was not, however, a drunkard.

I witnessed a surprising scene at the funeral of an old lady. My friend Dr. Beckwith took me there in a buggy drawn by a fine, spirited horse. He and a number of others hitched their horses in a group of oaks around the dwelling of the deceased, while the company attended the burial in the family graveyard about two hundred yards off. Suddenly there was a cry that a hive of bees in the yard had been overturned. At once in entire disregard of the funeral ceremonies there was an excited stampede of all the equine owners present. They were afraid that the bees would attack their horses and run them wild, the vehicles would get smashed, and the owners have to find their way home on foot. I was gratified that my escort the doctor won the race to the horses but all succeeded in averting the danger.

This incident reminds me of the Nantucket man who saw a flock of wild geese flying overhead at the burial of his wife. Being the most skilled honker in the settlement, he stopped the proceedings and honked at the aerial game so well that they paused in their flight and fluttered down to the nearest pond. His wife had been an economical woman and would no doubt have highly approved his course, as certainly did the neighbors.

After dinner at Lilesville I would take a nap, then write to my

Visits to My Brother at Lilesville 261

wife and answer letters which had been forwarded. After supper my brother's three daughters, Mary Lindsey, Lucy Martin, and Pattie Viola, would join him and me in singing old comic songs and others that once were popular. His excellent wife and his mother-in-law were good listeners, and neighbors half a mile off declared that our music was very pleasant. Sometimes but not often visitors would drop in.

My brother was a good conversationalist, with no tendency to disputation. With my high approval he was willing to be the leader as we drove along. As for eleven months my work required interviews with all sorts of persons and I was really fatigued with talking, it was a delight to me to be a listener. Taciturnity was a good medicine.

One day at a rock quarry between Lilesville and Wadesborough I had a most interesting experience. A blast was about to be exploded. A flat car stood within about a hundred feet of the blast. By dodging under the car before the shattered stones could descend, I was able to witness the effects of the explosion. The stones all went upward, none laterally, so that I was in no danger.

Once a party was made up to sleep in the open air on the banks of the Pee Dee after witnessing the hauling in of a seine. The torchlights gave a lurid aspect to the flowing water and the trees on the banks, and the half-naked negroes shouting out their weird melodies reminded me of pictures of Central Africa. The fish caught were mainly catfish. They were placed in piles equal to the number of the haulers of the seine. Then one man stood with his back to the fish and another with a stick touched a pile and asked, "Whose is this?" The other man without looking around assigned it to one of the gang. And so on with all the piles. After the distribution our party bought what they wished.

Another day I went fishing myself in the Pee Dee. My brother dressed me in a suit of old clothes and put worms in a gourd in my pocket. With fishing pole and line I waded into the stream. The bottom was of rock, very uneven, the water in some places up to my neck. It was a novel experience but I was not rewarded with a bite. The catfish were not running that day. But I didn't mind much. According to my taste, which is uncommonly catholic, these fish are not in any shape very attractive and made into soup are execrable.

I recall my visits to the Pee Dee with much pleasure. Since those days capitalists have erected mighty dams for the creation of power to be used in manufacturing and mining. Great industrial centres will spring up on the banks of this interesting river. It flows over a rocky bed and has the appearance of depth, although ordinarily it is only four or five feet to the bottom. Along one stretch the river is dotted with islands. These islands, appropriately called Grassy Islands, are clothed with green grass and shubbery, and are very beautiful. Sometimes there are mighty freshets, which play havoc with lowland crops and carry down houses that were near the banks. Not long before my visit a chicken-coop was seen floating down with a gamecock on its roof crowing as if for a recent victory.

The water of the Pee Dee being shallow and safe, people in ruder days used to indulge often in bathing and swimming. I was told that a number of ladies were once engaged in this recreation, unencumbered with bathing dresses. A man of the neighborhood approached on horseback and seeing that he was unobserved could not resist imitating Actaeon of classic story. He came near sharing Actaeon's fate. He was detected by an observant eye, wild shrieks arose, clothing was snatched up, and he was only saved from wrathful pursuit by the speed of his horse.

I made some interesting acquaintances at Lilesville. Among them were Charles and James Lindsey, Jesse Smith, Dr. Beckwith, Elijah Sanders, Edward P. Liles.

Smith told me interesting incidents of the war. For example, one of our brigades, commanded by Gen. Bryan Grimes, was at rest in the main street of Warrenton, Virginia. A fashionably dressed lady came out of the front door of a handsome residence. A spruce-looking gentleman bade her farewell and kissed her. A private in the company opposite called loudly: "Come out of that bonnet. I know you are in thar." General Grimes was very indignant, rode in front of the regiment demanding the name of the offender, but of course there was no answer.

Smith said there was a conscripted soldier in his company, an honest, well-to-do farmer, who went through all the toils and dangers of the Virginia campaigns, loaded and fired according to order, but positively refused to fire at the enemy. He was not a Quaker but was conscientiously opposed to killing a human being. Some of his comrades knew of his conduct but respected his character so much that they refrained from reporting him to his officers.

My niece Mary and I spent a day once with John Wall and his wife who was her sister Lucy. We went in a top buggy with the top removed. On the way down I left the buggy to get the mail. As I alighted, an unnoticed projection caught my pants and tore off nearly the whole of one side. The rest of the journey I hid the vast rent without difficulty but as John's pants were too small for me, I was compelled to bide a wee in my bedroom while Mary kindly sewed up the ragged edges and made me presentable. I had a delightful visit. Walking on the banks of the beautiful river about a mile from the house, watching the building of the Bluett's Falls dam and the adjacent works, inspecting the well-cultivated farm, and chatting with my kinfolks were extremely agreeable. It is sad that after several children were born to the Walls, the head of the family died. Lucy, ably assisted by her son William Battle usually called Battle, has managed the farm with true American pluck and wisdom.

My companion Mary, after marrying Professor Collier Cobb was the victim of tuberculosis, caught from a sister of her husband whom she nursed in her last sickness. She left three promising children. It is not safe to form hasty judgments of human character. When about to bud into womanhood Mary visited us at Chapel Hill. She was reticent, quiet, apparently emotionless, and did not show the talent we expected from her reputation at St. Mary's School. We were disappointed. We did not make allowance for her being in a manner awed by the atmosphere of a university town, of which she had heard so much. When I next saw her in Lilesville, I found her a different being. She was a popular leader, president of a literary club, a promoter of picnics, prominent in church and social singing, a self-possessed, agreeable, and lovely woman.

One day my brother had some business in Wadesborough, and we spent the day there. We called on Judge Ashe and his partner Col. R. T. Bennett. The colonel was on the floor, from an attack of rheumatism, studying a lawbook. We were most cordially met, the judge taking us to dine with him. His wife and daughters were most agreeable. His wife was a granddaughter of John Burgwyn, prominent as a business man before the Revolution. Judge Ashe was a grandson of Governor Samuel Ashe, of Revolutionary War fame.

When my brother Richard married Judge Ashe's daughter Annie in 1860, I was present at the wedding with my sister Mary. We went by stage from Salisbury. As the weather was pleasant and we were alone in the stage, the journey was delightful. On this trip I saw the operation of a country post-office. It was in Stanly

County. The mailbag was brought in to the rear room of the store kept by the postmaster. Ten or a dozen neighbors followed. The contents of the bag were poured on the floor and the official handed out letters and papers to the bystanders. What remained was placed on a shelf to await callers.

The wedding festival was very pleasant. The bride and groom were favorites in the village. I was in high good humor and joked and talked foolishness to my heart's content. I was complimented for my help in breaking up the stiffness of the party.

Judge Ashe and his wife were fine specimens of the Cape Fear aristocracy. The judge reached his judgeship after the war. During the war he was a representative in the Confederate Congress. In Reconstruction days he was selected by the anti-Republicans as a candidate for the governorship but the disfranchisements caused him to be beaten. He was one of the noblest men I have known. I mention for the encouragement of young speakers, that when at Hillsborough he rose to make his first speech at the bar, he lost his presence of mind and was dumb. County solicitor Priestly Mangum saw his predicament and said, "Will the gentleman give way a few minutes for me to call some witnesses to go before the grand jury?" By the time he had finished, Ashe was ready to make a creditable speech.

His father was unfortunate in business and he began life a poor man. Once, when he had occasion to visit Raleigh, the Wadesborough agent of the Bank of the State asked him to take $5,000 to the mother-bank at Raleigh. He made the trip in an old-fashioned one-horse sulky. When he reached his hotel, the package of money was gone. He was in agony, and rode back at once. After a few miles he met an old negro. "Uncle, have you seen a package lost on the road?" "Yes, master, I picked it up a mile back. I didn't look to see what was in it. Here it is." Mr. Ashe had a keen sense of honor and the permanent loss of so large a sum, which he was totally unable to replace, would have destroyed his happiness.

I went home from my brother's wedding by way of Cheraw. While at supper there I heard a happy retort to a gasconading South Carolinian who was abusing the United States, of course having the Northern states in mind. He sneeringly said, "It took the United States six years to put down a few hundred Seminole Indians in Florida." W. E. Smith of Anson quietly answered, "Yes, and they had South Carolina to help." It is impossible to imagine the hot feeling in South Carolina at that time. The people seemed crazy with anger against the North. David F. Caldwell, one of our North Carolina judges, an elderly dignified gentleman of the old school, while travelling through South Carolina, was grossly insulted for expressing an opinion against hasty action. My informant even feared that he might be mobbed.

43. Educational Addresses

SOME OF MY VISITS TO SCHOOLS AND COLLEGES for making addresses were very pleasurable. One of the most memorable was to the University of South Carolina (then called South Carolina College), at Columbia. I was entertained by Dr. J. M. McBryde, the President, one of the most sensible and agreeable men I have known. One of his faculty had written me that there was a movement to divert the agricultural and mechanical Land Scrip fund from South Carolina College and establish a separate college. As our University was in the same status, he suggested that my address should be to some extent in opposition to the separation. Accordingly I advocated the necessity of educating the hand as well as the head. The speech was well received. It was published with commendations in full in the *Charleston News and Courier* and a thousand extra copies were ordered for the use of the College. It was copied also in three North Carolina newspapers. Years afterwards I received a letter from a distinguished citizen of Richmond, Virginia, stating that my address determined him to change his plan of education and thus influenced his life. He asked for a copy that he might republish it in a pamphlet for the use of some of his young friends. This gentleman is Hon. John Skelton Williams, Comptroller of the Currency at Washington.

Although my address was successful in some directions, separate agricultural and mechanical colleges were established in both the Carolinas. In North Carolina the political triumph of the farmers' party, the Grangers, made the opposition to the separation of no avail. In South Carolina the devise by John C. Calhoun's grandson of the Calhoun plantation for the purpose of establishing a separate college was a potent factor. Dr. McBryde was so indignant that he resigned his presidency, whereas I comforted myself with the opinion which I have always had, that it is best for both the University and the Agricultural and Mechanical College that they should be separate.

It was a hard blow to Dr. McBryde as he had many agricultural experiments on hand and was especially interested in that branch of his work. He went as President to the Agricultural and Mechanical College and Polytechnic Institute of Virginia at Blacksburg.

In Columbia I met Rev. Dr. Woodrow, about whom there had been much controversy among Presbyterians of old-fashioned orthodoxy on account of his views about Darwinism. He did not appear at all disturbed by the opposition.

I spoke at other times in South Carolina at Walhalla, Spartanburg, and Charleston. At Walhalla, at the school closing of Rev. Dr. Hugh Strong, a graduate of our University, I received a unique compliment which I value highly. An uncle of the John S. Verner who married my cousin Mary Phillips, was in front of me, sitting by his nephew. I was advocating the education of farmers. Among other arguments I ridiculed them for their unintelligent purchase of fertilizers. They buy potash when the land needs phosphates, and so on. They show as much carelessness in curing the diseases of their land as a physician would who would prescribe arsenic, quinine, or strychnine for a sick child without seeing the child or inquiring whether he had measles or whooping cough or plain stomachache. I noticed the old gentleman, much amused, whisper to his nephew, who afterwards told me what he said. "Don't he call us damn fools nice?" The truth is that then and afterwards my strictures were deserved. The establishment of agricultural experiment stations and the extension of agricultural education have much enlightened the farmers since then.

One of the most delightful of my trips was to Charleston, South Carolina, to make the address at the closing of the South Carolina Medical College. I stayed with Dr. Francis Parker, the President, and found him and his wife charming hosts. Mrs. Parker took me to see the historic mansions and to an exhibition of Colonial and Revolutionary relics collected for some local charity. I was astonished at the display of uniforms, china, jewelry, and the like, indicative of the wealth and fashion of the progenitors of this once prosperous city. It was sad to look over the harbor and see not one vessel sailing in or sailing out or quiet at anchor. I met large numbers of the best citizens and at night had the theatre full to listen to my address, which was reported in full in the leading journal. By way of introduction I told of my visit to Charleston during the war.

Another memorable trip was to Sparta in Alleghany County, where I delivered two lectures before the Teachers' Institute. Sparta is the home of one of my best friends, ex-Lieutenant Governor R. A. Doughton, who was in my law class in 1879-1881, when I acted as Professor of Law until the coming of Hon. John Manning. The journey from Winston by way of Yadkinville was by horse conveyance, but the roads and weather were good and the ride not unpleasant. I spent one night delightfully at Elkin at the hospitable home of Mr. Chatham on the invitation of his worthy sons, Hugh and R. A. Chatham. The little town of Sparta was overrun but I had a comfortable bed in the parlor of the hotel, the boarders conveniently retiring early. One of my students, George W. Edwards, insisted on my spending a night at his father's home about six miles west of Sparta and I had a charming evening. His father had tried his fortune in California but preferred his farm in our mountains. I have always been favorably impressed with the mountain people. The ordinary notion of their want of culture is a mistake. Some may lack the refined manners of the low countries but they are kind and hospitable and many are shrewd. Some of our ablest men and most attractive orators were reared in the mountains.

On my return I took dinner at a wayside inn owned by a good-looking man said to have led a hard life as a deserter during the last year of the war. Among our company was Rev. Dr. Turrentine, lately one of my students. At dinner he asked me to say grace, which I did. This made my host misconceive my calling and when I offered to pay for my dinner he said, "No, sir, I never charge preachers." I replied, "I am not a preacher, only President of the University." He pushed back my money, "I never charge them nuther." I was probably the only president he ever met but my asking a blessing at the request of a preacher impressed him.

Coming down the mountains, I rode with Hugh Chatham in his top-buggy. The scenery was magnificent. A vast extent of piedmont country lay before us, with various mountain peaks in the distance. There were scattered rainstorms with thunder and lightning at different points in the region below. I counted seven storm centres in sight at one time, of a circular shape and limited in extent. I told this to a mountain friend. He replied, "I once counted thirteen." Before reaching Yadkinville, after parting from Mr. Chatham, I passed through one of these storms. The downpour was heavy and the thunder terrific. The lightning struck a tree so near us that I smelt the ozone. One of the horses was so frightened that he tried to run but the other horse and the skillful driver held him in.

The negroes in old times called this ozone brimstone and they thought that the odor came from a solid body, a thunderbolt. I heard a story, believed by the narrator to be true, that one of these bolts ran down the tree which it struck and buried itself in the ground. A man dug it up and put it into a "chist." Whenever a rain came on, the bolt rolled and tumbled about in the chist but couldn't get out.

The journey from Yadkinville to Winston had some ludicrous features worth recording. I had a top-buggy, a white driver, and a mule. For nine miles we progressed harmoniously. Then the road forked, the branch to Winston deviating from the one familiar to his muleship. He positively refused to change his habit. Persuasion, blows, swearing, loosening of harness, were tried in vain. Towards Winston he would not go. Then a tall yellow-haired man came along, with blazing blue eyes. Confidently he said, "You don't know how to manage a mule. I can make any mule go." He took the reins and spoke in gentle tones to the animal, cajolingly, persuasively, dulcetly. The mule walked briskly ten steps and stopped, obstinately, defiantly. The stranger forgot his previous teachings. His milk was turned to gall. Without any apology for his want of consistency he hissed, "Do you know what I'd do with that mule if he was mine? *I'd kill him!*"

Then I told the driver to ride back to Yadkinville and borrow or hire a horse. While he was gone, I sat in the buggy and wrote a letter to my wife. He did not go to Yadkinville. He met a wagoner who was confident he could make any mule under heaven go anywhere. He looked like it. He was a short, thickset man with dark features, black eyes, short black hair, thin lips, quick movements. He said, "I was raised breaking mules." He had what is called a bull-whip. The handle was about two feet long, the lash of thick leather tapering to the end, with a vicious looking cracker, the whole eight or ten feet long. He adjusted the harness and ordered the mule to go. At the same time he rained rapid and ferocious blows on all the after half of the animal, on the tenderest parts above and below. The vicious lash knew no mercy. I had not realized the possibility of such violent, incessant, pain-inflicting blows. Nor had the mule. He was conquered. The current of his thoughts was changed. The old road was forgotten. He had only one thought—to go forward and avoid the painful stings of that terrible whip. My driver looked on with admiration. He had taken a lesson from a master. He spoke to the stranger deferentially, "What will you rent me that whoup for to Winston?" "Ten cents." The bargain was struck and we reached Winston in season.

44. Visit to New York in 1884

IN THE SUMMER OF 1884 I WAS ALMOST BROKEN down with hard work. The University income was too small to allow me an amanuensis. I wrote all letters with my own hand. In 1884 the building of our new auditorium was about to come to a standstill for want of funds. I conceived the plan of raising money by placing tablets on the walls to the memory of those who had been prominently connected with our history. Their families were called on for contributions of $125 for each tablet, netting for the edifice $100. A printed circular would not have secured attention. It was necessary to write a personal letter detailing the plan and the connection with the University of the ancestor proposed to be honored. I wrote with my own hand some two hundred such letters. The success exceeded expectations. I secured over $10,000 for the completion of the hall. After repeated mistaken estimates by the architect, $8,000 was still needed, which Mr. Paul C. Cameron supplied by a loan, changed by his family after his death into scholarships of $1,000 each.

This hard work added to my other duties—the cares of the presidency, the teaching of political economy and constitutional and international law, a Bible class on Sunday, misbehavior on the part of the students, had about worn me out. My son Kemp was in the U. S. Marine Hospital Service and stationed on Staten Island, New York. He had a spare bed and invited me to spend some weeks with him. I gladly accepted his offer for three weeks and it was the making of me. One symptom of my trouble was a disposition to avoid acquaintances. I needed absolute rest with objects of interest to occupy my mind. While my son was engaged in hospital duties, I was at liberty to go where I pleased and when I pleased alone.

I reached New York one Saturday afternoon and next morning went to service at St. Bartholomew's Church. The rector and most of the choir were taking their summer holiday but we had a satisfactory service. After it was over, I strolled through the aisles and by the chancel to see the pictured windows and other architectural features. While doing so I heard behind me, "Hello, Battle, I'm glad to see you." I felt a nervous shock at being recognized. It was the brother of a classmate. We talked a few minutes. Then he said, "My friend and I are going to Central Park to enjoy the music. Won't you join us?" I had myself intended to go to Central Park

Visit to New York

but at once changed my mind. "No, I thank you. I wish to see St. Patrick's Cathedral." So I inspected that grand building and then went to High Bridge.

An excellent choice I made. I did not meet a soul whom I had met before but I had the good fortune to see a large section of sporting New York in its Sunday afternoon enjoyments—boating, swimming, diving, etc. I had, too, an excellent lunch of crabs. Then I boarded a little steamer carrying seven or eight passengers and had the pleasure of racing with a crew of young men in a cedar or paper boat. They rowed well but did not have the endurance of steam. It was refreshing to watch the crowds of well-dressed people, with occasional companies of half-naked athletes, and not be called on to speak to anyone. I was struck with the good behavior of the crowds. They seemed to be happy but made no sounds of boisterous merriment. And after the sun declined to his western home, the boat ride across New York Bay to Staten Island was as always a delight.

I had read so much in the papers about modern baseball that I determined to witness a game. I did not find it amusing, but the by-standers, or rather by-sitters, were intensely interested. The ball, if hit at all, was caught at once and neither side scored until at last one Kelly was lucky enough to knock the ball over the fence and thus make a home-run. As a result of this game, for once in my life I was a hero. When I reached home, my boy friends were so full of admiration of Kelly's knock over the wall that when I told them that I was an eyewitness of the feat, I was invested with a portion of the glory.

One morning I went to the Cunard Line office and showed my railroad pass given me as president of the University by the president of the Southern Railway Company, and asked for a permit to visit the "City of Rome," then the largest Cunarder. It was granted at once. I was surprised that I was allowed to visit without an escort every part of the vessel. I investigated public rooms, staterooms, machinery. I even went down into the engine rooms. In fact I went everywhere I wished. After a while three or four ladies came but they were allowed to see nothing except under guidance. This may have been from deference to the sex. The confidence shown in me came, I think, from my being a public officer. There was in that day no fear of bomb explosions.

Once my son found leisure to go fishing with me to a place about twenty miles out called Cholera Banks, on the southern shore of

Long Island. The sail to the fishing grounds was charming, but when the anchor was thrown out, there was a monotonous swinging motion of the boat which soon made me sick. My plan of avoiding nausea is to lie on my back, shut my eyes tight, and live through it. I tried the plan once on Lake Ontario, from two o'clock P.M. until nine next morning, and again all the way from opposite Atlantic City to Norfolk harbor. I succeeded in both these cases in preventing the worst feature of the trouble. This time I met my Waterloo. A waiter was constantly handing around iced lager beer, "Cool drink! Cool drink!" I concluded to try a glass. As long as it was cool it was not unpleasant, but when the warmth of the body abstracted the coolness, the beer refused to abide longer in the stomach.

But the trip ended with good luck. As soon as we began to sail home, the upsetting motion of the boat ceased and my stomach resumed its normal condition. Presently we had a remarkable experience. Officers of the army were practising at a mark across the bay with large guns. The shells flew over our heads as we approached the city. We could hear the peculiar hurtling sound of the shells flying through the air.

The pleasantest trips I took during my sojourn in New York were to Glen Island, at the entrance into Long Island Sound from the East River. The steamboats thither were large and comfortable and it was a delight to watch with my field-glass the beautiful residences and lawns on both sides of the river. I hope that the owners of such carefully created adornments are not actuated solely by selfish motives but also by the altruistic desire to give pleasure to the public. Wandering over Glen Island and watching the happy groups of strangers were of great benefit to my tired nerves. On the western side I noticed a rocky islet with a picturesque bridge leading to it. At the entrance was a sign "Klein Deutschland." I walked over, seated myself at a table on which were glasses. A waiter appeared with a white paper cap on. I determined to play German and as if I were on the banks of the Elbe ordered "ein Glas Bier, bitte." That was my first and last visit to Deutschland.

People had not stopped talking and thinking about the sad fate of Charlie Ross, the Philadelphia boy who was stolen and never heard of afterwards. Probably his abductors finding detection imminent put him to death to secure safety. I was surprised on speaking pleasantly to some children on the boat to notice that their parents discouraged my advances. There was an evident look of suspicion and of course I became as rigid as a wooden post.

I had a golden opportunity to realize the beauty and pleasantness of a summer home in the Catskills between West Point and Newburgh by spending a night with the family of Dr. Albert R. Ledoux. The clear air, the lovely flowers on the eminence on which his house stood, the glorious mountain scenery, and the cordial welcome of the host and hostess, made it a visit never to be forgotten. The only son of Dr. and Mrs. Ledoux was three or four years old—a handsome little fellow, more grave than children of his age usually are. I was interested in his delight over a cuckoo clock recently purchased for him, whose imitations of a cuckoo in striking the hours could be heard all over the house. Since then he has grown up and published poems of high merit.

I was driven next morning the three miles to the river in company with Mrs. Ledoux's father, a fine looking, well-built, intellectual-looking man. He was rather reserved in his manners, giving the impression of thoughtfulness and strength. On our way down the mountain a rollicking Irish driver passed us in an almost racing trot, barely grazing our wheels. It was really dangerous. I noticed that my companion was very angry but he indulged in no vituperation. After reaching the river, I saw him taking down the name of the driver. I never heard whether he prosecuted the offender, but certainly admonition, if not dismissal or a fine, had been fairly earned.

After coming down the Hudson past the picturesque Palisades, I visited an immense grain elevator. It was interesting to turn over in my mind the changes caused by canal and railroad in bringing the wheat lands of the northwest to the teeming city, whence merchant vessels carry cargoes to all the ports of all the oceans.

45. Visitor at West Point in 1886

WHILE MY PRESIDENTIAL DUTIES BROUGHT much anxiety and labor, there were occasional compensations. One of the chief was my fortnight's sojourn in 1886 at West Point as an official Visitor by the appointment of President Cleveland on the nomination of Gen. William R. Cox, then a representative in Congress.

On the last day of Commencement I left the duties of presiding officer to Dr. A. W. Mangum. Even so I was a day late at West Point and the Visitors had already organized by the election of General, afterwards Governor, Nichols of Louisiana as chairman. The members who attracted my attention were first of all General Nichols; then General Bragg of Wisconsin, representative in Congress, a general of volunteers in the war; Professor W. G. Sumner, a Yale professor of political economy; Hon. A. J. Cummings, a representative in Congress from New York City. There was little for the board to do except examine the accounts and pass upon the recommendations of General Merritt, the superintendent, which in turn were based largely on the reports of his professors and officers. The superintendent was, it appeared to me from his manners, ill at ease as being in a measure subordinated to an ex-Confederate officer. He gave no general reception to the board, nor did I hear of any invitations to his table except one to Mr. and Mrs. Cummings and me. His wife was handsome and agreeable but he was silent and unsocial in manner and his conversation was chiefly with the ladies.

Presently General Philip H. Sheridan came along on an official visit and General Merritt had a reception in his honor. There was a stream of visitors for two or three hours. General Sheridan went through the ordeal with the usual resignation. I said a pleasant word or two to him but I am sure that he did not hear me. The general may have been more attractive on other occasions. On this he appeared silent, unappreciative, bored. His wife was handsome in person and attractive in manner. I liked her much.

I dropped in for a few moments at the closing dance and had a pleasant chat with Mrs. Merritt and Mrs. Sheridan. The dancing ladies did not appear particularly attractive. Most of them seemed older than those at Chapel Hill balls.

I attended also the final supper, at which the Visitors were honored guests. The presiding officer, Major Alfred Mordecai, a son of North Carolina, who graduated number one in the class of 1823, was a fine-looking old gentleman. He had been a fellow pupil with my mother at the school of his father, Moses Mordecai, in Warrenton. He was very cordial, gave me a seat next to his own, and offered to call me out for a speech, but I declined the honor. I preferred to listen. Besides I doubted if I could do myself justice by a speech entirely impromptu. The speeches did not sparkle with wit but were of the sober variety. General Bragg spent his force in lauding the part taken by the volunteer army in the war. He felt bound to do so because he was surrounded by West Pointers.

The chief advantage enjoyed by the Visitors was their opportunity of free access to every part of the Academy and its functions. My front seat enabled me to admire to the full the skill of the cadets in horseback riding, jumping on and off the horses at full speed, adhering so closely to the sides of their mounts while in motion as to be almost invisible to one stationed on the opposite side, and so forth.

But I enjoyed most the opportunity of inspecting as closely as was agreeable the firing of artillery of all arms. The target for the heavy guns was distant about a mile on the mountain side. I was profoundly interested in watching the black missiles in their swift and graceful course through the air until the dust near the target showed the accuracy of the aim. I was surprised that my eye could trace the course of the Minié balls. I asked an officer the explanation. He said it was partly from the evaporation of the oil around the ball, but chiefly the compression of the air in front of the ball and the rarification of the air behind it. The gun used was named after its inventor, Richard Gatling of North Carolina.

I was surprised at the want of social attentions to the Visitors. The professors generally did not seek introductions to members of the board, and except where old acquaintances met there was no visiting, no seeking of opportunities for conversation. Of course all due politeness was shown when we were brought face to face with officers but after the necessary duty was done, the intercourse was ended. A good illustration may be given from my attendance at the official supper. Apart from the kindness of Major Mordecai to me because of family relationship, no other officer sought an introduction to me. It might be supposed that my experience was unique because of my being exceptionally unknown, being not only a stranger but having no military or naval title. But the Visitors were all at the same hotel and I could see that we were all treated alike. I must state however that an officer was detailed to attend to our comfort, and he was most efficient. We lacked nothing. My criticism is only of social attention.

There was very little discussion among the members of the board. We soon agreed in endorsing the conduct of the Academy and there was no effort to change the curriculum of studies. My modest suggestion that the study of Latin, as being the foundation or large constituent of so many languages, might advantageously be added, did not meet with a second. We cordially endorsed proposals for new buildings which have since been erected.

There was very little bonhommie among the members of the board. There was little disposition to indulge in general conversation, no effort to be agreeable. I was never thrown with a stiffer body of men. Professor Sumner once was moved to an anecdote and I replied with another. These were the only invasions of the decorous gravity of our meetings.

General Nichols was the only member who won my heart. He was still suffering from a wound in battle—I think he lost a leg. His sincerity, manners, countenance, geniality, kindly interest in the conversation of others, marked him as a most lovable man. I was not surprised afterwards to learn that he was elected Governor of Louisiana or that he had resisted the continuance of the Louisiana Lottery, notwithstanding the great pressure brought to bear on him. Millions of dollars were lost to the state by its discontinuance, but the cause of gambling received a severe blow.

46. Visits to William and Augustus Van Wyck

MY BROTHER-IN-LAW WILLIAM VAN WYCK some years after the death of my sister Mary married a wealthy lady of Baltimore, and being of good estate himself had bought a handsome country place on the Hudson opposite West Point. I was urged to pay a visit to them and my niece Mary Battle Van Wyck, who lived with them, and happily I was able to spare three days for it. I had the warmest of welcomes, the most agreeable of companionships. We drove behind spirited horses over admirable mountain roads amid the unexcelled scenery of the Highlands, or walked through the woods down to the river bank. I saw for the first time the luxurious mode of life of wealthy New Yorkers. And I was a painful witness of the impossibility of full happiness in the absence of physical health. The house abounded in beautiful and costly furniture, pictures, and china. The servants were well trained and respectful. The children, a girl and a boy, were uncommonly winning in manners and lovely in person. The situation was beautiful, the grounds covered some twenty acres, sufficient for dilettante farming under a skilled gardener. With all this, the lady of the house was afflicted with chronic rheumatism. And returning from a walk of a few hundred feet ascent from the river with my brother-in-law, I noticed him suddenly stop and with an expression of pain on his face press his hand on his breast. In about a year he was dead. His wife did not care to live in the mountain villa without him. It was sold and she returned to her old home in Baltimore. She did not live long afterwards.

I noticed another cause of worry to my brother-in-law. He and his brother Augustus were law partners, having an office on lower Broadway. They both were active members of Tammany, the powerful Democratic society then controlling the city and the state. Murphy was the boss. William hoped for a judgeship but was told by Murphy that his time had not yet come. He was much chagrined. Augustus, probably on account of living in Brooklyn, was more fortunate. He was elevated to the Supreme Court bench at a salary of $14,000. I was credibly informed, though not by him, that Tammany required a payment of $7,000 for expenses, i.e., one-half of the first year's salary.

When Judge Augustus Van Wyck delivered the baccalaureate address at the University in 1886, he and his excellent wife with their daughter were our guests. He considered it a great favor although it really was not, it being our habit to have every room full at Commencement anyway. Since then convenient railroad trains and autos and the inauguration of a general alumni dinner to which others than alumni are freely invited, together with closing the exercises on Wednesday instead of Thursday, have relieved the people of Chapel Hill of much of their ancient, really burdensome hospitality.

Judge Van Wyck was so urgent in insisting that I should be his guest in New York that I was glad to give him two days. They certainly were White Days. His family was in Virginia and we did not stay at his home, but there was nothing of interest or curiosity which was not furnished me with cordial care. The first night we spent at one of the most famous hotels, the Murray Hill. Of course we went to the theatre. The next day we attended the sweepstake races, the judge being a member of the racing society. I was introduced to a number of the best men about town. I was surprised that the horses ran so closely together. To my eye they appeared to be almost a solid mass and the mud thrown up from a track recently softened by a shower well nigh concealed the animals from view. I suppose that if I had placed a bet on a runner, I would have been more interested. As it was I could get up no enthusiasm. In the words of Disraeli, I could find no fun in seeing one horse outrun another.

That night we spent at Coney Island, the judge taking me to sundry shows—up to the top of a lofty wooden elephant, around in a rotary machine, to small theatricals, etc. Of course I took a swim in the incoming waves of the Atlantic. It is impossible for me even to enumerate the curious scenes and objects of interest to which he treated me.

The next day, as he had a case in court, he turned me over to his son William. We went first to see a wonderful picture by a Roman painter of a wedding dinner. It was skillfully arranged for exhibition, the lamps bringing out the gorgeous colors and all the facial expressions with a brilliancy that amazed me. He then took me to a famous restaurant to see other remarkable paintings. We conformed to the custom of the restaurant by ordering something to drink, to wit, glasses of lemonade at twenty-five cents a glass. I did not ask the flavoring components but the result was superb.

47. An Address at Round Lake, New York, in 1888

I PAID ANOTHER VISIT TO NEW YORK AFTERwards under delightful auspices. Rev. Dr. C. F. Deems, Pastor of the Church of the Strangers in New York City, invited me to deliver an address before a society founded by him, called the American Institute of Christian Philosophy. The meeting was at Round Lake, New York, a beautiful sheet of water not many miles northwest of Albany. There is a village on the brink which is the summer home of about 2,500 people, mostly Methodists, who gather for recreation and instruction. The lectures delivered by prominent men chosen by Dr. Deems were in the forenoon, the rest of the day being devoted to recreation and occasional meetings of societies and exhibitions of stereopticon views.

My lecture was on the Trials and Judicial Proceedings of the New Testament. I tried to show that St. Paul at Athens was not tried by the Court of the Areopagus nor was he merely giving his views before a miscellaneous crowd, making as it were a stump speech, but was under a preliminary investigation at the instance of university professors (Stoics and Epicureans) to ascertain whether he should be put on trial for the crime for which Socrates suffered. I also endeavored to show that Pilate, a hard and cruel man, was not actuated by pity for our Lord, but was endeavoring to induce the people to allow Barabbas, a rebel against Roman authority, to be punished. I showed that the young and ambitious Agrippa was working to secure from the emperor the province of Judea which had been under his father, that he was seeking to make the best impression possible on the assembled high Jewish and Roman officials. His remark to St. Paul and his rising to close the assembly are what might be expected of the ambitious young king, whereas the assertion in the King James Version that he publicly announced that he was almost converted to Christianity is, if taken literally, inconsistent with his character, his ambition, and his subsequent history.

I also contended that Gallio, brother of Seneca, a Roman judge in a great city, did not wink at the beating of Sosthenes but ordered his lictors to inflict the whipping, that being the usual punishment of a prosecutor bringing a trivial charge, whereas our judges make him pay the costs. My paper was published in a journal called *Christian Thought* and was complimented by eminent scholars.

Several days were most pleasantly spent at Round Lake among agreeable companions. I noticed that the waitress at our table was a pretty girl, well-mannered, evidently well raised, and was told that it was the custom for girls of good family to make pocket money and have the pleasure of an outing in this manner at such resorts as Round Lake.

My intercourse with Dr. Deems and his family gave me renewed admiration for his amiability and zealous following after the Master. He seemed totally devoid of envy, hatred, and malice. His work at the Church of the Strangers in New York was of great value. His procuring me an invitation to lecture before so widely known a body as the Institute of Christian Philosophy was of course mainly because of my official connection with the University. His interest in the University, of whose faculty he was a member in his youth, was shown long before by his establishment of the Deems fund and his inducing William H. Vanderbilt to increase it by a gift of ten thousand dollars. The principal is loaned to students in order to help them through the University. As borrowers give security and pay interest, the fund is constantly growing. No man has encouraged me in my work for the University more than Dr. Deems.

[Here end the Memories of an Old-Time Tar Heel. There was much of interest in his life still untold, but he was drawn away to other fields. Recent events had less attraction for him than those of long ago. After all, why record what people all around him still remembered?—EDITOR]

Chronology of Kemp Plummer Battle

IN THIS CHRONOLOGY AN ATTEMPT IS MADE TO give first the main life-facts of Kemp Plummer Battle (KPB) and his wife Martha Ann (Patty) Battle (Mrs. KPB); second to set down a few of the more outstanding men and events that shaped their lives from 1831 to 1919. These eighty-eight years saw amazing progress and revolutionary changes, extending from handicraft to mass production by machinery, from the stagecoach to the airplane, from patriarchal slavery to communism. The chronological approach is intended to keep clear the gradual course of development.

1829-1837. Andrew Jackson President of the United States.

1830. Steam railroad traffic inaugurated between Liverpool and Manchester, England.

1830. Revolution of July in France. Charles X dethroned and Louis Philippe King of the French.

1830-1831. First steam railroads inaugurated in the United States (South Carolina; Maryland).

1830-1832. Montford Stokes (Democrat) Governor of North Carolina.

1831, June 21. Capitol at Raleigh destroyed by fire and with it Canova's statue of Washington.

1831, December 19. Birth of KPB at Oakendale Plantation near Louisburg, son of William H. Battle and Lucy Martin (Plummer) Battle.

1831. William Lloyd Garrison establishes *The Liberator*, an abolitionist paper, in Boston.

1831. Nat Turner's slave insurrection in Virginia.

1831-1852. Levi Silliman Ives Bishop of North Carolina.

1832. Nullification in South Carolina.

1832. Passage of the Reform Bill by the British Parliament.

1832-1835. David Lowry Swain (Democrat) Governor of North Carolina.

1833, February 14. Birth of Martha Ann (Patty) Battle, daughter of James S. Battle and Sally Harriett (Westray) Battle, at Nashville.

1833, November 13. Magnificent shooting stars. "The year the stars fell."

1833. KPB's father, William H. Battle, moves from Oakendale Plantation to Louisburg.
1833. Abolition of slavery in the British Empire.
1834. Wake Forest Institute opened. In 1838 it was changed to Wake Forest College.
1835. State Constitutional Convention meets demand of the western part of North Carolina for greater representation in the State Government.
1835. Death of Joseph Caldwell, President of the University (born 1773).
1835. Revolver made practical by Samuel Colt.
1835-1837. Richard Dobbs Spaight, Jr. (Democrat) Governor of North Carolina.
1835-1868. David Lowry Swain President of the University.
1836. Independence of Texas from Mexico.
1837, June 20. Death of William IV, King of England, and accession of Queen Victoria.
1837. Davidson College opens.
1837. Widespread financial panic.
1837-1841. Edward B. Dudley (Whig) Governor of North Carolina.
1837-1841. Martin Van Buren President of the United States.
1839. KPB's father, William H. Battle, moves from Louisburg to Raleigh.
1839. Passage of the first public school law by the General Assembly.
1839. Goodyear devises a process for the vulcanization of rubber.
1839. Daguerre makes photography practicable.
1840. Population of Raleigh 2,244.
1840. First steam locomotive enters Raleigh (over the Raleigh and Gaston Railroad).
1840. New Capitol at Raleigh dedicated.
1840. State public school system set in operation.
1840. Log Cabin and Hard Cider Campaign for the presidency of the United States.
1840. Introduction of penny postage in the British Isles by Sir Rowland Hill.
1841-1845. John M. Morehead (Whig) Governor of North Carolina.
1841. William H. Harrison President of the United States.
1841-1845. John Tyler President of the United States.

Chronology of Kemp Plummer Battle 283

1842. Ether used in surgery by Dr. Crawford Williamson Long of Georgia.
1842. Ashburton-Webster Treaty settles northeastern boundary between United States and Canada.
1843. KPB's father, William H. Battle, moves from Raleigh to Chapel Hill.
1844. Death of Judge William Gaston (born 1778).
1844. Telegraph line inaugurated between Washington and Baltimore.
1845, March 1. Annexation of Texas by joint resolution of Congress.
1845. KPB enters the University.
1845. State School for Deaf, Dumb, and Blind opened at Raleigh.
1845. Death of Andrew Jackson (born 1767).
1845-1849. William A. Graham (Whig) Governor of North Carolina.
1845-1849. James Knox Polk President of the United States.
1846. Greensborough Female College opened.
1846. Oregon Treaty fixes boundary between United States and British Columbia at the forty-ninth parallel.
1846. Sewing machine made practical by Elias Howe.
1846. Repeal of the Corn Laws by the British Parliament.
1846-1847. Famine in Ireland and vast Irish emigration to America.
1846-1848. Mexican War.
1846-1868 and 1876-1879. Judge William H. Battle, father of KPB, Professor of Law at the University.
1846-1878. Pius IX Pope.
1847. James K. Polk, President of the United States, attends Commencement at the University.
1848. Completion of the Chapel of the Cross, Chapel Hill, parish church of Judge William H. Battle 1846-1868 and 1876-1879 and of KPB 1876-1919. Both were active members.
1848. Due mainly to the efforts of Miss Dorothea Dix of Boston and Hon. James C. Dobbin a State Asylum for the Insane is established in Raleigh and its site named Dix Hill.
1848. Treaty of Guadalupe Hidalgo adds 522,955 square miles of territory to the United States.
1848. Discovery of gold in California.
1848. Widespread revolution in Europe.
1848. Louis Philippe, King of the French, dethroned and Second Republic established in France.

1848. Abdication of Ferdinand I and accession of Francis Joseph I as Emperor of Austria and King of Hungary.
1849. KPB graduates at the University with the honor of the valedictory.
1849. Death of Edgar Allan Poe (born 1809).
1849-1850. KPB is Tutor in Latin at the University.
1849-1851. Charles Manly (Whig) Governor of North Carolina.
1849-1850. Zachary Taylor President of the United States.
1850. Population of Raleigh: free white, 2,253; free colored, 456; slaves, 1,809; total, 4,518.
1850. Compromise of 1850 relieves slavery question for a time.
1850. Death of John C. Calhoun (born 1782).
1850. Death of William Wordsworth (born 1770).
1850. Death of Honoré de Balzac (born 1799).
1850-1853. Millard Fillmore President of the United States.
1850-1854. KPB is Tutor in Mathematics at the University and studies law under his father, Judge William H. Battle.
1851-1854. David S. Reid (Democrat) Governor of North Carolina.
1851. Death of James Fenimore Cooper (born 1789).
1851, December 2. By a *coup d'état* Louis Napoleon makes himself master of France and in 1852 becomes Emperor of the French as Napoleon III.
1852. Death of Henry Clay (born 1777).
1852. Death of Daniel Webster (born 1782).
1852. Mrs. Harriet Beecher Stowe's *Uncle Tom's Cabin.*
1852. Death of the Duke of Wellington (born 1769).
1852. Power elevator made practicable by Elisha Otis.
1853. Calvin H. Wiley made first State Superintendent of Public Instruction in North Carolina.
1853. Completion of Christ Church, Raleigh, R. M. Upjohn architect. KPB was an active member of this church from 1854 to 1876.
1853. Gadsden Purchase adds some 45,000 square miles of Mexican territory to the United States.
1853-1854. Commodore Perry visits Japan and concludes a treaty between Japan and the United States.
1853-1857. Franklin Pierce President of the United States.
1853-1881. Thomas Atkinson Bishop of North Carolina.
1854. KPB begins the practice of law at Raleigh in partnership with Quentin Busbee.

Chronology of Kemp Plummer Battle 285

1854-1855. Warren Winslow (Democrat) Governor of North Carolina.
1854-1856. Crimean War. Florence Nightingale brings about a revolution in nursing the sick.
1855-1859. Thomas Bragg (Democrat) Governor of North Carolina.
1855, November 28. KPB and Martha Ann (Patty) Battle, daughter of James S. Battle and Sally Harriett (Westray) Battle, are married at Cool Spring Plantation, Edgecombe County.
1855-1881. Alexander II Czar of Russia.
1856. North Carolina Railroad completed from Goldsborough to Charlotte.
1857. Great financial distress.
1857. Death of Professor Elisha Mitchell (born 1793) on the mountain named after him.
1857. Dred Scott decision.
1857. Hinton R. Helper's *The Impending Crisis.*
1857-1861. James Buchanan President of the United States.
1857-1858. The Indian mutiny.
1859. James Buchanan, President of the United States, attends Commencement at the University.
1859-1861. John W. Ellis (Democrat) Governor of North Carolina.
1859. Trinity College opened in Randolph County, succeeding a Normal College (1851). Moved to Durham 1892. Now part of Duke University.
1859. Death of Washington Irving (born 1783).
1859. John Brown attempts to start a slave insurrection in Virginia.
1859. Darwin's *Origin of Species.*
1859. Natural oil is discovered in Pennsylvania. Oil lamps soon supersede candles.
1860. KPB runs for the General Assembly and is beaten by three votes.
1860, November 6. Abraham Lincoln elected President of the United States.
1860, December 20. South Carolina secedes from the Union.
1860. Population of Raleigh: free white, 2,693; free colored, 466; slaves, 1,621; total, 4,780.
1861, February 8-9. Confederate States of America organized at Montgomery, Alabama, and Jefferson Davis elected President.

1861, March 4-1865, April 15. Abraham Lincoln President of the United States.

1861, April 12. Confederates fire on Fort Sumter.

1861, April 15. President Lincoln calls for seventy-five thousand troops to coerce the seceding states.

1861-1862. KPB member of State Constitutional Convention which passes Ordinance of Secession May 20, 1861.

1861-1862. Henry Toole Clark (Democrat) Governor of North Carolina.

1861, July 21. First battle of Manassas or Bull Run.

1862. General Council of the Protestant Episcopal Church in the Confederate States meets in Augusta, Georgia. Judge William H. Battle was a deputy from North Carolina.

1862-1865. KPB president of the Chatham Railroad Company.

1862-1865 and 1877-1879. Z. B. Vance (Whig, later Democrat) Governor of North Carolina.

1862-1868 and 1874-1919. KPB trustee of the University.

1862. Death of William Makepeace Thackeray (born 1811).

1863, January 1. Lincoln's Emancipation Proclamation.

1863, May 3. Battle of Chancellorsville. Death of General "Stonewall" Jackson.

1863, July 1-3. Battle of Gettysburg.

1863, July 4. Grant captures Vicksburg.

1864. Death of Nathaniel Hawthorne (born 1804).

1864-1865. Bingham School moved to Mebane, where it was attended by sundry Battles.

1865, January 15. Capture of Fort Fisher by Northern forces.

1865, April 9. General Lee surrenders at Appomattox.

1865, April 13. Sherman's army enters Raleigh.

1865, April 14. President Lincoln shot by John Wilkes Booth and dies next day.

1865-1869. Andrew Johnson President of the United States.

1865, April 26. General Joseph E. Johnston surrenders near Durham.

1865. W. W. Holden Provisional Governor of North Carolina.

1865-1868. Jonathan Worth (Conservative) Governor of North Carolina.

1865. KPB and his father, Judge William Horn Battle, are deputies to the General Convention of the Protestant Episcopal Church in Philadelphia memorable for the restoration of the southern dioceses to their ante-bellum status in the Church.

Chronology of Kemp Plummer Battle 287

1865. State Constitutional Convention repeals Ordinance of Secession and abolishes slavery in North Carolina.

1865. Thirteenth Amendment to the U. S. Constitution prohibits slavery.

1865. Lister introduces antiseptic surgery.

1865-1877. Period of reconstruction of the seceding states. President Johnson seeks to restrict federal control of the South and to restore the several states to their normal functioning as rapidly as possible with due regard to the protection of the now freed negroes. The Republican party through control of Congress overrides the President, enfranchises the negroes, and disqualifies from voting large numbers of white people. The resulting corruption and mismanagement grievously hamper and delay the recovery of the South from the prostration brought about by the widespread destruction of life and property in a four years' war, which ended in the South's total defeat.

1865 ff. Drain of wealth from the South by tribute to the North involved in the payment of high tariff duties protecting northern manufactures, of interest on the national debt incurred in the conquest of the South, and of pensions to soldiers in northern armies. Southern farming interests are gradually strangled; the plantation owners one by one go down. KPB and the Edgecombe Battles die poor. Little of the land owned in slavery times belongs to the Battles of today. What wealth is now to be found in North Carolina is mainly due to the development of manufacturing—cotton, tobacco, furniture, rayon.

1866. Death of Judge George E. Badger (born 1795).

1866. Inauguration of submarine trans-Atlantic telegraphy.

1866. War of Prussia and Italy against Austria and Bavaria. Defeat of Austria at Sadowa (Königgrätz).

1866-1868. KPB State Treasurer. John H. Wheeler states that "his official reports are considered models of financial ability, conciseness, and accuracy."

1867, March 2. Reconstruction Act passed by Congress over the President's veto.

1867, March 11. Gen. Daniel E. Sickles is made Commander of the Second District (North and South Carolina).

1867, June 19. Maximilian, Emperor of Mexico, shot by order of Juarez at Querétaro.

1867. General Assembly transfers to the University the land scrip granted the State by the Morrill Act of 1862 for an agricultural and mechanical college.

1867. KPB as chairman of a committee of the trustees of the University with ex-Governor William A. Graham and S. F. Phillips, later Solicitor General of the United States, makes an elaborate report called "The University Plan," which is adopted by the Board of Trustees, but because of the Reconstruction Act not put into operation.

1867. Andrew Johnson, President of the United States, attends Commencement at the University.

1867. Death of Professor James Phillips, Professor of Mathematics at the University 1826-1867, in the chapel at morning prayers.

1867. KPB as its treasurer assists in the inauguration of St. Augustine's Normal School and Collegiate Institute (for Negroes) at Raleigh.

1867. Purchase of Alaska from Russia.

1867. Establishment of the Dominion of Canada.

1867. Karl Marx's *Das Kapital*.

1867. Second Reform Act greatly extends suffrage in Great Britain and Ireland.

1867, August 26. General E. R. S. Canby succeeds General Sickles as Commander of the Second District (North and South Carolina).

1868, August 11. Death of David Lowry Swain, Governor of North Carolina 1832-1835, President of the University 1835-1868 (born 1801).

1868. Under Congressional Reconstruction, Republican party gains control of North Carolina.

1868. New Constitution adopted in North Carolina under Congressional Reconstruction.

1868. Under Congressional Reconstruction, Judge William H. Battle loses his position as a member of the Supreme Court, moves to Raleigh, and begins the practice of law in partnership with his sons KPB and R. H. Battle.

1868. The trustees and faculty of the University are removed from office by the Reconstruction government of North Carolina, and the University is closed.

1868. Fourteenth Amendment to the U. S. Constitution secures to freedmen rights of citizenship, validates the national debt,

Chronology of Kemp Plummer Battle 289

and regulates the basis of representation in Congress and disqualification from office.

1868. Impeachment and acquittal of President Johnson.

1868-1870. W. W. Holden (Republican) Governor of North Carolina.

1868. C. S. Sholes makes a practicable typewriter.

1869. Opening of the Suez Canal.

1869. First transcontinental railroad completed (Union Pacific and Central Pacific companies).

1869-1875. Rev. Solomon Pool President of the University under Reconstruction government. He is legally President even though the University is closed.

1869, March 3-1870, June 9. The University open under Reconstruction government. Thirty-five students enroll the first year, of whom twenty-five are in the preparatory department. The second year there are fifty-three students, twenty being in the preparatory department.

1869-1877. Ulysses S. Grant President of the United States.

1869-1872. KPB is president of the State Agricultural Society and leads in reviving the State Fair at Raleigh.

1870, October 12. Death of General R. E. Lee (born 1807, January 19).

1870-1871. Governor W. W. Holden is impeached and removed from office.

1870. Fifteenth Amendment to the U. S. Constitution provides that the right to vote shall not be denied because of race, color, or previous condition of servitude.

1870. Death of Chief Justice Thomas Ruffin (born 1787).

1870. Population of Raleigh: white, 3,696; colored, 4,094; total 7,790.

1870. Death of Charles Dickens (born 1812).

1870-1871. Franco-Prussian War.

1870, July 18. Proclamation of Papal Infallibility by the Vatican Council.

1870. Napoleon III dethroned and Third Republic established in France.

1870-1876. KPB president of the North Carolina State Life Insurance Company.

1871, January 18. William I proclaimed at Versailles German Emperor.

1871. Unification of Italy under Victor Emmanuel II.

1871-1873. Thiers President of France.
1871-1874. Tod R. Caldwell (Republican) Governor of North Carolina.
1871-1873. KPB a commissioner of the city of Raleigh.
1873. Adoption of an amendment to the State Constitution, providing again for the election of trustees of the University by the General Assembly.
1873. Devastating financial panic.
1874-1876. KPB Secretary and Treasurer of the Board of Trustees of the University.
1874-1877. Curtis H. Brogden (Republican) Governor of North Carolina.
1875. As chairman of a committee of the trustees to raise funds for the revival of the University KPB secures about $18,000.
1875, September 6. The University is reopened with Professor Charles Phillips as Chairman of the Faculty.
1875. Death of William A. Graham (born 1804).
1875. Pictet devises a practicable ice-making machine.
1876. Revised Constitution adopted in North Carolina by popular vote.
1876-1891. KPB President of the University and Professor of Political Science and Constitutional Law.
1876, October 3. Inauguration of Johns Hopkins University, marking a new era in graduate instruction in the United States.
1876. Alexander Graham Bell develops a working telephone.
1876-1877. KPB buys from his father the old family home at Chapel Hill, a charming tract of six acres with the University campus in front and the forest on two sides. He enlarges and repairs the sadly dilapidated house. He names the place Senlac.
1876-1877. KPB advocates the establishment of an agricultural experiment station in North Carolina by addresses in eighteen counties and before the General Assembly. This address was the introduction of the subject into North Carolina.
1877. Phonograph made practicable by Thomas A. Edison.
1877. Gas engine made practicable by Nicholas Otto.
1877. Reconstruction period in North Carolina ended by the inauguration of Z. B. Vance as Governor.
1877-1881. State Agricultural Experiment and Fertilizer Control Station operated in connection with the chemical laboratory

Chronology of Kemp Plummer Battle 291

at the University, though for want of funds only the Fertilizer Control part of the work could be carried out. Dr. A. R. Ledoux is Director 1877-1880, Dr. C. W. Dabney 1880-1887. In 1881 the Station was moved to Raleigh.

1877-1881. Rutherford B. Hayes President of the United States.

1877-1884. University Summer Normal School for the training of teachers.

1877-1887. KPB member of State Board of Agriculture by virtue of his office as President of the University.

1878. Congress of Berlin.

1878-1903. Leo XIII Pope.

1879-1885. T. J. Jarvis (Democrat) Governor of North Carolina.

1879, March 14. Death of KPB's father, Judge William Horn Battle, at Chapel Hill, in his seventy-seventh year.

1879. Incandescent lamp made practicable by Thomas A. Edison.

1879. Henry George's *Progress and Poverty*.

1879-1881. KPB Acting Professor of Law at the University in addition to his duties as President and Professor of Political Science and Constitutional Law.

1880. Western North Carolina Railroad reaches Asheville.

1880. Population of Chapel Hill, 831; Raleigh, 9,265; Rocky Mount, 552.

1881. The University secures from the General Assembly its first annual appropriation ($5,000).

1881. James Abram Garfield President of the United States (assassinated 1881).

1881-1885. Chester A. Arthur President of the United States.

1881. Revised version of the New Testament.

1881. Death of Thomas Carlyle (born 1795).

1881. Death of Benjamin Disraeli, Earl of Beaconsfield (born 1804).

1881. Assassination of Alexander II, Czar of Russia.

1881-1894. Alexander III Czar of Russia.

1881-1893. Theodore Benedict Lyman Bishop of North Carolina.

1882. University Railroad opened from University Station (on the North Carolina Rail Road between Durham and Hillsborough) to Chapel Hill, largely through the efforts of KPB. For several years KPB was president of the University Railroad Company.

1882. Death of Ralph Waldo Emerson (born 1803).

1882. Death of Henry Wadsworth Longfellow (born 1807).

1883. Establishment of the Elisha Mitchell Scientific Society, mainly by the efforts of Dr. F. P. Venable, Professor of Chemistry in the University.

1884. Mergenthaler develops the linotype machine.

1885-1889. A. M. Scales (Democrat) Governor of North Carolina.

1885-1889 and 1893-1897. Grover Cleveland President of the United States.

1885. Erection of a gymnasium at the University adjoining the campus to the west on Cameron Avenue by a stock company composed of alumni and friends. The immediate compelling motive was to provide a place for the Commencement Ball hitherto held in the Library but lately excluded therefrom by the trustees in deference to the objections of those opposed to dancing. A prominent feature of the decorations at the Commencement Ball of 1885 was the legal maxim in huge letters: *Cujus est solum ejus est usque ad caelum.*

1885. Revised version of the Old Testament.

1885. General Assembly increases annual University appropriation from $5,000 to $20,000.

1885. Dedication of Memorial Hall at the University as an auditorium for large gatherings.

1885. Death of Victor Hugo (born 1802).

1886. Electric welding is devised by E. Thompson.

1887. General Assembly takes away from the University the $7,500 income from the lands appropriated by the Morrill Act of Congress for the promotion of education in agriculture and the mechanic arts and gives it to a new Agricultural and Mechanical College at Raleigh.

1888, March 8. Death of William I, German Emperor, and accession of Frederick III.

1888, June 15. Death of Frederick III, German Emperor, and accession of William II.

1889-1891. Daniel G. Fowle (Democrat) Governor of North Carolina.

1889-1893. Benjamin Harrison President of the United States.

1889. Centennial celebration of the granting of the charter of the University. Endowment of the Alumni Professorship of History.

1889. Opening of the North Carolina College of Agriculture and the Mechanic Arts at Raleigh. Generally known as State College, it is now a part of the Greater University.

1889. Death of Jefferson Davis (born 1808).
1890. Population of Chapel Hill, 1,017; Raleigh, 12,678; Rocky Mount, 816.
1891-1893. Thomas M. Holt (Democrat) Governor of North Carolina.
1891-1896. George T. Winston President of the University.
1891-1907. KPB Alumni Professor of History in the University. "Under his wise and sympathetic direction the department has enriched and invigorated the intellectual life of the University. The historical instinct, the love and aptitude for historical research, the power to collect, arrange, deduce, and vivify historical data are entering into the equipment of University students. History is no longer with us merely informational and conventional, but is a department of the great science of sociology. In the days to come the commonwealth shall not lack for those able to tell the story of its spirit, its genius, and its progress." (Edwin A. Alderman, President successively of the University of North Carolina, Tulane University, and the University of Virginia.)
1892. Opening of the State Normal and Industrial School at Greensborough, later North Carolina College for Women, now a part of the Greater University.
1892. Death of Alfred, Lord Tennyson (born 1809).
1892. Automobile gasoline engine made practicable by Otto Daimler.
1893. Great financial panic.
1893-1897. Elias Carr (Democrat) Governor of North Carolina.
1893-1932. Joseph Blount Cheshire Bishop of North Carolina.
1894-1917. Nicholas II Czar of Russia.
1895. Centennial Celebration of the opening of the University.
1895. Death of Louis Pasteur (born 1822).
1896. Marconi makes wireless telegraphy practicable.
1896. Free Silver campaign of William Jennings Bryan for the presidency.
1896-1900. Edwin A. Alderman President of the University.
1897-1901. Daniel L. Russell (Republican) Governor of North Carolina.
1897-1901. William McKinley President of the United States (assassinated 1901).
1898. Spanish-American War. Cuba freed; Porto Rico, Guam, and the Philippines ceded to the United States.

1898. Annexation of Hawaii.
1898. Death of W. E. Gladstone (born 1809).
1898. Death of Bismarck (born 1815).
1899-1902. South African War.
1900. Population of Chapel Hill, 1,099; Raleigh, 13,643; Rocky Mount, 2,937.
1900. Assassination of Humbert I and accession of Victor Emmanuel III as King of Italy.
1900. A species of mosquito (*Aëdes aegypti*, earlier known as *Stegomyia fasciata*) is proved to be the carrier of yellow fever and the conquest of this terrible scourge is assured.
1900-1914. Francis Preston Venable President of the University.
1901, January 22. Death of Queen Victoria.
1901-1910. Edward VII King of England.
1901. American Revised Version of the Bible.
1901. Inauguration of the Commonwealth of Australia.
1901-1905. Charles B. Aycock (Democrat) Governor of North Carolina.
1901-1909. Theodore Roosevelt President of the United States.
1903-1904. President Roosevelt promotes the independence of Panama from Colombia and a treaty for the construction of the Panama Canal.
1903-1905. Airplane flight made practicable by the Wright brothers on the coast of North Carolina.
1903-1914. Pius X Pope.
1904-1905. Russo-Japanese War.
1905-1909. Robert B. Glenn (Democrat) Governor of North Carolina.
1907. Financial panic.
1907. Grant of an annuity to KPB by the Carnegie Foundation for the Advancement of Teaching.
1907. KPB publishes *History of the University of North Carolina*, Volume I, From the Beginning to the Death of President Swain, 1789-1868, pp. ix, 880. He was awarded the Patterson Cup for the best historical work published in North Carolina in 1907.
1907-1919. KPB Professor of History Emeritus in the University.
1909 ff. L. DeForest makes practical wireless telephone or radio.
1909-1913. William W. Kitchin (Democrat) Governor of North Carolina.
1909-1913. William H. Taft President of the United States.

Chronology of Kemp Plummer Battle 295

1910-1936. George V King of England.
1910. Inauguration of the Union of South Africa.
1910. Population of Chapel Hill, 1,149; Raleigh, 19,218; Rocky Mount, 8,051.
1910. Death of Mark Twain (born 1835).
1912. KPB publishes *History of the University of North Carolina,* Volume II, From 1868 to 1912, pp. viii, 875.
1912-1913. First Balkan War.
1913-1917. Locke Craig (Democrat) Governor of North Carolina.
1913, February 18. Resolution of thanks and appreciation for the services of KPB, introduced by Speaker George W. Connor, adopted by both houses of the General Assembly, on the completion of his *History of the University of North Carolina.*
1913, March 13. Death of Martha Ann (Patty) Battle, daughter of James S. Battle, wife of KPB, at Chapel Hill, in her eighty-first year.
1913. Federal Reserve Bank Act passed by Congress.
1913. Sixteenth Amendment to the U. S. Constitution allows Congress to levy taxes on incomes.
1913. Seventeenth Amendment to the U. S. Constitution provides for direct election of senators by the people.
1913. Second Balkan War.
1913-1921. Woodrow Wilson President of the United States.
1914-1918. Edward Kidder Graham President of the University.
1914-1918. World War I.
1914-1922. Benedict XV Pope.
1915, May 7. Sinking of the "Lusitania" by a German submarine.
1916. Death of Francis Joseph I, Emperor of Austria.
1917-1921. Thomas W. Bickett (Democrat) Governor of North Carolina.
1917, April 6. Declaration of war against Germany by the United States.
1917. Purchase of the Virgin Islands from Denmark.
1917. Russian Revolution.
1919, February 4. Death of KPB at Chapel Hill in his eighty-eighth year.
1919, February 6. Funeral service held for KPB at 8 A.M. in Gerrard Hall at the University. In charge of the service was the Rev. R. M. Marshall, Rector of the Chapel of the Cross. Addresses were made by Chairman of the Faculty H. W.

Chase and the Rev. W. D. Moss, Pastor of the Presbyterian Church in Chapel Hill.

1919, February 6. Burial of KPB in Oakwood Cemetery, Raleigh, from Christ Church. The service was conducted by the Right Rev. Joseph Blount Cheshire, Bishop of North Carolina, the Rev. R. M. Marshall, Rector of the Chapel of the Cross, Chapel Hill, and the Rev. M. A. Barber, Rector of Christ Church, Raleigh. The General Assembly adjourned for the funeral. The Supreme Court attended in a body.

www.ingramcontent.com/pod-product-compliance
Lightning Source LLC
Chambersburg PA
CBHW021118300426
44113CB00006B/199